DATE DUE 28563

#47-0108 Peel Off Pressure Sensitive

RETHINKING

DEMOCRATIC
EDUCATION

RETHINKING

DEMOCRATIC
EDUCATION

The Politics of Reform

David M. Steiner

The Johns Hopkins University Press
Baltimore and London

© 1994 The Johns Hopkins University Press
All rights reserved
Printed in the United States of America on acid-free paper

The Johns Hopkins University Press
2715 North Charles Street
Baltimore, Maryland 21218-4319
The Johns Hopkins Press Ltd., London

ISBN 0-8018-4842-3

Library of Congress Cataloging-in-Publication Data will be found
at the end of this book.
A catalog record of this book is available from the British Library.

*For my parents,
and in memory of my grandparents*

Contents

Acknowledgments

A book such as this one draws on many sources, both intellectual and personal. My fascination with political theory can be traced to three years of privileged tutoring from Alan Montefiore and Steven Lukes at Balliol College, Oxford. The idea of considering political theory and educational reform together I owe only to a perverse instinct—the thought was still unfashionable when I undertook the doctoral work that eventually became this book. Nevertheless, Judith Shklar's seminar on the Enlightenment at Harvard University introduced me to the works of Rousseau, and it was she who supervised my initial research. Professor Shklar's recent death has left American intellectual life in general, and this book in particular, without one of its most rigorous critics.

My work at Harvard brought new friendships. Wallace MacCaffrey always offered a home away from home. Dan, Joanna, and the entire Rose family extended wonderful, and until now unacknowledged, hospitality. Shelley Burtt and Joshua Dienstag, both of whom now teach in the field of political theory, have been generous and exacting discussants and readers. With others, paths crossed to my inestimable benefit—William Griffith, Ann Blair, Jack Trumpbour, Kamilla Bren. The transition to a life of teaching led me to the South and to new sources of support. It is in no small measure due to the confidence of Richard Teichgraeber and Thomas Langston that I undertook to transform my doctoral thesis into a book. Tom willingly undertook a detailed reading of many sections of the present manuscript. From that same period came my friendship with Ellen Konowitz, who offered the gift of unstinting and enduring confidence in my work.

That work was completed at Vanderbilt University. Thanks go to Jean Elshtain, who brought me here, to my department colleagues, and to Timothy Cloyd, who has added his name to the list of readers and friends with whom I have shared my writing. Financial support in the shape of a Vanderbilt Research Council Grant helped to provide invaluable time for writing. Paul Conkin generously read the entire manuscript and offered detailed comments on the Dewey chapters. William Race of the Department of Classics has tried patiently to insure that my thinking about ancient Greece was not entirely a fantasy—but he will welcome the assurance that he is entirely free of responsibility for the results. The same thanks and proviso go to my sister, Deborah Steiner. Finally, my thanks to another classicist, Myles Burnyeat, whose exactitude of thought and example of careful reading have always set a humbling but heuristic example.

The work and arguments of Amy Gutmann, Benjamin Barber, and Stephen Macedo have most obviously helped to frame my own considerations about contemporary education. Those considerations have benefited too from the hard work of my editor, Henry Tom, and my copyeditor, Elizabeth Gratch. I am deeply grateful for their efficiency and tactful support.

Evelyne Ender and Leslie Kirby, present at the inception and completion of this project, know that this book would not have been written without them. Given the subject matter of this work, it is natural that my most profound debts are to those who tried to educate me. My parents provide an example that is, happily, impossible either to emulate or to ignore. Their conviction that the most honorable life is to be spent in the company of ideas, of literature, and of inquiry has been the highest and most troubling gift of all.

Introduction

This book addresses some fundamental problems facing education in contemporary America. The goal is to offer a fresh conception of education which is sensitive to political fundamentals, to the fact that in the United States political authority is ultimately vested in every citizen.[1] My allegiance, therefore, is to a model of democratic education, though not one necessarily based on a populist approach. Democratic education must often take issue with the preferences of parents and political authorities, at least as these groups currently view their pedagogic responsibilities. Rather, I suggest that a democratic education should be grounded in and justified through an account of language, experience, and growth. It should be possible to link an analysis of these critical elements for any education with the unique demands and opportunities placed before citizens in a democratic society. The result would be a form of learning in which epistemology, political theory, and educational practice could be brought into powerful harmony. Imperfectly realized, that harmony is the goal of this book.

The nature of the argument separates me from certain widely maintained views of the American academy. The idea of defending public policy by reference to epistemological argument is not currently fashionable. In an era of philosophical skepticism political theorists often assume that only conservative thinkers upholding visions of timeless truths could find in philosophy a natural ally. While I distance myself from the Neoplatonism that some reformers embrace, I do not share the liberal theorists' antipathy for philosophical argument. Eschewing both positions, I lay out a model of education that rests neither on a consensus of public intuitions nor on a metaphysical idealism.

I distance myself too from the view that a political theory of education has a legitimate interest only in questions of political authority and rights. I argue that telling teachers not to discriminate against nor to repress their students cannot constitute a fully compelling conception of education. Certainly, issuing such guidelines to educators is important; in America border disputes between claims of liberty and equality, between respect for universal rights and protection for fragile communities, are inescapable. In its organization and practices public education must forever balance such claims against each other. But the necessary debate about the exact position of these frontiers, ably undertaken in the existing literature, cannot enlighten us about the political importance of what is to occur within those frontiers. It is such activity that makes up the vast majority of educational practice.

Cognizant of the widespread debate about the authority of the "canon," I nevertheless ask the reader to join in a rereading and rethinking of old texts firmly located within the tradition of Western thinking. I believe that the results of such a review need not be insensitive to contemporary questions of gender, ethnicity, and identity. Indeed, effective methods of thinking about such issues are not necessarily exhausted by the vocabulary within which they are currently discussed. The consequences of considering such questions from an oblique perspective may lead to ideas that cut across the entrenched antinomies of contemporary rhetoric. The reader will judge whether my choice of material fulfills this pedagogic responsibility.

Finally, I take issue with the common conviction that education should focus on the goal of a more efficient and more competitive work force. Convinced that predicting the required skills over a relevant time frame is extraordinarily problematic, I argue that technical education is best done in close conjunction with particular occupations and cannot form the heart of a democratic education for all citizens. An economically determined focus on education blinds us, in my view, to other more critical and attainable educational goals. I follow Friederich Nietzsche in his rejection of a model of education in which "the task is to make men as useful as possible, and to approximate him, as far as possible, to a an infallible machine."[2]

The argument of this book has its origin in another suggestion of Nietzsche's, when he celebrates those long derided targets of Socratic irony, the ancient Sophists. With characteristic confidence, Nietzsche proclaims that "every advance in epistemological and moral knowledge has reinstated the Sophists" (*Will to Power*, par. 428). Building on the best known of sophistic dictums, I will argue that a seminal, forgotten but redeemable promise of a democratic society to its next generation is that every citizen be capable of becoming "the measure of all things." The capacity to create and re-create an identity, to negotiate and renegotiate its components in a social setting, to judge the merits of public choices as they intersect with self-understanding and social needs, to engage in aesthetic experience and to develop intellectual habits equal to the task of discriminating among inescapably incommensurable demands; these capacities constitute the ends of a democratic education.

Through an examination of contemporary education and the rhetoric of educational reform, the first chapter considers why many contemporary proposals for educational reform do not further these ends. Drawing selectively from a vast literature that encompasses school choice, testing, the economy, issues of parental involvement, religion, and other matters of curriculum, I argue that something vital is missing—namely, a model, or at least a conception, of what it is that makes a citizen worthy of the epithet "educated." Without denying that practical reform along lines currently suggested in American political and academic forums would somewhat improve test scores and reduce dropout rates, I suggest that the crisis of American education is of a different order and would thus not be fundamentally altered by these recommended changes.

What follows this introduction is an exercise in the recovery and reforging of a vocabulary for democratic education to make vivid a road (currently) not traveled. The possible components of such a vocabulary are, of course, multiple: from constitutionalism to individualism, from community to transcendence and beyond. My choice to juxtapose Greek political discourse, the imaginative spaces evoked by Jean-Jacques Rousseau, and the naturalism of John Dewey should strike a discordant note. Plato's enmity to a democratic polity is legion, the relevance of ancient Greece to contemporary America doubtful. Some perceive Rousseau and John Dewey as the evil forefathers of "permissive" educational chaos.

I choose writers and texts because of the thesis I defend. An adequate conception of democratic education must fuse together critical arguments advanced by Rousseau and Dewey and also account for tensions that remain once that synthesis is effected. The discussion of Platonic texts and Greek politics is necessary to sketch out a framework within which such a synthesis can take place. Since I have selected these writers in order to advance an argument that belongs to none of them individually, it should be clear that I do not intend to defend all, or even most, of what they wrote. The argument that follows stands on its own merits. This is not to say, however, that the textual interpretations that follow are without constraint. Much of the benefit from rereading Plato, Rousseau, and

Dewey lies in the detailed identification of claims to be found within each of their works. The legitimacy of such a reading is itself now suspect, especially in the view of many "deconstructionists." While my interpretive methodology is informed by their work, what follows will certainly strike the committed deconstructionist as overly traditional.

The first textual exegesis begins with a brief reconstruction of a democratic sensibility in ancient Greece. This account is motivated by the conviction of the contemporary importance of classical political argument for our overly proceduralist, epistemologically impoverished political vocabulary. I am persuaded, as are other students of antiquity, that Greeks "understood that the only human qualities that can secure well being are precisely those which prompt and enable man actively to order the world, thereby increasing the risks to well being, and to reflect on his own condition and situation, thus destabilizing and fragmenting the social order on whose integrity his well being depends."[3] If this is an adequate sketch of the aspiration of the first democratic theorists, it also powerfully indicates the extent of their ambitions. Democritus, a key figure among this group, argued that education "shapes" man and thus "makes his nature."[4] Linking this assumption with the goal of preparing human beings to be the constructors, interrogators, and negotiators of their world places a great burden on democratic education.

The evocation of ancient Greek thought in my work focuses on the contribution of the Sophists. The politics of public speech as it emerged in the encounter between citizens in the assembly form the immediate context of their work. It was the Sophists who trained the orators, the political elite whose proposals in the assembly constituted the political choices of the citizens. It is because the structure of Greek politics made the assembly an educative exercise in the role playing and judgment that I will be able to defend the democratic legitimacy of the Sophists and use their insights: "When they addressed the demos, or a fraction of it, members of the educated elite participated in a drama in which they were required to play the role of common men. . . . Only if they played their democratic roles well were the elite political orators allowed to 'step out of character' and assert their claim to special consideration."[5]

The role that concerns me is that of the political debater as well as the education in rhetorical technique upon which his skills depended. It was in providing this education that the Sophists justified their profession (an account of why this is so appears in chap. 2). My intention will be to show that Protagoras and his followers, in their concern with political language and its use, have something vital to teach contemporary democrats about the development of educated judgment.

The theme of an education in judgment is further developed in subsequent chapters on Rousseau and Dewey. I reinterpret the infamous paradoxes and antinomies of Rousseau's thought as so many exercises in the assessment and measurement of self, society, and their fluid yet often stubbornly opaque intersections. Rousseau's rich imagination, erudition, and mastery of diverse literary styles enabled him to measure the promise and the tragedies inherent in a plethora of possible social and psychological environments. The juxtaposition of history, political theory, and a vocabulary of eroticism in Rousseau's multiple measurements suggest an initial vocabulary for contemporary education. But his example goes further: Rousseau's complex techniques of constructing heuristic psychological reactions in his readers lead me to a reevaluation of the role of the teacher and the relationship between teachers and other citizens.

Dewey's contribution to a model of democratic education takes a very different form. Rather than constructing multiple perspectives from which to imagine human possibilities, Dewey attempted to develop an overarching and unified picture of human experience in experiential and aesthetic terms. In a vocabulary as multidimensional as Rousseau's, Dewey integrates his understanding of philosophy, science, politics, and organic behavior into a vision of democratic life. Dewey was not the facile or naive optimist of the popular imagination. But he was convinced that democracy as a political order emerges seamlessly from the conditions of natural growth and development, at least once these conditions are correctly understood. In Dewey's democratic faith are to be found a commitment to the experimental, to the provisional, to the dynamic—at the level not only of personal but also of public life. Dewey calls for a society in which "the ever-expanding and intricately ramifying consequences of associated activity shall be known in the full sense of the word, so that an organized, articulate Public comes into being. The highest and most difficult kind of enquiry and a subtle, delicate, vivid and responsive art of communication must take possession of the physical machinery of transmission and circulate and breathe life into it."[6] Democracy, for Dewey, is experience correctly understood: the environment created by democratic politics is one in which the individual can construct and take responsibility for an identity.

Two principal elements emerge through the textual analysis in these chapters. The first is an ideal model of democratic education. Such an education will equip its citizens to place themselves in the social environment of which they are an integral part, to understand its forms of speech, its symbols and images, and its silences. An educated citizen will be ready to question the agreements, both historical and contemporary, which match his or her aspirations to a set of social possibilities and prohibitions. A democratic sensibility will hold fluid and in question the relationship between the finite spaces of political interaction and the potentially infinite arena of the private imagination. It will be prepared to undertake a lifelong negotiation between the temporally immediate and the claims of the domestic, the political, and the ethical, which may intersect with, or put in question, the demands of the moment.

The second element is an argument that this ideal is not merely the accidental product of an idiosyncratic set of readings but also the consequence of recovering the core meaning of democratic politics. Many forms of collective life encourage sustained self-reflection, perhaps most vividly those that ground the constraints and freedoms of behavior on religious grounds. But as the analysis of Greek thinking will suggest, only a democracy must try to make good the conviction that citizens "are the measure of all things." Without that conviction democracy is but the provisional construction of the political economist: an argument that the most efficient production of social goods takes place in circumstances in which multiple preferences can be freely expressed. Rousseau, perhaps more than any other thinker, points out the paucity of such a political idea and the possibilities of achieving self-understanding it undermines. Dewey, returning to the original and deeper understanding of democracy as the capacity to measure reflectively and judge acutely, encourages us to rethink the challenge of educating the democratic citizen in contemporary times.

In the final chapter I lay out some steps in that rethinking. There I suggest how to recast the language of educational reform, remodeling the sacred cows of core curriculums and tests along lines that reflect the promise of democratic politics rather than the frustrations of contemporary reformers. Most of the work of application remains: those who are familiar with the technological resources, the Byzantine structures of local education, and the politics of educational reform, will, I hope, be encouraged to build on the groundwork I sketch. The principle task of the chapter is one of translation, from the theoretical language that delineates the ideal of a democratic education, to the more practical and incremental steps that would bring us closer to that ideal. To offer no such translation would encourage the erroneous conclusion that ideals have no constructive place in politics. To go too far would be to claim an expertise in technical matters of education which lies beyond the scope of my treatment.

It is one of the peculiarities of American education that almost every citizen has a view on the subject and one that he or she often aggressively defends against outside interference of any kind. The causes for such behavior are multiple, but many emerge from the uniqueness of the American founding, with its extraordinary blend of belief in providential destiny and practical experimentalism. The magisterial incompatibilities encompassed in the phrase "we hold these truths to be self-evident," have haunted the history of American education. The resulting tensions are vividly captured in George Washington's double assertion that "no people can be found to acknowledge and adore the Invisible Hand . . . more than those of America" and that "the preservation of the sacred fire of liberty . . . [is] justly considered, perhaps, as deeply, as finally, staked on the experiment entrusted to the hands of the American people."[7] This book is focused on that experiment, the education of a citizen responsible for the construction, interrogation, and reconstruction of private and public space. It would be reassuring, indeed, to believe that the invisible hand will sustain such an experiment.

Abbreviations

Jean-Jacques Rousseau's Writings

CC	*Correspondance complète de Jean-Jacques Rousseau.* Edited by R. A. Leigh. Geneva: Institut et Musée Voltaire, 1969.
Conf.	*The Confessions of Jean-Jacques Rousseau.* Edited by J. M. Cohen. New York: Penguin Books, 1953.
Corsica	*Political Writings.* Edited and translated by Frederick Watkins. New York: Thomas Nelson and Sons, 1953.
Dialogues	*Rousseau juge de Jean-Jacques* [sic]. *Dialogues.* In *Oeuvres complètes.* Vol. 1.
E	*Emile, or On Education.* Translated by Allan Bloom. New York: Basic Books, 1979.
FD	*First Discourse.* In *The First and Second Discourses.* Translated by Roger D. and Judith R. Masters. New York: St. Martin's Press, 1964.
Fragments	*Fragments politiques.* In *Oeuvres complètes.* Vol. 3.
Geneva	*Geneva Manuscript.* In *On the Social Contract* with *Geneva Manuscript* and *Political Economy.* Edited by Roger D. Masters. Translated by Judith R. Masters. New York: St. Martin's Press, 1978.
Heros	*Discours sur cette question: quelle est la vertu la plus nécessaire au heros.* In *Oeuvres complètes.* Vol. 2.
L	*Letter to D'Alembert.* Translated by Allan Bloom. In *Politics and the Arts.* Ithaca, N.Y.: Cornell University Press, Agora Editions, 1960.
MEW	*The Minor Educational Writings of Jean-Jacques Rousseau.* Translated by William Boyd. New York: Bureau of Publications, Columbia University, 1962.

Mountain	Lettres écrites de la Montagne. In Oeuvres complètes, vol. 3.
Narcisse	Preface to Narcisse. In The First and Second Discourses and Essay on the Origin of Languages. Edited by Victor Gourevitch. New York: Harper and Row, 1986.
NH	Julie, ou la nouvelle Héloise. In Ouevres complètes. Vol. 2.
OC	Oeuvres complètes. 4 vols. Paris: Gallimard, Bibliotheque de la Pleiade, 1959–69.
Poland	The Government of Poland. In Political Writings. Edited and translated by Frederick Watkins. New York: Thomas Nelson and Sons, 1953.
Political	Political Economy. In On the Social Contract with Geneva Manuscript and Political Economy. Edited by Roger D. Masters. Translated by Judith R. Masters. New York: St. Martin's Press, 1978.
Reveries	Reveries of the Solitary Walker. Translated by Peter France. New York: Penguin Books, 1979.
SC	Social Contract. In On the Social Contract with Geneva Manuscript and Political Economy.
SD	Second Discourse. In The First and Second Discourses. Translated by Roger D. and Judith R. Masters. New York: St. Martin's Press, 1964.
Third Letter	Third Letter to Malesherbes. In Oeuvres complètes, vol. 1.

John Dewey's Writings

AAE	Art as Experience. New York: Perigee Printing, 1980.
DE	Democracy and Education. New York: Macmillan Publishing, 1966.
ED	Ethics of Democracy. In The Early Works of John Dewey, 1882–1898. Vol. 1.
EEL	Essays in Experimental Logic. In The Middle Works of John Dewey, 1899–1924. Vol. 10.
EN	Experience and Nature. New York: Dover Publications, 1958.
ENF	On Experience, Nature, and Freedom. Edited by R. Bernstein. Indianapolis: Bobbs-Merrill Co., 1960.
EW/MW/ LW	The Early Works of John Dewey, 1882–1898; The Middle Works of John Dewey, 1899–1924; The Late Works of John Dewey, 1925–

	1953. Edited by Jo Ann Boydston. Carbondale: Southern Illinois University Press, 1967–93.
HNC	*Human Nature and Conduct.* In *The Middle Works of John Dewey, 1899–1924.* Vol. 14.
I	*Impressions of Soviet Russia.* New York: New Republic, 1932.
ION	*Individualism Old and New.* In *The Later Works of John Dewey, 1925–1953.* Vol. 5.
Logic	*Logic: The Theory of Inquiry.* New York: Henry Holt and Co., 1938.
"Nature"	"Nature in Experience." In *Philosophical Review* 49 (1940).
PC	*Philosophy and Civilization.* In *The Later Works of John Dewey, 1925–1953.* Vol. 6.
PP	*The Public and Its Problems.* New York: Henry Holt and Co., 1927.
QC	*Quest for Certainty.* In *The Later Works of John Dewey, 1925–1953.* Vol. 4.
RP	*Reconstruction in Philosophy.* In *The Middle Works of John Dewey, 1899–1924.* Vol. 12.
School	*The School and Society.* Chicago: University of Chicago Press, 1915.
ST	*Schools of Tomorrow.* In *The Middle Works of John Dewey, 1899–1924.* Vol. 8.
Studies	*Studies in Logical Theory.* In *The Middle Works of John Dewey, 1899–1924.* Vol. 2.

RETHINKING
DEMOCRATIC
EDUCATION

1

The Politics of Reform

LOCAL EMBARRASSMENTS can reveal more profound difficulties. Eastern Europe, in the process of constructing market economies, naturally turns to Western Europe, to Japan, and to the United States for assistance and advice. Judged by the norms of political economy, America no longer has a monopoly on resources or expertise. But when Eastern Europe focuses on the concurrent development of democratic institutions, America still provides a compelling example. In particular, faced with preparing a new generation for a new politics, Eastern Europe is seeking our educational expertise. The nation that made democratic citizens from the peoples of the earth must, it is supposed, have something to teach the Old World about the process.[1]

We should have the good grace to be faintly embarrassed. Fifty years ago Mortimer Adler doubted that anything could be done about American education; today we are still trying to take the first steps.[2] Once viewed as the benign melting pot of American identity, public schools stand accused by media and government of splintering the population into groups of apathetic or violent illiterates. The public schools' vaunted record of reducing what a contemporary liberal would label the prejudices of racism or religious bigotry is in question.[3] Seen as no longer fulfilling their task of socialization, schools become yet more vulnerable to the charge that they are doing a poor job of basic education. Time studies and comparisons with apparently more successful foreign systems suggest that literacy and numeracy rates in America are low and stagnant, dropout rates are high, and morale is poor.[4] Business leaders and politicians complain that students are inadequately prepared for future employment, a condition that threatens our national survival.[5]

The educational profession responds to such criticisms by accusing the culture of malign neglect. Its members point to a critical paradox: at a time when the political and social support for many urban public schools is so weak, the demands laid on them has never been so extensive. Fighting for decent wages, basic sanitation, security, and educational materials, the teachers and children in many schools, unsurprisingly, adopt a bunker mentality.[6] Educators protest that the good news gets swamped by the bad: innovative programs and remarkable examples of commitment fail to affect the near indifference with which the public treats the teachers of its children.[7]

Educators blame the public and the state, politicians blame the educational establishment, and the children are left in the middle. In such circumstances one response to the East Europeans would be to reassure them that some semblance of a democracy is possible despite, not because of, the education we offer to our citizens. This is, so to speak, the $250 billion question: Does our constitutional regime require a particular substantive educational curriculum, or do broad institutional arrangements that limit overt discrimination suffice? Do we simply need to do a better job on the margins, strengthening vocational training and basic literacy levels, or must we rethink the whole nature of education? To put the question another way: Should the principal focus of education be determined by economic criteria, in particular the need for an adequately prepared work force, or is a radically different emphasis required?

Currently, the political, business, and academic elite largely answer this last question in the negative. In the post–World War II years, when Mortimer Adler could confidently identify American democracy with "the authority of reason," the challenge was to mobilize that philosophy of reason, or logic, on behalf of a substantive model of education for democracy.[8] Philosophical conviction and educational vision were confident partners. But such confidence in a philosophical consensus diminished, and the academy has renegotiated the vision. Take Joseph Schumpeter's modest yet influential definition of *democracy:* "a certain type of institutional arrangement for arriving at political—legislative and administrative—decisions . . . [characterized by] a competitive struggle for the people's vote." Schumpeter's model requires minimal partnership between education and democracy. So long as the electorate could express their most basic preferences in an election, educators would have fulfilled their political obligations to future citizens.[9]

The convergence of a widespread perception of educational malaise with the retreat of a philosophical or moral confidence within the educated elites has produced a distinct situation. On many fundamental issues of educational reform I will detail the substance of a consensus among an influential group of academics and politicians. While disagreements do exist, they are largely confined to traditional arguments over available dollars and to a difference of views about the value of "choice" in education. What unites these thinkers is their focus on efficiency and rationality as the key issues in educational reform. They support slashing the educational bureaucracy, higher teacher incentives, greater parental involvement, tighter standards, and increased business participation. Defense of these measures is partly based on intuition, partly on a plethora of case studies in which various combinations of these factors have unquestionably raised test scores and reduced dropout rates. While the difficulty of agreeing on the content of a national curriculum or the form of national testing might seem to undercut the confidence of reformers, the reverse seems to be the case. Increasingly, opposition to institutional reform smacks of intellectual Luddism.

If there is only modest disagreement among this group over the means toward better education, there is scarcely more concerning the end sought. It is a citizen who will enable America to be more competitive, whose education in the sciences and mathematics will no longer be a source of national embarrassment.[10] The demand is for "literate," drug-free, and disciplined citizens educated in schools that have returned to an emphasis on the "basics." Reformers pay lip service to the need for citizenship education, but the translation of this idea into practical goals occurs in the vocabulary of Wall Street: "To be successful, the new agenda for school reform must be driven by competition and market discipline. . . . Business will have to set the new agenda."[11]

It is not surprising that educational reformers who defend the use of market analogies largely ignore writers with socialist, neo-Marxist, or "postmodernist," sympathies.[12] It is more striking that academics unsympathetic to all of these approaches, including the market model, have been slow to enter the debate; until 1993 Amy Gutmann's *Democratic Education* stood alone as the only extended theoretical counterweight from a "liberal" or "democratic" theorist in the American academy.[13] In such circumstances the academy left advocates of reform centered on efficiency, measurement, output, and testing largely undisturbed. Despite the 1993 transition in Washington, these prescriptions remain the focus of national educational reform.

The appeal of this "efficiency school" has its origins in our present cultural condition. A broad literature has documented the dislocation of community, the breakdown of the nuclear family, and the psychologically isolating impact of contemporary technology.[14] No doubt there is some mythmaking at work in these treatments, but even myths of lost Edens have a seductive appeal.[15] In the writings of the efficiency school one finds a vigorous effort to recover and reenergize a conception of pedagogy with a distinctly Victorian flavor. The note is almost contrite; we have sought too much in the way of nonacademic outcomes from our educational system. We have blamed it for the failures that manifestly have their origins beyond the school wall, in the incapacity of American citizens to preserve their emotional and ethical self-discipline. (Attendance at secondary school, we are reminded, typically occupies but 9 percent of a child's time during those years).[16]

The efficiency school offers a powerful synthesis between pedagogic and moral or cultural concerns. Chester Finn, onetime advisor to Lamar Alexander, President Bush's secretary of education, argues that "we would . . . do well to save some of the beliefs and attitudes about human behavior that characterized an earlier culture. Responsibility is a term too often scorned today." Finn's practical recommendations are interspersed with scoldings about modernity: we must recall "that taut thighs, a nice smile, Monday Night Football, a fax in the den" are no replacement for the "once upon a time" of "tradition, family [and] religious faith." Reformed schools must be "refuges from a tumultuous environment" in which modernity can be made noble again.[17] His desire is to return the school to a purer form, to reemphasize academic training. In a mood at times Foucaultian in nature, the emphasis is on longer school years, lower dropout rates, and constant monitoring through testing.[18]

Perhaps the most striking aspect of Finn's sharply worded work is its tough-minded impatience. His solutions are really quite straightforward—some form of choice, more testing, longer and more school days, and a proper core curriculum. It takes Finn a mere page to outline the reforms, several hundred to point out our Neanderthal reluctance to embrace them. While he claims that debates about the curriculum are "worth having," he does not discuss them; after all, Finn believes that "most Americans strongly affirm those 'traditional values and beliefs about education' that researchers deplore."[19]

The efficiency school interprets "traditional values" as family based. Citing studies that show a linkage between parental involvement and student performance, and (less clearly) between community support networks and academic progress, reformers such as those at Boston University are putting this theory into practice, structuring schools so that they embrace community practice. Schools in Chelsea, near Boston, are implementing programs that emphasize parental involvement, adult education, outreach programs, and links with the local medical and social services networks.[20]

James Coleman, whose research on public and Catholic school performance has been highly influential, is one of the few to pursue these ideas to their full extent. In a largely unnoticed remark Coleman suggested that America faces a stark choice between the reassertion of parental discipline and the greater supervision of its future citizens. Where the discipline of parental authority has crumbled, Coleman argues, the only plausible alternative is boarding school.[21] As is the case with the policymakers he has influenced, Coleman justifies his conclusions on pedagogic grounds: chaos in the home, mirrored in the classroom, does not make for educated citizens.

The second strand of support for these efficiency reform proposals has its origins in a loss of political faith. Widespread resistance to local government spending on education suggests that Americans have diminishing confidence either that fellow citizens share their basic preferences or that the public authorities can forge effective compromises among divergent views. Dissatisfaction with public services, including education, has led to the demand for a closer match between consumer tax payments and how that revenue is spent. In such circumstances it is unsurprising that calls for the reduction of educational bureaucracy and the advocacy of various choice schemes have resurfaced.[22] Only by promising the individual parent a school that mirrors that parent's own preference can the state insure that funds will still be available for the education of the next generation. Granting greater parental control over the design and institutional culture of the school means the reprivatization of public policy.

Curiously enough, therefore, the very discord about social mores contributes to the appeal of the efficiency school. Market-oriented reformers urge the state to withdraw to the role of umpire. The same reformers encourage the schools to secure their futures through direct appeal to consumers. But there is a second dimension to the call for reform. By placing their weight behind public and publicized testing, politicians and reformers are trying to balance the call to localism with a measure of national discipline.[23] By insisting on national accountability, reformers hope to influence local pedagogic practice through the back door.

A program that combines deference to parental authority with the creation of national standards and an expansion of the scope of the classroom thus reflects as much a political as a pedagogic intent. Confronted by an economy that cannot promise advancement for its children, and which drastically limits the time and energy that parents can commit to their children, the reformers' response is predictable. They argue that a school system that can reengage parental allegiance will have to be one that safely houses children for longer hours and more days in activities that can at least be assumed to be unharmful.[24]

The only element of these efficiency reforms which has caused deep division is the call for more choice through a voucher system. Private schools, the argument runs, have outperformed the public institutions not only in cases in which they were favored by more financial resources and indigenous populations but also those in which they have served the same clientele with fewer financial resources than the public schools.[25] If public schools were the object of parental choice, the argument goes, they would be forced into superior performance by the threat of losing their students to a rival school.

Local education authorities would encourage parents to pay their local taxes by assuring them of greater control over the selection of their children's schools. Choice would grant financial relief to religious groups, no longer doubly taxed by the burden of paying for parochial and public schools. Indeed, for all those using secular private schools there would be some form of voucher support or tax concessions.[26] Choice schemes would encourage every parent, no matter what his or her convictions, to become discriminating consumers, with schools competing for their business by advertising social, educational, sporting, and geographical particularities.[27]

The Democratic party and a majority of American teachers and teaching administrators have been opposed to private choice plans. Otherwise, however, they have had remarkably few counterproposals with which to take on the efficiency school. Since this school forged the vocabulary of most reform proposals—"choice," "national testing," "decentralization"—the Democrats are inevitably on the defensive in the debate. Against choice they argue for less of it; against national testing they urge slowness and caution. They join conservatives in celebrating the family, only urging more economic help for the disadvantaged and the marginalized. While choice and testing schemes seductively flatter the sovereignty of parents and appeal to the economic consequences of poor national performance, the Democratic response is caught in a time warp. The stress is on preschool programs, prenatal care, higher teacher pay, more choice within the public school sector, and greater fairness in the distribution of economic resources across district lines.[28]

Unsurprisingly, therefore, the intellectual heritage of the Clinton administration's educational positions is a watered-down copy of the efficiency school's model. Once a participant in President Bush's own blue-ribbon educational reform team, Clinton has insured a large degree of continuity through the selection of Secretary of Education Richard Riley. Like Clinton and Lamar Alexander, Riley was a participant in the National Governors' Association's "Time for Results" education initiative. In common with Clinton and Alexander, Riley is a onetime governor of a southern state, a tough-minded reformer sympathetic to the doctrine of more schooling (including mandatory kindergarten), more accountability, and the establishment of national standards.[29] While the administration is giving deference to doubts about vouchers, its sole innovation to date has been a modest social service plan for those seeking federal dollars for higher education. The efficiency school is in good shape.

The Theory of Reform

What has the response of political theorists been to this barrage of apparently practical common sense about education? Diverse theorists recognize that much of the force of reform proposals comes from their focus on the family—and that the family is not a comfortable target for attack. Theorists who are sympathetic to the teaching of eternal verities have had to face an uncomfortable dilemma: if they follow the reformers who call for expanding choice, they must simultaneously renounce their search for a republic of virtue. Perhaps families will, in perpetuity, choose schools that promote what Thomas Pangle has called "a passionate loving commitment to civic participation in a just political order," or a "reverence for republican tradition"—but surely one cannot rely on such an outcome. After all, as Pangle himself affirms: "Aristotle is correct in insisting that private and familial moral or religious education lacks the authority to sustain itself without direct public reinforcement."[30]

Those theorists who have by contrast focused on the goal of social equality in education are likewise in difficulty. Turning away from a sixty-year tradition that championed the enlightening impact of federal intervention, a number of theorists are rediscovering their private roots. In the thought of John Locke, after all, the privileging of family as the necessary locus of education is legion. By contrast with Hobbes and Filmer, who "give the ruler the power to 'instruct' the ruled, . . . Locke gives education solely to parental power and not to civil government." Certainly, Locke is at pains to distinguish parental authority from political power: the former does not extend to life and death and is by necessity limited by the fact that the child's reason will at some point insure his or her independence.[31] But in the years of childhood it is the home that provides the legitimate source of pedagogic authority.

In recent years concern about segregation and poverty interrupted the otherwise consistent suspicion with which theorists in the Lockean tradition have regarded political intervention in the private sphere. Today such bluntly interventionist political strategies as busing are out of favor, and the family is championed once again. In Stephen Macedo's words, "Families and the particular moral and religious communities with which they identify must remain the places where private people reflect upon and live according to their own best conceptions of what is good in life."[32] While theorists such as Macedo are concerned that families may inculcate intolerance, they are more worried that the public school will undermine belief in anything at all. In these circumstances it is natural that liberals are split on the legitimacy of political claims raised on behalf of religious fundamentalist education.[33]

Liberal theorists acknowledge that American schools have lost their way in an increasingly desperate bid to be all things to all people. Sustaining pluralism depends on treating equally the diverse claims of ethnicity and tradition, which claims are in turn dependent on forms of historically produced exceptionalism and exclusivity. Too strong an insistence on equality of treatment may undermine this fragile dependency. While some regard the destruction of exceptionalism as an example of the force of rationalism, many have their doubts.[34] As Macedo reminds us, liberalism is not just about the "Socratic virtues (critical reflection, insistence on evidence and public reasons)" but equally on "Millian values (the range and depth of choices available . . .).[35] The very value of choice is diminished if students regard the options that remain as interchangeable. In William Galston's words, "The greatest threat to children in modern liberal societies is not that they will believe in something too deeply but that they believe in nothing very deeply at all."[36] It is a fine line, indeed, between teaching mutual respect and inculcating universal apathy, and a large constituency argues that the schools have crossed it. Theorists summon the family to redress the balance.

The writings of many communitarian theorists make the embracing of family yet more attractive. Jean Elshtain has argued that the escape from the family represented a wrong turn: a retreat into the arms of technocracy, surveillance, and dependency on welfare. The tone of Elshtain's remarks is suggestive of a wider frustration with elitist interventionism: "Inside this picture [of dominant liberalism] one is stuck with more and more of what has helped to sicken us in the first place: final rationalization and disenchantment of all aspects of social life; deeper dependency of the self on anti-democratic bureaucracies and social engineering—and now genetic engineering—elites; a more complete stripping away of the last vestiges of . . . traditional identities (construed as irrational and backward), and so on."[37] The celebration of the family dovetails nicely with a renewed interest in granting parents more choice over educational options. Communitarian advocacy of greater choice thus combines a distrust of political micromanagement and a potent reassertion that the family is the critical as well as the natural locus of educational direction.

What, finally, of political theorists whose first allegiance is to the promise of democratic education itself? The vocabulary of democratic theorists was once based on the argument, common to both Joseph Schumpeter and Robert Dahl, that some very limited forms of social training were a necessary supplement to democratic political structures.[38] Dahl, in particular, seemed to affirm that some political education was necessary to sustain American constitutional practices, or "polyarchy," as he termed it. While his language was deliberately descriptive—"polyarchy is a function of consensus. . . . Consensus is . . . a function of the total social training"—one can detect around the edges of Dahl's language a concern that some minimal level of such training is necessary.[39]

The successors of Schumpeter and Dahl have gone one step further, suggesting that a sufficient democratic political education could be provided by the political structures alone. Born into democracy, citizens develop the requisite political skills. It is in this spirit that George Kateb can appeal to the "impersonally educative force of political and legal procedures and processes."[40] Theorists are reluctant to advocate any more direct political education.[41] In a climate of cultural as well as philosophical pluralism, we no longer find proposals of an education for democracy. Rather, there are theories of "democratic education," models that extend the procedures of democratic politics to issues of political authority over education.

The difficulty with such theories is that, while they embrace democratic procedure as a sufficient goal, proceduralism alone underdetermines educational content. Take Schumpeter's definition once again: "That institutional arrangement for arriving at political decisions in which individuals acquire the power to decide by means of a competitive struggle for the people's vote."[42] What education for the people is implied by this procedural definition? Modestly restricting the realm of any theory of democratic education to issues of authority fails to solve the problem. We still need to ask what kind of "struggle" for the people's vote is involved: Must the people understand the issues, see through the rhetoric, appreciate short- as against long-term trade-offs, grasp the complexity of self-interest correctly understood? A different theory of democratic education is implied by different responses, and thus the essential justification for any particular education is absent.

The most compelling recent models of democratic education recognize this difficulty and go beyond the mere translation of process into educational theory. Amy Gutmann, who has articulated the most developed version, offers an extensive guide to thinking about authority and democratic education. Gutmann argues that, since we can agree only that each citizen should have an equal capacity to shape his or her world, democratic education should promote such a capacity, even where parents resist that goal. When she turns to the provision of that capacity, Gutmann argues for a tripartite division between parent, school, and state, arguing that a division of authority can restrict repression and discrimination against a student, while each group can promote its own respective values.

Gutmann offers the goal of "conscious social reproduction" as the "core value of democracy" and thus the litmus test of sound educational politics.[43] Divided as democratic citizens are, there is in Gutmann's view a shared commitment to distribute educational authority that nurtures the capacity of each future citizen to contribute to future policy formation. She seeks to translate this commitment into educational policies. Here Gutmann's recommendations take the following form. First, educational policy must satisfy conditions of nondiscrimination and nonrepression (essentially the liberal component of her theory); second, it must encourage public discussion about the rest (the democratic component).

What is not clear, however, is on what grounds Gutmann selects (or could select) any particular points of transition from constrained to open discussion. In general terms Gutmann's desire to start from minimal, nonmetaphysical premises and to end by avoiding any commitment to a particular curriculum leaves her theory somewhat underdetermined.[44] Take the example of an orthodox Jewish citizen who argues for the right to educate her child, in school and out, in the traditional faith. Gutmann's understanding of "self-conscious social reproduction" rules out such demands. A theory that was supposed to embody the "deepest convictions" of democratic citizens does not endorse this particular desire. Gutmann's explanation is that "the same principle that requires a state to grant adults personal and political freedom also commits it to assuring children an education which makes those freedoms both possible and meaningful in the future." What Gutmann means by "possible" and "meaningful" is suggested by her claim that the state must not allow a religiously committed family to "insulate their children from exposure to ways of life or thinking that conflict with their own."[45]

The implication of Gutmann's remarks is that the political freedom of a devout Jew who has not been exposed to conflicting belief systems is not "possible," let alone meaningful. It would be useful to be able to argue on Gutmann's behalf that democratic debate can determine this contested definition of freedom. But the conception on which she implicitly relies necessarily predetermines the content of what counts as legitimate democratic process. Her policy prescriptions rest on the view that an exposure to alien life-styles is necessary for self-conscious deliberation. Without a defense of such claims, her resulting theory of democratic education will remain fragile. Although theorists might hope otherwise, citizens of the United States do not agree that democracy demands "conscious social reproduction," especially when it conflicts with the transmission of communal or religious values. Moreover, *conscious* is a loaded term; religious fundamentalists are capable of both introspection and social activity, even if they do not choose exposure to every alternative life-style or belief.

Moreover, Gutmann cannot easily maintain her commitment to restricting herself to procedural educational recommendations. Although she consistently declines to suggest to teachers "how rather than whom to teach," Gutmann goes on to argue that our educational system must end up "permitting (indeed obligating) professional educators to develop in children the deliberative capacity to evaluate competing conceptions of good lives and good societies."[46] Even setting aside the thorny issue of what counts as "rational deliberation," Gutmann again assumes that an undiscussed agenda has been resolved. What is the standard of "evaluation"? Is the better life or society the more "democratic"? If the teacher starts from the premise that the democratic is rational, what is left of the freedom to conceive of alternatives?

In sum, Gutmann's antifoundational commitments limit her willingness to identify the core value of democracy, and the result of that difficulty is a paucity of detail on curriculum. For filling in the details of an educational program would reveal a leaning toward a particular understanding of the good in democracy which she is constrained from identifying. Such lacunas handicap a vision of education which must compete in the marketplace of other, often less democratic, visions. The absence of a compelling substantive vision of educational goals cannot help the morale of those educators already combating adverse monetary, professional, and social circumstances.

The second prominent theory of democratic education emerges from Benjamin Barber's writings on democracy and, more recently, on education. Barber argues that we find ourselves "enshrouded in ambivalence, in a world constrained to reject a Thrasymachian ideology of pure interest without being able to achieve Socratic philosophies of pure right." The promise of democratic politics, correctly understood, is that it can cope with this situation (with "the presence of conflict and the absence of private or independent grounds for judgment") because the justification for a democratic decision is that citizens arrive at it through a democratic procedure. In Barber's case this means that every (sane) adult must be an informed and contributing party to any political decision. An involved citizen will learn what needs to be learned about politics. "Direct political participation" is the best democratic education. The process of public involvement which represents the ends of democratic politics is identical to the (educational) means.[47] One may applaud Barber's clarion call for a polity in which the citizen is more involved in the construction of the public agenda. But even in his most recent writings Barber says little about the nuts and bolts of education, its organization, or its testing.

Gutmann's and Barber's work make important contributions. Nevertheless, I am convinced that educators should fundamentally reconsider the project of democratic education from the ground up. Gutmann's democratic theory is heavily concerned with the moments at which education becomes overtly discriminatory in its basic procedures, while Barber's focus is on maximal participation. Neither provides a full alternative to the efficiency view. Neither bloodless proceduralism nor pious hopes for a change of the American psyche will have much impact against a reform movement dominated by populist appeals to choice and educational standards. It will require a wholesale rethinking if democratic theory is going to be heard above the cacophony.

Revisiting the School
Revising the Theory

That rethinking should begin by revisiting the site of education itself and proceed by exploring and recovering the intellectual resources for the reconstruction of a democratic theory of education. While attention to the second task will occupy the remainder of the book, I want to suggest in the balance of this chapter that the messages of reformers and the popular media alike have produced a somewhat distorted picture of education in the mind of theorists and reformers. Reformers have selectively packaged and then oversold the empirical evidence that is supposed to back up their proposals. The following section will make these claims specific through an analysis of the major planks of the efficiency school. The view that children in most public schools lack choice is blinkered, while the argument that their parents' exercise of choice is severely limited is misleading. The celebration of the contemporary American family as the natural source of authority for educational reform is often myopic, based on wishful thinking and contradictory uses of evidence. The data that proves that private schools freed to select their consumers do far better than public schools that cannot is surprisingly weak. Most important, the idea that we are in desperate need of a more literate work force is simplistic. Finally, even in their own terms the sum package of reforms do not make better sense than their constitutive parts. The blending together of family authority, testing, curricular reform, and even limited choice, far from being a powerful synthesis of the best in commonsense thinking, represents a somewhat incoherent package.

To generalize about the educational practice of American schools is a risky but unavoidable task for theorists of educational reform. Within school boards and their roughly eighty-four thousand public schools can be found an almost infinite variety of pedagogic experiments, from high-technology emporiums to prisons, from luxury hotels to communities of John Dewey's remaining disciples.[48] Nevertheless, certain characteristics are common enough to warrant note: the critical one for our purposes is the buffet-style curricula offerings increasingly common in today's schools. As a very recent study put it, "freedom of choice is a ubiquitous characteristic."[49] One example captures the tone: "Dr. Nelson, an experienced guidance counselor, celebrated his school's 'deep, deep commitment and concern that we don't dictate the program to the kid. The kid builds the program around his or her needs.' He emphasized that the catalog's clear commitment was not idle rhetoric. It embodied the democratic ideal at its very best."[50] The course offerings at many high schools are in the hundreds, the possible combinations that make up a single "education" in the thousands. Crisscrossing the plethora of course offerings are tracks and groupings with their own mixtures of constraint and flexibility. For the ambitious "best" and the trouble-making worst there is the least choice: advance placement tracks and remedial warehouses bracket unstructured school offerings for the vast majority. Public Law 94-142 mandates special programs for the disabled, but for the average student there is choice and more choice.[51]

While local economic circumstances can place harsh restrictions on curricula choice, it is clear that, as a whole, educational choice is pervasive in the United States. Those who are calling for more choice in public schools (almost everybody) or between public and private schools are in fact referring not to choices made by students but, rather, by their parents. But this is often a distinction without a difference. Much of the available evidence suggests that, if a parent intervenes in the public school curricula choices of his or her child, that school leans over backward to accommodate through fear of appearing to discriminate. Indeed, schools often operate on the comforting assumption that all parents are choosing, even when they are aware of the contrary. Meanwhile, many parents assume that the school's multifarious course offerings add up to coherent educational packages.[52] The arguments around extending choice must thus implausibly assume that parents who are otherwise content not to intervene in the nitty-gritty of educational programs within a school building would exercise pedagogically astute judgment between alternative school programs and buildings.

It is nevertheless the case that many parents would welcome the chance to exercise more control over the educational choices of their children. At the time of this writing California has just rejected a voucher system, but no doubt other states will continue to wrestle with this issue. The question is whether, as a matter of national policy, giving parents more ways in which to opt out of the public school system is a good idea. This question itself has two components: first, how will parents use such choices? and, second, will the private schools that they patronize with their voucher dollars offer a better education to the nation's children?

The case for returning to the family as the primary source of educational authority is perhaps most vividly put in the following terms. Public schools, administered as they are by entrenched bureaucracies and educational unions, leave many individual parents deeply frustrated. Reformers suspect that such lack of involvement greatly weakens the family structure itself: remove parents from the center of their child's education, and you greatly diminish the moral capital that affords that family its natural justification. Finally, the research data suggests that the disintegration of the family is an influential determinant of the child's educational potential. The result is a vicious circle of social and educational atrophy. Why not turn the circle around? Reintroduce parental authority over the substance of a child's education. This will reinforce parental responsibility, aid in the reaffirmation of the importance of the family structure, and in turn help the child succeed in school.

The issue is not so straightforward. First, the statistics on family views of the public school system indicate low-level contentment, not seething despair. In the vast majority of cases parents are not overly concerned with the academic content of their children's education.[53] Those who argue for choice assume that marketing will insure that parents will become more involved and more discriminating consumers of education on behalf of their children. Freed to choose (or even create) their own schools, parents of both secular and religious inclinations are expected to insist that academic standards be maintained. Schools, on pain of losing parental backing, will compete for future enrollment by doing the best they can with the students they get.

But it is clear that the capacity of parents to absorb such information will depend not only on the unregulated willingness of those schools to provide relevant information but also on the educational background of the parent.[54] Moreover, evidence from existing choice experiments indicates no obvious escape from the correlation between income, education, and parental involvement.[55] The language of choice points to the empowerment of individuals, the calling to account of bureaucracy and teachers. But as the reformers well know, that reempowerment will reflect and flatter the electorate, and its consequences will in turn reflect the contemporary conditions of indifference toward purely academic standards. Fear about violence and concern about ethnic, racial, and religious tensions can go hand in hand with flattery of consumer sovereignty. Parental distrust of outside neighborhoods, ethnic groups, or divergent communities of faith may nicely blend with the force of the market. But the result is as likely to be a resegregation of the next generation as it is an improved education.

The second difficulty with choice-based reform is that the evidence for the damaging consequences of single-parent families, consequences that promote a demand for more schooling, is far more ambiguous than the common wisdom appears to realize. Many studies inadequately control for income effect, and many fail to note that the difference in the child's performance is far smaller in the case of black or poor (often black and poor) families than it is in the case of the white middle class. Moreover, longitudinal studies indicate that the differential between children of two-parent and one-parent families (usually female-headed) households diminishes over time.[56] In any event there is something paradoxical in arguing that the new source of educational authority is to be the family while arguing that the breakdown of the family structure lies behind much of our educational woe. One fails to see how putting more pressure on families to choose the right schools will strengthen them as a source of pedagogic support, unless that tactic is backed up by a comprehensive package of social supports and adult education.

For those who have the inclination and the education to intervene in the schooling of their child, then, there are many options within the public system. For those who do not, adding choices and increasing authority is unlikely to repair torn family fabric or create intense parental interest in the new, "chosen" school. One final argument for choice remains, namely that private schools simply work better. If this were true, then, irrespective of family issues, the case for vouchers would be strong. But once again the survey data is ambiguous. John Chubb and Terry Moe, whose work on this issue has shaped all academic and much of the policy debate, rely on a data set whose findings are open to radically different readings.[57] In that data it was found that private school students of comparable racial and socioeconomic background to their public school peers had between a 0.12 and 0.29 standard deviation in achievement. As Henry Levin records, "longitudinal results based on sophomore to senior changes found even smaller estimated private school effects"—from nothing to 0.10 standard deviation. These differences are so trivial (they amount to a 10-point difference on an SAT [Scholastic Aptitude Test] for which the range is 200–800) as to suggest that educational reform cannot simply rely on the solution of choice.[58] If one is convinced that the test scores measure educational achievement, the real tragedy of American education is not that the public schools dramatically underperform the private schools but, rather, that both types perform almost equally poorly.

One further element of the reform proposals remains: As suggested above, educational policymakers hope to stir national testing of a core curricula into the potpourri of educational reform. As David Kearns admits, there is an immediate tension in the position of those who want to increase choice on the one hand and regulate further on the other.[59] But proposals such as Chester Finn's incorporate a subtle balance between the two competing pressures, a balance that is geared, simultaneously, toward popular support and central control. Finn's suggestion is that we think of education as it will be once reformed as a series of intersecting ovals, in which each oval represents an individual school.[60] The core area of intersection will be secured by the national curriculum and reinforced by national testing. What goes on in the school outside that area is a matter left up to the school itself, and thus the individual family, who will have the option of selecting a different school (or oval) if it prefers that school's offerings. Not all schools, of course, will have to include that area of intersection: Finn has no intention of banning a private school that opts out of the system. But such a school will be cut off from public support.

There is much shrewdness in proposals of this kind, particularly the way in which they deftly walk the tightrope between choice and control. It makes little sense to argue about Finn's scheme in the traditional terms of whether it grants more authority to the "public" or the "private" sphere than the current distribution of authority. Local education authorities will have reduced authority, the nationally mandated curriculum designer will have more. The wealthy will have much the same choices as always. Under some choice schemes religiously committed families will receive more financial backing from the public for their more specialized vision of education in return for opting into a public testing scheme, but they need not so opt. (Is this a more public or less public policy?) Nationwide testing in literacy and mathematics, history and geography, will control school curricula. Thus, Finn's proposals blur traditional public-private distinctions by implying that parents (the private element) will "choose" schools (either public or private) that do better on nationally approved tests (the public element). National standards and national testing will deftly control schools and eliminate those that emphasize unsuccessful "idiosyncratic" programs. The resulting pressure will be toward greater conformity. The public, it is assumed, will have little patience for pedagogic experimentation, or the complexities of quotas if Johnny's test scores are at stake. Rather than forcing citizens together through busing, the intent is to weld them together by allowing them to learn the same thing, only separately.

I have already suggested doubts about the efficacy of family-based educational choices and the celebration of private schools as educational meccas. Does Finn's addition of national testing of a core curriculum turn the sow's ear of choice into a silk purse? We have already touched on the issue of choice: the difficulty with choice schemes is that the economically poor student of average or weak academic ability will be at the mercy of schools of last resort, schools ready to take voucher money for the education of children other schools have rejected. It is unlikely that forcing students at such schools to take more standard tests will improve their education. On the other hand, under at least some choice proposals, parochial schools, which often cater to the poor, will receive additional public funds for the education of their children. To some degree the performance of the better of these schools might rise when they are forced to publicize their results along standard measures. On these terms the combination of choice and testing cuts both ways.

The pedagogic issue of national testing is a staple of debates inside the education profession.[61] American education is awash in testing: what we need to know is what new ideas for yet more testing the efficiency school has in mind. The honest answer is that, so far, they are still in the process of disagreeing.[62] In his proposed "Modern Red Schoolhouse" Chester Finn joins William Bennett in designing a "classical education, time tested and proven."[63] Other reformers critique the traditional tests, calling them "a scandal," and demand European-style tests based on essays.[64] Still others champion various forms of "outcome-based" monitoring, focused on projects, exhibitions, and presentations in which students synthesize particular academic subjects into interconnected packages.[65] Everybody wants accountability, yet few can agree about how our future citizens are to be held accountable.

Professional analysts on both sides of the testing issue tend to remove their discussion from the social and economic contexts that give it substance. Since testing and its accompanying curricula are supported by both political parties and consistent popular majorities, one might wrongly assume that these contextual issues are clear. The critical question that arises about any form of testing is its purpose: What kind of hurdle does a test represent, and what does being able to pass it promise? Answering such questions leads us back to the heart of what was termed above the efficiency view: the conviction that America needs far more workers with high levels of mathematical and scientific literacy to stay competitive and that properly designed tests can help produce the required results.[66]

But the truth about this critical issue is far more opaque. The historical record indicates very little success in predicting the compulsory match between public school performance and future economic needs. Joel Spring, for example, points out that the economic mission reformers give to the public schools tends to change every decade. In the 1950s the concern was over technology, in the 1960s it was poverty, in the 1970s it was unemployment, and in the 1980s it became technology again. Spring argues that there is no evidence to suggest that the reforms associated with these concerns alleviated any of the problems. Instead, the economic prescriptions of one reform movement rapidly became the target of the next as perceptions of economic needs changed. Spring concludes that the only result of tying reform policy to the whim of economic wisdom has been to place the public schools "in a state of flux and chaos."[67]

Current evidence suggests that more recent efforts to teach those making up the future job market are similarly mistargeted and that the accompanying language of praise for "high-tech" preparation is overstated. The U.S. Department of Labor predicts that the American economy will generate 18.1 million jobs between 1988 and 2000. While the computer processing sector will grow, a detailed review of the data suggests that such highly technological employment opportunities will represent relatively small portions of new job creation. The projected 520,000 new jobs in computer and data processing are fewer than those for eating and drinking establishments (1.5 million) and grocery stores (560,000) and only barely outpace new hotel service jobs (410,000).[68] When the figures are broken down by occupation as opposed to industry, the results are equally instructive. The next decade will produce more jobs for retail salespersons, janitors, waiters, secretaries, truck drivers, and cashiers than for computer programers.[69] If the United States needs vast numbers of workers in low-skill jobs, it is not astonishing that the system operates to provide them.[70]

The attention paid to new jobs also tends to distort the picture of the economy as a whole, in which job openings actually depend more on regular turnover than they do on new jobs created. If, for example, during the twelve years covered by the government projections, one fourth of the job force retires (a conservative estimate), thirty million replacement openings will appear. Hence, the lion's share of job prospects for the next decade will remain in purely traditional sectors. Analyzing the trend reported by the Labor Department, Lawrence Mischel and David Frankel conclude that "the jobs of the future will not be markedly different then the jobs available today."[71] They suggest that, while education and skill requirements for the work force may rise, this change will be extremely slow: the median years of schooling rising by only 0.4 years in the next decade. This actually represents a dramatic slowdown in the rate of increase in the 1970s and 1980s.[72]

These job trends would be irrelevant to the argument, however, were it the case that American schools fail to meet even the present market's educational requirements. But this argument also seems

off the mark. As David Paris notes, "Surveys of business have not shown shortages of qualified people for technical and engineering kinds of jobs." Paris goes on to point out that currently 70 percent of jobs require a high school degree or less but that half or more of young people attend college.[73] What effect does this have on the job market? The Congressional Research Service acknowledges that "competition for entry level jobs could lessen and improve the employment prospects of workers with limited education."[74]

In fact, the economic concern for academic improvement is for a specific and remarkably narrow band of the work force: those whose lack of sophisticated mathematical or scientific skills are a drag on national innovation. In the words of Harold Howe, former U.S. commissioner of education, "Economic advancement is the engine that is driving the present school reform movement. . . . School reform is back to the serious business of rescuing our corporations from Japanese competition."[75] For such students testing is an efficient method of identifying talent: educational authorities can then track such students more efficiently into magnet schools or shift them by use of vouchers, parental income, or scholarship to the better private schools.

As for the rest, the evidence that a more regulated traditional core will represent the answer to our economic woes is completely unpersuasive.[76] One might go further: the arguments that connect educational reform to economic necessity are extraordinarily misleading. They enable all parties to focus on goals that are in critical ways out of touch with the conditions of the American economy and to bypass the question of what education might consist of if it were not fixated on myopic assumptions about the job market.

Choice and testing are the twin pillars of Finn's proposals. But there is still a third element—a behavioral ethics—which is implicitly sustained by these two. That vision of ethics is tied to the concern with economic competitiveness but in an understated way. Traditionally, conservative critics of America's educational system have pointed to the breakdown of "ethical values" as the key to the disintegrating standards of educational performance. It is surprising to note, therefore, the relative silence of the current thinking on the issue. A number of explanations are possible: it may be that reformers are uneasy at the prospect of dictating morality at the same time as advocating a model of free choice in education. (Is the market moral as well as efficient? Conservatives may not wish to decide.) Perhaps this is why two leading proponents of choice leave open the question of "racial integration, religion, funding equalization, [and] the educationally disadvantaged."[77]

The most compelling explanation for silence on ethics, however, is that the reformers believe that the ethical program they favor is included in their preferred model of curriculum and testing. Competition between schools, publicity about results, and employment pressures will discipline the American child. Putting it another way, discipline will become the core morality; so long as children are working hard, the rest of their behavior and beliefs are of little interest to the state.

But discipline per se is not a morality. The subject matter of the curriculum will critically affect the ethical nature of any educational program. This is certainly clear to the proponents of a "traditional" core curriculum. What they intend, presumably, is a selection of material and a form of testing which will produce a "good American."[78] By focusing on the efficiency and discipline-enhancing nature of national testing and a national curriculum, the consensus model hopes to bracket, or presuppose the issue of, what exactly being a good American consists of. But the question begging is a little transparent. A conception of education which obfuscates the multiple sources of its own nature by focusing attention on the form rather than the substance of its proposals may be politically shrewd. But in the long run, as policymakers hammer out the nature of the core, the tests, and the contours of choice, they will sorely test the coherency of Finn's synthesis of Allan Bloom's Platonism, business rationality, and Victorian discipline.

Educational Reform Reconsidered

There is no magic bullet to be found in the current bundle of educational reform proposals. Reformers emphasize family responsibility while decrying the collapse of the traditional family, celebrate choice as if our private schools have solved the problem of education, and call for a core curriculum and national testing while pretending that a consensus exists on the content and structure of each. The package has more chance of political than pedagogic success: it blurs distinctions between public and private and speaks to the publicly controlled revitalization of the family sphere. Middle-class frustration and economic red ink are driving national reform efforts. What gets shunted aside is our incapacity as a nation to decide how to educate our future citizens.

Naturally, one committed to the education of these citizens cannot simply ignore the political and economic context that has driven the politics of educational reform to date. Confronting an economic situation that drastically limits the time and energy they can commit to their children, and an education system that does little to reinforce family cohesion, American parents have reacted in several ways— not only by departing from the public system but also in taxpayer revolts against school budgets. This fiscal revolt has been further fueled by the reliance on property taxes which penalize cities, less affluent suburbs, and rural areas.[79] Unless the schools of tomorrow offer safer foster homes for their children, the middle class will further dismantle the traditional public school system.

Second, the economic cost of dropouts, most especially those who dropout inside the schoolroom by muddling through with minimal achievement, is extremely high. The Committee for Economic Development, in a well-known study, estimated that each year's class of dropouts costs the nation more than $240 billion over the lifetime of those students. In part this comes from the loss of those who would have added to the national product, in part from the price to be paid in "crime control, welfare and other social services," to deal with those whose schooling and/or economic prospects did not give them the incentive to prepare for a life of minimal self-management.[80]

Third, the current practices of public education do not fare well against the standard of a commonsense review. Placing a twelve-year-old student in front of several hundred course offerings, or in a class taught in run-down schoolrooms by substitute teachers, is the way the school avoids pedagogic responsibility and political controversy. As a result, child and teacher negotiate ad hoc, minimal-resistance paths through high school and call it a democratic enterprise. Placing the same child in a public or private school that predetermines a single pedagogic route defined along traditional academic lines is little better: perhaps on balance any closed structure produces slightly better tests scores but little more.

It is the combination of these three empirical factors, above all else, which in fact motivates current reforms and shapes their content. Market-oriented reformers are right to criticize our current system of education and shrewd to take advantage of the confusion. Their proposals are tempting to family and corporation alike: a quiet contract between parents and state to supplement, and even replace, a crumbling domestic space with a lengthier school day, a longer school year, and an academic program that incorporates economic reality by allowing children to earn a living while they are at school.[81] The extensive introduction of computer technology into educational settings as well as adherence to a merit system to determine which teachers should be hired and fired, can certainly raise SAT scores.

It would be churlish to reject out of hand the improvements that good management can bring to crumbling schools. Private companies such as Educational Alternatives have delivered hope and better performance to public schools at no increased cost to the taxpayer. Moreover, such organizations remain, ultimately, under the control of the public authorities who hire them, an arrangement that represents a hopeful compromise between the efficiency of the market and the responsibilities of democratic authority.

It is, however, unclear that the majority of current proposals have much to do either with the real conditions of the economy or with equipping our future generations with the characteristics or capacities that underpin a liberal democratic society. David Kearns, once President Bush's undersecretary of education and former CEO of Xerox Corporation, asks: "Who will choose and what will the core consist of? It must be chosen by the wise and the judicious, the penetrating and the discerning, the discriminating and the disciplined."[82] It is at least ironic that a businessman-king summons Plato's ghost to rescue American democracy and the American school. I do not believe that a recipe of boarding schools run by capitalist entrepreneurs, focused on the efficient production of *homo economicus*, represents the answer to our educational problems. But what alternative is being offered? As we have seen, liberal and democratic theorists are strangely silent on the pedagogic crisis in American schools. Faced with the program of the efficiency school, they have continued to agonize about the boundaries between school, state, and families rather than focusing on the substance of the educational curriculum.

Dissatisfaction with the vocabulary of the prevailing reform proposals prompted this book. The promise of a democratic education is both more extensive and more demanding than that represented by granting every parent an unbridled license over the education of their children.[83] The conception of democratic education which I describe is intended for the audience of educational reformers and political theorists alike, to prompt them to raise their aspirations by reminding them of the high promise of democratic politics. The democratic educational ideal voiced earlier, "to honor the individuality of each child," has never been in more need of reinterpretation and support. Rather than trying to find a lowest common denominator on which to build consensus, democratic education should offer citizens a chance to wrestle with the complex and multivarious issues that confront their polity. Opposed to the assumption that the majority are suited best for mindless productivity or a life of politically acquiescent technological contributions, an authentic democratic education implies that schooling provides citizens with the skills to question the basic assumptions of their society. Such a preparation is, of necessity, severe. Rather than chasing a downward spiral toward insuring that citizens are equipped to follow instructions, it points to an ascending set of challenges that assume a high potential to negotiate and shape a considered life.

Few would take issue with such goals, but contemporary reformers have been content to pay lip service to them, treating them as vacuous truisms. A theory for democratic education must give these goals substance. It should not ignore either the importance of contemporary reform proposals or the political conditions that give them appeal. Against the extraordinary (but intellectually flattering) juxtaposition of Plato and market rationality, democratic education can display an intellectual heritage as ancient and perhaps more powerful. Against reformers who want to "take charge," who pine for more productive workers and safer streets, democratic reform will offer an education for citizens in a republic whose productivity is directed toward goals they can interrogate and streets whose environment they can reconstruct.

But one who supports a theory of democratic education cannot simply offer a rival conception and argue point for point with the controlled market view of educational reform or reverse its current monopoly on the interpretation of popular slogans. Rather, one must argue that what is at stake is the nature of the polity itself. A revitalized vocabulary for democratic education is required because the efficiency school draws its strength from a conception of citizenship and politics which citizens should reject on the authority of careful consideration. The particular proposals of administrative reform, of testing and choice, exhibit immediate difficulties. But the weaknesses of those contemporary proposals go beyond their specific parts to the vision of the program as a whole—to its view of society, culture, and the potential of democracy. Those who affirm a democratic political theory must contest this view, defend an alternative conception, and in so doing reassert the legitimacy of their voice in public affairs.

What substantive education does a liberal democratic state owe to its future rulers? Neglecting the tradition of democratic political theory and its debates about the relationship between education and democracy, the liberal and democratic theorists cited earlier have sidestepped or bracketed this question. Making a virtue of philosophical self-effacement, these theorists have sought to avoid questions of curriculum content. They have devised ever more sophisticated strategies for delineating public and private spheres of power, grounded on the counterfactual assumption that the popular consensus comes complete with the basic self-understanding that can suffice as a foundation for education. The result has been a chorus of "thou shalt not"—to the family, the state, the teacher—but very little on "thou shalt."

I fully endorse Gutmann's important plea for a shared social responsibility for a fair distribution of educational resources, for attention to the disadvantaged and concern for the suppression of educational freedoms. But theorists interested in improving American education cannot bracket questions of what will be taught. Silence on this issue has left the field to the celebrants of the market and the eulogizers of the family.

Another approach to reform is possible, and this one on behalf of democratic citizens who, in Protagoras's simple but decisive words, will be the measure of all things. Here I will develop a substantive conception of education befitting sovereign citizens. I envision a day when every citizen will judge among competing conceptions of the polity, about his or her place within it. Without the practice and the vocabulary to engage actively with such questions, the capacity of judgment will wither, and citizens will too often live their lives without critical thought. Much in the culture today mitigates against the development of such capacities, but the task is not an impossible one. The aim of a democratic education may be high, yet it need not be utopian. But the journey of intellectual recovery takes us first to the plain of Argos, twenty-three centuries ago.

2

The Buried Triangle

Democracy, Philosophy, and
Education in Ancient Athens

MUCH OF the contemporary educational reform movement is focused on test scores. At best it offers to spread more statistically satisfying school results to poorer performing institutions. Its proponents are unwilling to ask basic questions about the relationship between education and political theory or about the constitution of an educated democratic citizen. Since such questions seem irrelevant to the task of reform, the efficiency school focuses its energy on improving the techniques of educational management. Although experts disagree about the shape of educational reform, they concur on the product. The delivery system alone, it would appear, is at fault.

Since this book defends a very different approach to educational reform, it must offer an extensive counterargument to this assumption. In the first chapter I pointed to the social milieu of the United States and asked, partly rhetorically, whether reforming the administration of schools would have much impact on the most intractable difficulties, the most enduring disappointments, of the American experiment in education. Nevertheless, a negative response to this question is of limited value unless one has something to put in the place of current reform proposals. All else being equal, there is, after all, no reason to argue against a more efficient administration of educational resources or more parental involvement in schools.

In this chapter I outline the contours of an educated democratic sensibility at a considerable distance from the present thinking. The fact that I recover this sensibility from a reading of ancient Greek sources raises immediate questions: Are arguments from the ancient world relevant for our own age? Can one wrench them from their historical and philosophical contexts without doing violence to their content? Is it possible to reconstruct the "democratic sensibility" of ancient Greece?

It is a commonplace to note that the textual evidence of antiquity is both fragmentary and multifarious. No simple or single view of "ancient Greece," or even "ancient Athens," is secure. Within the two hundred years (fifth and fourth centuries B.C.) from which we draw our evidence, the constitutions, mores, and cultural understandings were extraordinarily dynamic. More pertinent to my investigation, the testimony gathered from funeral orations, grave markers, and public records or from theatrical, forensic, oratorical, and philosophical sources is markedly silent with regard to any political philosophy of democracy. Even as an antithesis to aristocratic political thought, one must reconstruct references to democratic predispositions from the fragmentary evidence or from unrecorded assumptions. "It is curious that in the abundant literature produced in the greatest democracy of Greece," A.H.M. Jones writes, "there occurs no statement of a democratic political theory."[1]

By contrast with the paucity of discussion of democracy in the ancient sources, there is a multitude of material on the subject of education. The pressing concern with the maintenance and sustenance of the polis produced a mass of didactic writing. It may be true that the multiple accidents of loss and survival have determined what we have inherited, but in the available material the Greeks extensively probed the relationships between habit and political constitution, political power and ethical norms, civic responsibility and individual passion. The histories of Greek international relations make clear that the character of the citizen represented a critical concern in policy debates. Sparta and Athens were rivals first and foremost as representative pedagogues of their citizens; the most intractable irreconcilables lay in their educational systems. Thucydides's Pericles called Athens a democracy in a speech in which he tried to teach the citizens of the city what democracy meant while celebrating those who died to defend it. In the process he drew an explicit comparison with Sparta.[2]

The ancient clues to an education fitted to a democratic sensibility are multiple if often problematic. Obviously, my aims in this chapter stand in open opposition to those who argue that present America should ignore the thought of the ancients lest it promote "despotic archaisms."[3] Nevertheless, I believe that we learn little by simply tearing threads out of the tapestry of ancient sources so as to reassemble them by whim or according to contemporary interest. To give one example, I see Protagoras as one who began the construction of a democratic theory of education. But we cannot read Protagoras directly, since almost none of his writings survive. Plato's "Protagoras," our principle source, is not the historical Protagoras, and Plato reshaped certain if not most of Protagoras's positions.[4] Second, Protagoras's allegiance to a democratic form of government is in question. The fact that he probably undertook certain populist reforms in the Antenian colony of Thurii, and that he was almost certainly a confidant of Pericles, can be interpreted as political opportunism.[5] There is no direct evidence that Protagoras intended to construct a theory legitimating democracy. The point of analyzing his thought, nonetheless, is to argue that the coherence of Protagonist principal sayings and activities depends on, and in turn promotes, the development of democratic political structures.

To put the matter in different terms, the hermeneutic approach I adopt rejects the view that one can recover the pure self-understanding of the ancients but resists the temptation to ignore the grammar, vocabulary, or historical context of their work. Richard Rorty suggested that interpretations should be classified as historical reconstruction or rational reconstruction—the former category reserved for philological and historical exegesis, the latter treating the sources as a springboard for contemporary theorizing.[6] I think such a separation is unhelpful: if a contemporary theorist can interpret the words of antiquity in any way whatever, that theorist has emptied that particular source of any independent significance. Conversely, no scholar can obliterate the history through which his or her reconstruction will operate.[7] Hans-Georg Gadamer is particularly convincing when he suggests that both extremes represent intellectual chimeras. It is of critical importance to be aware of the temporal distance within a tradition of thought and to "make conscious the pre-judgments governing our own understanding": "Hermeneutics must start from the position that a person seeking to understand something has a relation to the object that comes into language in the transmitted text and has, or acquires, a connection with the tradition out of which the text speaks. On the other hand, hermeneutical consciousness is aware that it cannot be connected with this object in some self-evident, questioned way, as is the case with the unbroken stream of a tradition."[8]

A contemporary classicist, Nicole Loraux, captures the spirit of Gadamer's position, underscoring her readiness to "deepen the gap that separates Athens from us."[9] Like Loraux, I am convinced that it is the strangeness of Athenian thought and the particularity of its democratic ethos which is precisely the source of its importance to us.[10]

One cannot reconstruct Athens in contemporary America. To assume the transference or immediate use of an Athenian model both trivializes the subject and obscures the value of the investigation. But one can extend the logic of arguments by focusing on the questions they raise for contemporary theory. Through an examination of relevant sources, theorists can recover certain pervasive concerns that link the questions of self-rule to those of education in ancient Greece. In addressing the Greek exploration of these concerns—an exploration that embraces epistemology, geopolitics, pedagogy, and problems of social hierarchy—one can locate rich resources for reevaluating our own conception of democratic education.

Too many political theorists who extol the importance of the Athenians are impatient with the need to balance careful textual scholarship with an awareness of the temporal gap that, as Gadamer indicates, both links and separates us from ancient Greece. Such impatience is evident both in general theoretical terms and in particular examples. Duly noting the reforms of Cleisthenes, Pericles, and Ephialtes, which enabled a wider attendance at the Ekklesia (the assembly) or in the Dikasteria (the jury councils), sympathetic theorists translate attendance into participation, participation into education, and education into a psychological, moral, and political *Aufhebung* in which the warrior-citizen becomes an ideal human being. We are confidently assured that "men become politically and morally changed and educated"[11] and that attendance at the Ekklesia "changed the nature of mass experience . . . to actively listening and judging the merits of complex, competing arguments [*sic*]."[12]

These interpretations may have merit, but the grounds for such sweeping optimism are fragile. Concerning the Ekklesia, such basic facts as attendance, the seating arrangements, and the voting patterns are still the subject of considerable and continuing debate. It is worth noting that the involvement of a wider number of citizens in the "public space" was actually purchased by the state: foreign tributes and the public purse financed Athenian participatory democracy.[13] Moreover, "debate was dominated by a small group of half- or fully professional orators," and neither speakers nor audience contained women.[14] Close scrutiny of the record of Athenian leaders suggests at least that the idealized vision of collective civic education needs tempering. After a detailed analysis of Pericles's funeral oration— an oration often cited as the defining moment of Athenian democratic sensibility—Gregory Vlastos concludes that "the idea of the masses engaged in the actual business of government . . . is suppressed throughout the whole of this speech."[15] In the course of her lengthy treatment of the *epitaphioi*, or funeral oration, Loraux argues that "no passage is devoted to that direct egalitarian exercise of citizenship represented by attendance at the Ekklessia."[16]

More generally, contemporary theorists engage in a form of "reception theory" with little sense of its complexities. To infer that the education and subsequent political and moral development of the Greek audience had a direct and positive relationship to the inherent sophistication of the material that some of them saw and heard is at least problematic. Nevertheless, such inferences form the core of contemporary accounts. Take an example from the treatment of Greek drama, often paired with the Ekklesia as the critical component of a democratic education. In a not unrepresentative argument, Peter Euben claims that Aeschylean drama portrays "reconciliation of diversity, reciprocal sharing of authority and mutuality of decision; recognition, in the sense of acknowledging the legitimacy of another, taking others into account, giving their choice and presence real consideration; judgment, the capacity to see an action, person or event from other points of view and thereby accept the human condition of plurality."[17] For this author the lessons of Greek tragedy offer an "immanent critique" of totalizing theories. It is perfectly legitimate to constitute a theory of justice and then declare its lineage to be Aeschylean. But Euben goes further to assure us that the influence of tragedy at the time was "pervasive" and that it helped to "qualify citizens to participate intelligently" in part by "dramatiz[ing] the necessity of democratic normalization and the need to disrupt the hegemony of such norms in the name of democracy."[18] The point is that we simply do not know what impact Aeschylean drama had on the thirty thousand to forty thousand Athenian citizens who had the opportunity to watch the plays. Guess work is driven not by the evidence but, rather, by a desire to appeal to authority and to read back into history one's hopes for reform.

The charge of unwarranted assumptions applies even more directly to contemporary treatments of the rhetors and Sophists. Commentators too easily transform these early professional teachers, whose livelihood depended on the largesse of a wealthy political elite, into a vital strand in a seamless web that links education to democracy, insuring "the continuity between public and private spheres."[19] I am sympathetic to the view that the Sophists and, in particular, Protagoras "produced for the first time in human history a theoretical basis for participatory democracy," though he might well have been surprised by the thought.[20] Far more dubious is the proposition that they promoted "complex processes and subtle currents of judgments which go to the making of the collective mind."[21]

It is sobering, in view of such persistent judgments, to recall that we have almost no direct source material of pre-Aristotelian rhetorical or sophistic reasoning and that the reported views of the Sophists were anything but sanguine about the wisdom of the demos.[22] In Plato's rendition, at least, the rhetor Gorgias is openly scornful of the Athenian citizen's hubristic presumptions about his ability to understand and judge political rhetoric (*Gorgias*, 464d). Gorgias's advertisement for his craft promises a very enigmatic form of democratic education, one that "brings freedom to mankind" only by bringing people "dominion over others" (452d.) The teacher of political rhetoric is an instructor in political mastery. If the Sophists' teachings can inform us about democratic education, it is not because the Sophists thought of themselves as directly educating the demos but, instead, because their insights present a challenge and resource to our own democratic sensibility.

My concern is that such commentators as Euben and Jarratt are overanxious to prove the contemporary relevance of ancient practice. As a result, the legacy of Greece becomes oversimplified, packaged as an invitation to communitarianism, to critical theory, or to a post-modernist pedagogical critique. The following treatment proceeds from a different set of hypotheses or prejudgments. My intention is to examine elements of Greek thought and history which illuminate the relationship between education, democracy, and philosophy. In this view Athenian discussions of *autonomia*, or self-rule, are remote from our present political and pedagogic debate; it is this very remoteness that makes them instructive for our time. We are, as Foucault ambiguously reminds us, "much less Greek than we believe."[23] This is the reason the ancient Greeks can teach us something about education.

Rereading the Sophists

The effort to recover a conception of democratic education finds a natural starting point in the consideration of the so-called Great Speech in Plato's dialogue the *Protagoras*. In that oration the Sophist Protagoras poses a critical question: "Is there not some one quality of which all the citizens must be partakers if there is to be a city at all?" (*Protagoras*, 324d). In the passage immediately following, Protagoras makes it clear that there is such a thing (or things) and that education must provide it (or them). The failure to learn "justice, and self-control and piety and, in a word, human virtue" can justly lead to punishment, exile or death (325ab). Protagoras here argues that there is an inescapable link between political survival, the universal mastery of certain social and intellectual habits, and the education that will inculcate the citizens of the polis with those habits. He suggests, in short, that education and politics are inseparably linked.

In the text that follows these introductory claims, Plato's Protagoras denies that the mastery of technical know-how (carpentry, pottery, and ironmongery are his examples) exhausts the educational agenda. Rather, he outlines the alternative program that, in his view, Athens employs to inculcate the sense of justice or virtue it requires of its citizens. That education concentrates on inducing correct "behavior" (325e) defined by the accepted social norms among those who have "the good qualities that men acquire by deliberate choice" (323d). The use of the plural *qualities* forces Protagoras to grapple with the thorny issue of the singularity or multiplicity of the politically vital virtue or virtues for which education is required. In response to Socrates's questions Protagoras confirms that in his view justice plus a sense of shame and holiness are all parts of the excellence he regards as the acme of Athenian pedagogy. In responding in this way, Protagoras makes clear that education and ethics are necessarily linked.

Having discussed the qualities of character which insure the survival of a polis, and having defined their broad outline, Protagoras must also justify his own role in the Athenian scheme of education he has just defended. He has to advance his claim (and those of his fellow Sophists) to offer special advice to the Athenian polis.[24] He has to make his insight into the processes of education consistent with his argument that anyone in Athens can be a teacher of virtue (*Protagoras,* 323a). If virtue is the habit to be taught, it stands to reason that the most virtuous will represent a source of instruction to the rest. "If there is anyone of us who is even a little better than others at helping men to attain [excellence] so much the better. I claim to be one such man" (328b). Protagoras implies that someone like himself who has analyzed the role of virtue in education will be useful in insuring that everybody else, as they teach their children and one another, has a standard against which to measure their success. He must square such an argument, however, with the democratic political structure of Athens. Must a democratic political society assume that all citizens are capable of mastering the minimally necessary virtues, or does it determine that capability during the educational process, thus producing a virtuous elite? Is that virtue a habit that the citizens can teach one another or, as Protagoras appears to suggest later, a knowledge that is "the preserve of the educated and talented few" such as himself?[25] In answering these questions, Protagoras is forced to clarify the link between politics, philosophy, and ethics.

Protagoras's Great Speech hints at a particular relationship between education, democracy, and philosophy. More fully analyzed, his is an argument for the necessary links of that triadic relationship: his understanding of and teaching about each of the triads depends on holding secure assumptions about the other two. Protagoras's triad depends, furthermore, on a precise delineation of each of its elements. Protagoras's claim is not merely about the interconnectedness of education, government, and principles. Rather, his speech implies a particular account of education, politics, and philosophy. That content, however, does not emerge instantly from the Great Speech—far from it. Protagoras's position is uncertain and incomplete. In particular, the ambiguities of the *Protagoras* rest upon its relative silence on philosophical, and especially epistimological, issues. To remove these lacunas will necessitate the consideration of other textual sources.

The difficulties with Protagoras's position are numerous. As we have seen, Plato's Protagoras claims that a certain set of abilities among the citizenry are the prerequisite of any political society.[26] But the text leaves ambiguous the question of what portion of these abilities are innate to human beings and what portion subject to education. Protagoras claims that, as a gift of Zeus, all men are endowed with an innate ability to learn basic justice, to experience shame (*dike* and *aidos*), and even to have "in common" "political excellence" (*Protagoras,* 323a.) But Protagoras subsequently lists a sense of justice among those qualities that every citizen must acquire through education. This indicates an ambiguity in Protagoras's account. It is unclear whether Zeus insured that citizens are innately just or that they can learn about justice on the basis of some other capacity.[27]

A second difficulty emerges about the role of Zeus in the myth. He bestows his universal gift—whatever it is—after that of technical competence, which Prometheus gives to men in unequal proportion. The problem is to understand how man could be unequally adept at technical matters, which include the mastery of language and communication (*Protagoras,* 322a), but be equally equipped for the skills of citizenship, or self-rule, that most demanding of tasks. Moreover, if one assumes that all citizens are capable of learning the skills of political involvement by teaching one another, as the text implies, then the Sophist would have no role to play in educating the polis.

Given these difficulties, it is clear that Plato has shaped Protagoras's Great Speech for self-destruction. In particular, the Platonic reconstruction undermines the coherence of the Sophist's activity in a democratic polis. Protagoras will be forced to make a distinction between activities that depend on levels of competency (like ship building), on the one hand, and the activity of politics—which involves wisdom—on the other.[28] The Sophist will then be unable to define that wisdom and thus, by obvious inference, will be incapable of teaching it. Cynthia Farrar tries to rescue Protagoras from the trap: "In the democratic polis . . . the most skilled and virtuous citizens teach everyone, via interaction in the assembly and on the council, and as a result everyone achieves the competence associated with the son of the craftsman, and *all* those who are naturally gifted, not merely sons of the gifted, achieve excellence. Thus Protagoras suggests . . . that the political realm unlike the technical or social is a realm of universal competence and equal opportunity to achieve excellence."[29] In Farrar's reconstruction, the "true" Protagoras would have had nothing to do with the distinction between technical know-how and objects of "true" knowledge. Whether the subject matter is politics or flute playing, there are simply different levels of expertise: in an Athenian democracy education prepares every citizen to be competent at politics and enables the gifted to achieve excellence.

The devil, unfortunately, is still in the details. Leaving aside for the moment the (implied) association between wealthy and gifted, we are still left with the critical problem of what it is that Protagoras teaches. While he argues that the acquisition of a sense of justice and shame is either a prerequisite of, or an educational achievement common to, all Athenian citizens, Protagoras offers himself as an expert in becoming "noble and excellent" (*kalos k'agathos*) (*Protagoras,* 328b). It follows that, when Protagoras argues of "justice and political excellence" (323a) that "all men have it in common" and goes on to remark "that they consider it to be a teachable thing," he is both ambiguous about its status and is not talking of his own form of instruction in "excellence," since he largely restricts that instruction to an elite.[30]

If, however, the teachings of Protagoras (whatever they are) are distinguishable by their nobility and excellence from the education required for the political participation of the average citizen, then the question arises about why those who have benefited from Protagorian expertise should submit to the will of the assembly. In Colby's words: "The sophistic teaching of the political art delegitimates democratic government. For no longer may the citizens of Athens distinguish between technical and policy questions. If Sophistry is truly an art of virtue teachable to others, then virtue is itself an art, *aretē* is *technē*, and all policy question are technical."[31] In Colby's view Plato's Protagoras has admitted that in questions of technical expertise the polis consults the experts. If political wisdom is another *technē*, then Athens should consult only the Protagorian experts. This is a critical point, for, if accurate, it would undermine Protagoras's position as the educator of an elite within a democratic Athens. An educational theory that makes Protagoras's views consistent with democratic practice will have to show why the common citizens have a veto over public policy, despite their lack of high expertise, and suggest why experts should accept this veto, even on highly technical policy issues.

The text, in short, presents us with two uncertainties that even Farrar's generous reconstruction leaves unresolved. First, Protagoras seems to suggest four sources of education, innate (as in Zeus's gift), social (the Athenians teaching one another), formal (the education the rich provide for their sons), and his own (the Sophist's education of the rich orators).[32] The first two of these instructions appear to overlap, and the relationship among all four is vague. Second, Protagoras leaves the content and status of his own teachings unspecified and undefended: we are given no sense of the manner in which the Sophist will better the life of the Athenian polis.

One could offer a political history to explain, though not to justify, Protagoras's ambiguities and silences. It would be the familiar account of the aristocratic rivalries which led in complicated ways to the extension of participatory rights to a wider body of the Athenian citizenry. Indeed, the teachings of Sophists such as Protagoras would have been redundant but for such political reforms, which in turn produced a demand for the mastery of the rhetorical skills of political persuasion.[33] Thus, one way of characterizing Protagoras's pedagogics is to view them as a gift of rhetorical effectiveness to those desirous of political influence. In this interpretation the Sophists teach their students to short-circuit democratic constraints for which there is in any case no extrapolitical, philosophical justification.

In such an interpretation Protagoras's myth, with its assertion of universal political competency, would flatter only to deceive. While encouraging the belief by the many that democratic politics was a value in itself, the Sophist would instruct his pupils to pay lip service to that democratic faith while bending it to their own particular wills. The many methods through which the rhetors shaped their political and forensic speeches for mass approval, and their complex tactics of affirmation and self-abnegation, would then be the Sophists' way to help maintain elite control.[34]

Plausible as it first appears, such a political-historical explanation of the Sophists' tactics has to overcome two insurmountable difficulties. First, it still leaves Protagoras's own role in a democratic politics inconsistent, dependent as that role is on the idea that the polis will grant the citizens political power despite the fact that expert management—of the kind the Sophists were intent on educating and promoting—was available. Democratic politics, in this sense, would stand revealed as a form of political compromise with common sense. In response, one could cite Protagoras's direct description of the citizen body, a cattle like body who "don't really notice anything, but just repeat whatever their rulers tell them" (*Protagoras*, 317a). But highlighting these moments still leaves Protagoras's Great Speech problematic. His dismissive view of the common citizen's capacities (reiterated at 353a) is less than consistent with Protagoras's assertion elsewhere that the masses have the requisite competence to judge political affairs.[35]

Second, the purely political account of Protagoras's teachings ignores his concern with knowledge and ethics, a concern much discussed in Plato's *Theaetetus*. The obvious rejoinder is that in the *Protagoras* itself there is little overt statement of a connection between the pedagogic message and these more theoretical issues. As one commentator puts it, "it is a perfectly plausible historical hypothesis that Protagoras did not in fact attempt any close integration of his popular teaching with his epistemological and ethical theory."[36] But this line of defense too is shaky. A famed teacher and epistemologist such as Protagoras would have been unlikely to separate the two concerns; thus, the fact that Plato forces him to link them in the *Protagoras* is scarcely illegitimate.[37] And force him he does: already at 329b–30b Socrates has led Protagoras to a discussion of the relationship between knowledge and justice, and at 334ac Protagoras must address directly the question of the nature of the good and the related question of what is good for man.[38] Even if only to deny the force of Socratic metaphysics, Protagoras must gesture toward his own epistemological position. At such moments he can no longer separate politics from philosophy.

Certainly, the fact that Plato leads his Protagoras into such territory does not prove that issues of teaching and epistemology were unavoidably related for Protagoras himself. But two points should be stressed. First, as we shall see, the historical Protagoras makes a claim—and a famous one—about epistemology, a claim that has strongly democratic implications. Second, one cannot adequately address even those assertions made directly by the Sophist in the *Protagoras* without confronting both education and philosophy. As we have seen, when Protagoras describes his own role as "better at advancing people along the path to excellence," of helping them become "noble and excellent," he is referring to something more than the inculcation of the basic habits necessary for the survival of any political community (*Protagoras,* 328ab). Earlier in the dialogue Protagoras speaks of teaching the citizen "good planning both of his own affairs, to the end that he would best manage his personal estate, and of the city's, to the end that he would be in the strongest position to conduct, in speech and action, the common business of the city" (318e). Now these phrases are at least ambiguous: Does Protagoras mean to equate excellence only with the achievement of individual power or with a power citizens will gain and use to the benefit of the polis? But if the latter, then we need to know in what, beyond mere political survival, that benefit lies, and how we are to measure it.[39]

In the absence of a political context within which their education could operate, Protagoras and his fellow Sophists would have lacked employment. They instructed a wealthy few in the skills required to hold power in a democratic political context that was both potentially and frequently actively hostile to the aristocracy. To have taught disdain for democratic norms would have been politically suicidal, as the Socratic exemplar dramatically indicated. But in asking for tolerance of its leadership, the elite had also to argue that its advice was of actual benefit to the city, that it saw its own excellence as indistinguishable from the caliber of its civic service. This is why it needed to offer a criterion for the identification of political betterment, for the meaning of progress. Moreover, Protagoras has to defend a political position that, as we will see, gave no overt support for the political sovereignty of an intellectual elite.

In such circumstances the strongest defense for the Sophist's education of the Athenian elite would be that it fused together the epistemology that Protagoras espoused and the democratic politics he claimed to serve. To put it another way, the teaching about education in the *Protagoras* would need to be reconciled with the philosophical arguments attributed to Protagoras in the *Theaetetus.* Such a reconciliation would have to indicate why Protagoras can speak of a sense of justice as both a precondition for political life and a subject for political education and make clear the justification for his own further educational contribution. In short, the two texts, when taken together, must resolve those questions the *Protagoras* alone posed but left unresolved. It is to such a resolution that we now turn.

As the *Protagoras* is haunted by the specter of philosphical argument, so the *Theaetetus,* overtly about philosophy, is filled with educational implications. Myles Burnyeat highlights the connection between the two themes and, in so doing, introduces Protagoras's most famous epistemological claim. "Protagoras, in the mouth of Socrates, undertakes to show that expertise can exist, and the activities of experts can be described, compatibly with the relativism of the doctrine that man is the measure of all things." Burnyeat continues:

> According to the Measure Doctrine, whatever we think or feel is true for each of us; so the state of mind which results from the expert's ministrations is not truer than our previous state of mind. But it is *better* (*Theaetetus* 167ab). . . . The meaning of better is disputed . . . most in accordance with the state of mind of a healthy subject or that which most agrees with the perception and thought of one's fellows, or that which is advantageous to the organism, or that which will seem better in the future.[40]

Notice that in each variant "there is a thing-quality (A is B) and a frame of reference that constitutes a 'measure' (A is B for C)."[41] The difficulty is to identify C and thus to uncover the reference measure that Protagoras intended. In the *Theaetetus* Protagoras proclaims "I call wise . . . the man who in any case where bad things both appear and are for one of us, makes a change and makes good things appear and be for him." (*Theaetetus,* 166d). Burnyeat offers the two most plausible readings. In the first, "better things appear and are for someone" means the same as "things appear and are better for him." In other words, things are better (and only are better) for the person who thinks so if and only if he considers them to be so. The first reading is illustrated in Plato's discussion of the doctor who makes the food of a cured patient taste sweet rather than bitter. (166e–67a). But there is a second reading, namely, that the expert or teacher is successful when the things that appear to me "are in fact better, regardless of whether they seem so to the person whose mind the expert changes." Now this reading also finds textual support, in the example of the politician, in which the "claim is not that the new conventions seem better but that better things seem just."[42]

These two readings echo the critical ambiguity in Protagoras's educational project. In the *Protagoras* what the Sophist promises to his students varies. In certain passages, as we have seen, the Sophist claims to instruct pupils to be successful in private and public affairs (318a, 318d–19a). But we find elsewhere the suggestion that what counts is whether the student regards himself as better off for the lessons received (316c, 328bc). Putting the two texts together with their two possible interpretations produces a choice of substantive interpretations: in the first what Protagoras achieves in his teaching is the wisdom "to change men so that the result seems good to them"; in the second he persuades the student to learn what is in fact the better course of action.[43]

The difficulty with accepting the first interpretation follows from the political nature of the sophistic education. One can plausibly argue that simply making the pupil believe that he felt better would be insufficient. In the words of one commentator, "that claim must be tested by actual results, the acquisition of wealth, position, etc."[44] But this is too quick. The successfully educated politician will measure that success by the degree to which he persuades others to grant him power, that is, to the extent to which his words suggest an interpretation of events which "seem" (and therefore are) satisfactory to them. In other words, it is possible to interpret Protagorian education as if it achieves what the doctor manages in the *Theaetetus* (166e–67a).[45]

The difficulty with the second interpretation is that it leaves Protagoras with the task of defending an objective measurement for "better"—a task for which he obviously has the greatest distaste. Indeed, the weakness of his position is most vividly marked in the *Protagoras* when he must concede the necessity of a standard of measurement independent of individual perception (356bc). But perhaps one can circumvent this difficulty also. As we have noted of the *Protagoras*, the argument of the Great Speech is that it is the individual habits of virtue, which are the product of education, which make possible communal life. In other words, the standard of measure is that of political viability, the strengthening of "order" and "common bonds of amity" (322c). It is better to have citizens persuaded of the legitimacy of a common sense of justice and shame since discord on such matters would undermine the possibility of political survival itself.[46]

The fact that one can construct a defense for both interpretations of the sophistic education suggests that one plausible interpretive solution is to regard them as complementary. Detailed scholarship on the grammar of Protagoras's measure doctrine lends further support to such a resolution.[47] What the Sophist does is to persuade people freely to accept as their preferred understanding of political insight what has proved itself to the perspicacious speaker to be politically better in the past.[48] More broadly, a reconstruction of the Sophist's educating role ties epistemology and democratic functionality together in the following way: each man is convinced that his own chosen convictions are the only convictions that are persuasive to him. But for the sake of political survival he must live in harmony with others whose convictions have the same force for them. Citizens with substantially clashing convictions will, if committed to those convictions, destroy the conditions of their citizenship. Thus, each citizen has an interest in being persuaded to embrace a set of convictions which he can choose, affirm, and hold in common with other citizens. But what sets of convictions are these? Those that permit him to accept a certain standard of justice and develop a degree of shame in the cases of his own transgressions against that standard. And why is this? Because a sense of justice means a readiness to conform to those public laws that insure the harmony of collective beliefs on behalf of communal survival and because a sense of shame will encourage such conformity. To the extent that the Sophists can further this set of social goals through their education their expertise will have merited a degree of democratic legitimacy. Or to put it in language now familiar, the Sophist's role is to generate a collective practice of affirming as better for each what the assembly judges to be better for all.

Such a reconstruction is, at this stage, quite abstract. It leaves open the question of the particular way in which the Sophist's education of a political elite prepares those individuals for the role of persuading other citizens of the better course of action. But even at this initial stage we can sense the triple nature of that educational enterprise. First, the politician will have to evoke and then appeal to the collective experience of his audience, to their preconceived understanding of their own history and the lessons it provides for contemporary problems. In a democracy in which every citizen is an equal measure there can be no other legitimate standard. As Farrar correctly argues, "The sophist or politician can only proceed from what the student or assembled *polis* know, believe and are. . . ."[49] Protagoras's assumption that the polis can assume a universal capacity for political participation suggests that the people of any political body must be collectively capable of maintaining a conception of themselves over time which could be the subject of such an appeal by their politicians. To the extent that such conceptions are multi-faceted, the politician will have to engage in a complex rhetorical effort to select, integrate, and privilege a particular perspective or narrative reconstruction. What he will appeal to is a particular interpretation of the men who will measure. He will have to make men self-conscious about the terms, the limits, the extent of their self-conceptions, so as to argue that those conceptions are best furthered by accepting his proposals. In short, he will attempt to educate his judges.

The second component is more difficult to conceptualize. The politician or rhetor who is going to remain powerful in public affairs must persuade citizens that his own message is indeed intended to present them with a self-understanding in which they have reason to have confidence. Now, in part, this second aspect of political practice is connected to the first: those whose rhetorical narratives utterly fail to connect with the preconceived understandings of the citizens will provoke suspicion. The procedures of the assembly require the citizens to judge not only the message but also the messengers. As Thucydides's accounts of the Mytilenean debates graphically suggest, rival members of the elite may conceptualize the same historical experience in ways that produce opposed policy recommendations. A common way in which to sway the audience toward accepting one's own version is to cast aspersions on the integrity of the opposing speaker.[50]

It was inevitable, therefore, that the citizens would constantly have to judge the ethical integrity of the politician. Just as he appeals to their collective desire for social survival and civic harmony, so they ask if his own intentions are communally motivated. He offers words to the polis as an interpretation of its better desires. In Athens the stakes were appropriately high: if the assembly was persuaded that their politicians had misrepresented the public law or interest or had sought private advantage in the guise of public-minded rhetoric, it could take them to court (through the *Graphe Paranomon*) or have them ostracized from the city.[51] Indeed, one of the features that most distinguished Athenian politics from any other Greek city-state was the constant suspicion of rhetoric and its effects.

Underlying these two broad themes there remains a third and perhaps most critical issue, that of the conception of improvement, or betterment, itself. In Protagoras's Great Speech the capacity of a community to teach itself the skills of civic survival are presupposed. In this context, to argue that the elite is concerned only with the brute existence of the polis makes no sense.[52] Embedded in the first two goals of a Protagorian education, it should be possible to identify a normative content, a pointer toward the qualitative improvement of public life. The certification of such improvement would have to be consistent with the claim that "man is the measure of all things" and that a highly educated elite has a role to play in the search for a finer polis. As we will see, it is in the fusion between making citizens self-conscious about the nature of "measure" and an elite's practice of a rhetoric capable of measuring its own claims that democratic education finds a place for the Sophists' teachings and justifies itself in democratic terms. Put another way, the Sophists' commitment to the functionality of the "measure doctrine" justifies, rather than undermines, his profession.

The Polis as Measure

What is presupposed by Protagoras's bold suggestion that a collective sense of justice is itself the necessary presupposition of political life? One familiar way of approaching the question is to suggest that the commitment to justice represents a partial transfer of allegiance from the private to the public arena. Such a transfer itself depends on the delineation, the identification, and finally the celebration of that public space whose "betterment" will in turn provide the standard of measurement when citizens must make public choices. Man remains the measure of all things, but in the realm of political judgment the self to which measure is returned for judgment is the civic self, its identity established by the contours of the polis. This transformation of the measuring rod is well captured in Socrates's argument "on behalf" of Protagoras: "for whatever things seem noble and just *to any particular city* are so for that city, as long as it thinks them so" (*Theaetetus,* 167c; emphasis added).

Classical scholarship reinforces the view that multifarious features of Athenian custom aimed at achieving such a transformation. Such customs encouraged the embracing of a civic identity by means of public ceremonials, which saturated the citizen with an awareness of the particular topography of Athenian civic space. Two examples will indicate what I am suggesting; the first is the *epitaphios,* or funeral oration, and second the evidence from Greek drama.

In Greek history, Homeric song had indelibly fused the praise of aristocratic courage displayed in deadly *agon* (the contest of war) to the life of *aretē* and *dikē*.[53] The challenge facing Athens of the later fifth and fourth centuries was to transform the conception of death, suffused with what had been aristocratic values, into a public, democratic, and civic celebration. In other words, the polis would have to teach men who had once died for themselves how to die for the polis. In her exhaustive treatment of the issue Nicole Loraux has detailed the subtlety through which the ceremonies of public burial and funeral oration served such a goal. As she suggests, these ceremonies "have a composite character" that evokes civic history, geography, and ethical acumen so as to glorify the dead and identify their sacrifice with the polis.[54]

Running as a unifying thread through such reconstructions is the pervasive concern to balance the ancient aristocratic conception of death with the demands of a democratic polis. This balancing act within the civic celebration of death is evident in every facet of the archaeological and textual records. In ancient Athens the path from the agora to the academy passed directly through the burial grounds, or *Kerameikos*. *Stelae*, or stones, which recorded tribe by tribe the names of the fallen citizens, lined the route. In such practices Loraux identifies "the democratic wish not to make distinctions among citizens buried in the *demosion sema* (public grave) whom the *epitaphioi* designate only as *hoi enthade keimenoi* (those who rest here).[55]

The democratic structures of burial found their counterpart in aspects of the Greek funeral oration, the *epitaphios*. As a rule, the orations reiterate the teaching that there could be no life beyond that generated by the polis: glory was due to those who chose freely to affirm that belief through the gift of their lives. It is in this context that Pericles asserted that glory "is to be attached more to the decision than to act of the dead."[56] In this way the *epitaphios* marks out the polis as the legitimating measure for the exercise of individual courage and the celebration of a worthy death. But in addition it integrates the occasion of civic sacrifice with a recasting of Athenian history. The immediacy of individual death is reconstituted as a narrative that conceives of "Athenian history between the fragmented time of battle and the paradigmatic timelessness of the citizen's valor."[57] The living and the dead are reunited in a civic myth of communal unity and timeless glory.

What is curious about these mythic constructions, however, is their relative silence about the democratic structures of the Athenian polis. What Gregory Vlastos remarks about the Periclean oration in *The Peloponnesian War* can be extended to the *epitaphios* genre as a whole: "the idea of the masses engaged in the actual business of government . . . is suppressed throughout the whole of this speech."[58] Through close textual analysis Vlastos reveals that the object of Pericles's oration is in fact a double audience—an audience that reflects the distinction between the *pleiones,* or the majority, and those capable of *epimelia,* an engaged concern with the affairs of the polis. Crawley's translation captures the spirit: "Our public men have, besides politics, their private affairs to attend to, and our ordinary citizens, though occupied with the pursuits of industry, are still fair judges of public matters."[59] As in Plato's *Protagoras,* the critical feature of Athenian democracy is the relation between politics and judgment; the central tension is between those who serve to offer up their version of political wisdom—the rhetors or politicians—and the many who will serve to measure the quality of that wisdom.

In an earlier moment of the Periclean oration Thucydides had already suggested the precarious nature of this relationship. There Pericles contrasts the formal egalitarianism of the law with the unequal consequences of individual judgment. In Vlastos's gloss: "To be sure, our constitution, being government for the people, is called 'democracy'; but while on the one hand we have equality in litigation, yet on the other hand each is preferred according to our esteem for him, not so much for his class as for his excellence."[60] Many contemporary commentators regard this passage as deeply antidemocratic in spirit.[61] But if our earlier readings of the *Protagoras* and the *Theaetetus* have merit, Thucydides's Pericles is accurately reflecting and reinforcing the complex messages of democratic education in Athens. The judgment of the many is indeed focused on the excellence of those to whom the public gives its ear and in response to whom the public will frame its judgments. The funeral oration retells the greatness of Athens through the celebration of its most devoted citizens, those fallen in battle on its behalf. The oration fuses the dead into the civic space, and into the ongoing story of civic history, reshaping the common vocabulary that offers itself up anew for the consideration of its citizens. In celebrating their dead, the citizens of Athens measured the limits of their polis and its worth.

It was left to the orator's skill to create these required conditions of civic renewal and self-judgment. The many listened as Pericles represented to them an idealized sense of their worth and offered them a vocabulary of collective self-measurement which would justify the individual effort to judge well in the assembly. The *epitaphios* of Gorgias, though available to us only thirdhand, suggests the vocabulary involved: "These men attained an excellence which is divine and a mortality which is human . . . believing that the most godlike and universal law was this: in time of duty dutifully to speak and to leave unspoken, to act <and to leave undone>, cultivating two qualities especially judgment <and strength>, one for deliberating, the other for accomplishing, giving help to those unjustly afflicted and punishment to those unjustly flourishing."[62] Gorgias invokes a vocabulary of measurement in which aristocratic strength blends with judgment, action is tempered by speech, and justice trims the mighty while supporting the weak. In other words, he reaffirms, at the moment in which the polis acknowledges the cost in lives of its survival, the qualities without which it could not celebrate those lives. As in the case of the other *epitaphioi*, Gorgias is silent about the democratic constitutional structures of Athens. The explanation, however, is not that the speech concealed antidemocratic sentiment but, rather, that its purpose was somewhat different: the articulation of the ethical preconditions for those political structures in just the way that Protagoras had done in the Great Speech.

One further point concerns the funeral orators themselves. As the interpreters of Athenian identity, they were not only being judged by the measure of their audience but also by their own. As Lysias acknowledges, his speech would "compete" with "the orators who have celebrated them [the dead] before [him]."[63] Through the repetition and variation of the traditional topoi of the *epitaphioi* (*topoi* of civic celebration), the orators allowed the citizens to judge their speeches against the rhetorical histories that the orators themselves renewed. The *epitaphioi* concern a measurement critical to civic identity, the worth of its citizens in the hour of their death, and the valuation of the limits of individual life in terms of its contribution to the history of the polis. Implicitly, the ceremony permits the citizens to assess the polis in terms of its most extravagant claim, that it is the measure of all things, even of individual lives. That claim, in turn, is measured by the polis, in the audience gathered to judge both itself and its orator historians as those who will preserve and define Athenian identity for the future.

The *epitaphioi* thus make up an important component in the reconstruction of Athenian education. But they represented, of course, only a single strand of that education: legal practice, religious custom, social behavior, sexual mores, and drama, with their multiple moments of intersection, would also prove fruitful grounds for the identification of sources of Athenian self-measurement. A full discussion of these topics clearly lies beyond the scope of the present study. Nevertheless, I would like to emphasize one aspect of measurement before returning to the details of the Sophists' pedagogic message: the measurement of political boundaries. If the *epitaphios* provided a temporal measure of the aspirations of the polis, other forms of civic life more immediately offered a vivid sense of the spatial frontiers.[64] As we will see, the awareness of such measures would greatly influence the Sophists' own contribution to Athens.

Greek drama and the physical structures of the city of Athens represented two principal sources of an education in civic awareness. It is a theme of recent classical scholarship that Athenian drama both relied on and raised questions about civic allegiance and the boundaries between behavior that the city could tolerate and that which might prompt exile. Drama made vivid the always fragile boundaries between the inner and outer realms. One recurring example was the topos of Thebes, a city that represented "the paradigm of the closed system that vigorously protects its psychological, social, and political boundaries even as its towering walls and circular ramparts close off and protect its physical space."[65] The god Dionysus exemplified the opposite extreme: "Dionysus is the fluidity of experience we confront every time we leave the everyday logic . . . of whatever Thebes we inhabit."[66] The Athenian audience confronted the problem of placing Athens somewhere between austere closure and bacchanalian chaos.

The very structure of drama, in which masked players transformed themselves into a variety of characters inside the *skene,* or concealing building at the back of the stage, suggested questions about the nature of identity. As Ruth Padel remarks of Aeschylus's *Agamemnon,* "this is the theater exulting in the possibilities of relating inside to outside, unseen to seen, and private experience to the external watching and gazing of others."[67] Greek drama brings the boundaries of self and of city into often painful view. In two related passages Peter Euben summarizes the effect:

> By portraying the establishment and disestablishment of bound-
> aries around and perhaps between spheres of activities drama
> provided an opportunity [for citizens] . . . to reflect on themselves
> as definers and redefiners. . . .

> [Drama] reveals the social demarcations that give people their
> identity and insists that such definitions are necessary to make a
> people at all. Bringing up from below and from outside forces,
> passions and strata otherwise ignored or excluded, it provides a
> more inclusive stage for reflection than do other public institu-
> tions. But it also reaffirms the need for limits whose limits it has
> just displayed.[68]

Again, the dramatic sense of political boundaries as portrayed at the drama festivals was complemented by a more mundane, but no less vital, education—that offered by the history and present geograph-ical circumference of the polis. The limits of that circumference represented a critical element in the identity of "citizen as measure." Sprung from the same etymological root, the Greek word *nómos* (law) and *nomós* (pasture) point to the interrelation between legal and political boundaries. The verb form *némo* refers to the act of dividing up according to agreement on the law.[69] One can hear similar echoes of political topography in the early meaning of the word *polis,* which designated the circle formed by the assembly.

Those who were admitted to such circles, the citizens of the polis, defined themselves against the outsider. The Athenians rarely granted citizenship to one whose origins lay outside the geographic boundaries of the city-state: it was a common topos of rhetoric to claim that one's opponent was not a citizen and thus lacked legal standing.[70] When the polis was able to contain outsiders, it admitted them both as guests and as evidence of its very strength as a cohesive political entity with nothing to hide. Thus, Pericles's famous boast that in Athens "our city is open to the world."[71]

There was, of course, a certain irony in such remarks. Partly in response to the advice of Pericles, an elaborate series of walled fortification surrounded Athens. E. R. Dodds summarizes the extent of the enclosures: "The original Long Walls, built between 461 and 456, linked Athens and Piraeus and Phaleron respectively, thus enclosing the city and two ports within a triangular fortification whose third side was the sea. Later . . . a third wall was built, within and parallel to the north or Piraeus wall, so as to enclose the military road from Athens to Piraeus."[72] These walls and their history figure prominently in the Sophists' education of men as measure.

The Sophists:
Architects of the Verbal Measure

Speakers before the assembly in Athens posed their advice against the traditions, ceremonies, and architecture that provided an audience with the criteria for evaluation. But what of their public words themselves, what was their history, their relationship to the city? From the dawn of democratic politics it was the possibility of public speech in the agora which demarcated both the security and the health of the polis. As Deborah Steiner has recently argued, the fortunes of this space offer an accurate barometer for the shifting fortunes of democratic government. For it is the agora that "not only plays host to popular and egalitarian debate but also guarantees that information can circulate unchecked."[73] As Steiner records, those opposed to democracy focused on the treacherous nature of open debate. Herodotus's King Cyrus speaks scathingly of those "who set aside a space in the middle of the city and there proceed to swear false oaths and to deceive one another." Indeed, it was Babylon's failure to maintain communication between its expanding parts which brought on its collapse.[74]

The linkage between speech and deceit is as powerful and familiar in classical thought as that between speech and politics. The rhetor Gorgias famously compared speech with magic, remarking on the power of words "to stir passions, and thereby to deceive."[75] Plato characterizes the Sophists as magicians and conjurors (*Sophist*, 235ab) and uses the "three notions of magic, sophistic and imitation . . . as being almost synonymous."[76] Words have the critical capacity to create *apate*, or powerful illusion, much like the voice of Orpheus, to whom Plato compares Protagoras.[77] But as de Romilly argues, Gorgias's originality went beyond the mere charm of his words. Gorgias claimed the ability to decipher the chemistry of verbal magic and to demonstrate that the production of persuasion was "something technical, and even scientific."[78] If education could provide the techniques of persuasiveness, and be used for political purposes, rhetoric and rhetorician would gain an immense power to shape the polis.

It is precisely this power that engages Socrates's attention as he discusses with Gorgias (in the dialogue of that name) the question of political authority in Athens. The subject in question is already familiar to us, namely the construction of the walls that enclosed the Athenian polis:

> *Gorgias:* Well, I will try, Socrates, to reveal to you clearly the whole power of rhetoric: and in fact you have correctly shown the way to it yourself. You know, I suppose, that those great arsenals and walls of Athens and the construction of your harbors, are due to the advice of Themistocles, and in part to that of Pericles, not to your craftsmen.
> *Socrates:* So we are told, Gorgias, of Themistocles; and as to Pericles, I heard him myself when he was advising us about the middle wall. (*Gorgias,* 455 d–e)

To preserve these walls Athens had withstood military catastrophe and starvation. In 404 Sparta forced a defeated Athens to demolish the walls, a duty that, as the historian George Grote suggests, was "the prominent mark of humilation."[79] But the destruction of walls built under the spell of rhetoric was not simply a humiliation. In Xenophon's account, at least, the "walls were demolished by eager hands, while flute girls played, and men thought that the day marked the beginning of freedom for Hellas."[80]

The reference to Themistocles further complicates the account. On the eve of Xerxes's invasion it had been Themistocles who persuaded the Athenians that the ships under his command represented the "wooden walls" that the Delphic oracle had pinpointed as Athens' last hope. Under Spartan influence at the time the oracle was almost certainly referring not to Athenian ships but, instead, to the isthmus wall under construction by the Spartans. Thus, Themistocles's advice, subsequently vindicated at the battle of Salamis, was necessarily based on a metaphorical reading of the Delphic pronouncement.

The spell of words, and the metaphors and histories that are its form and subject, can build and move walls, lose and win battles. In the *Republic* Plato offers a second image of the conflict over walls, this time in the form of an antidemocratic allegory.[81] He renders the final defeat for oligarchy as both a rhetorical and military drama. "False and boasting speeches and opinions ran up and seized" what Plato describes as "the acropolis of the young man's soul. . . . And if some help should come . . . those boasting speeches close the gates of the kingly wall within him" (*Republic,* 360bc). Once again the power of words are decisive in the battle for the fortifications of the city and the soul.

While the funeral oration, the drama, and the other social practices of democratic Athens played a vital part in demarcating the temporal and spatial measure of the polis, the citizens' interpretation of public speech was critical to its very survival, to the maintenance of its defense. It is to the precise nature of this speech, to the *technē* of the Sophists' verbal magic, that I finally turn. I argued earlier that in order for rhetoric, or the art of argument, to play a role in the education of man as measure, that rhetoric must contain within itself an education. While public speeches offered the demos arguments about how to be the measure of their city, those speeches had the second task of educating the citizens in the art of measuring rhetoric itself. In Athenian democratic deliberation rhetors aimed not only to advocate a policy but also to unpack the oratorical devices of rival arguments. In this manner each speech served as warning to the citizen that rhetors can manipulate words and that language is far from a neutral tool of deliberation.

By operating in this way, sophistic rhetoric can legitimate itself as a pedagogic tool. In particular, sophistic rhetoric opens itself to the judgment of its practitioners and the demos, displays its own forms and methods, and demarcates the boundaries of legitimate argument. Surprisingly, perhaps, it is in Plato's *Euthydemus* that we find the most revealing account of these qualities.[82] The traditional view of the dialogue sees Socrates as confronting and subsequently embarrassing his Sophist opponents, demonstrating the paucity of their own eristic, or argumentative, skill.[83] That skill, which has as its aim "not to educate but to refute and bewilder," is juxtaposed with the Socratic protreptic, which "leads to confidence, willingness to learn and actual progress."[84] In a recent revisionary work Michel Narcy has made this assumption problematic, arguing that the dialogue represents a serious philosophical defeat for the Socratic position. Without endorsing this claim, the following account shares Narcy's assumption that the position of the Sophists offers more to the reader than exercises in logical gymnastics.[85]

Plato's *Euthydemus* is a dialogue about education, language, and entrapment. Socrates challenges two Sophists, the brothers Dionysodorus and Euthydemus, to persuade a young man, Clinias, "that he ought to love wisdom and have a care for virtue" (275a). Their technique, later transferred to Socrates himself, is to force their student to deny the middle ground in any position. This Eleatic mode of argument forces the choice between antinomies: educated or ignorant, being or not being, beautiful or ugly. The technique rests in part on exploiting grammatical ambiguities in Greek, in part on the acceptance of certain rules of speech: respondents have to answer questions directly, without modification. Teachers toss the student horizontally from one absolute assertion to its opposite. The truth status of each assertion is equal and equally irrelevant: education consists in mastering the throws that force the interlocutor to embrace an opposite position to his starting one.

Socrates, whose responses are sandwiched by the Sophists' interrogations, offers Clinias a journey of ascent.[86] Relying on implicit rules of speech similar to the Sophists' own,[87] Socrates leads the young man from a celebration of material riches to health, to generalship, and, finally, to the political or kingly art of ruling other men. Socrates and the Sophists offer two strategies of education, two rhetorical instructions in the exercise of power. When Socrates and the Sophists turn to confront directly each other, each uses their technique to attempt to entrap the other. The prize for the victor is considerable: at stake is the nature of political education, the identification of those who will teach it, and the relationship between politics and philosophy.

The very structure of the *Euthydemus* suggests entrapment and claustrophobia. Socrates and Crito are engaged in a conversation that itself encloses two further conversations, that between Socrates, Clinias, Ctesippus, and the Sophists, which took place the previous day (273c–304b), and between Crito and an unnamed witness to that same conversation (304d–5d). Crito, who was present at the original event, himself interrupts Socrates's account of the conversation. Moreover, the substance of the conversations reinforces the sense of enclosure: Socrates opens his account in the *Euthydemus* with a request to Crito that he join with him as a paying pupil of the Sophists but it is the dialogue that follows that justifies Socrates's request: he starts, so to speak, at the end. Crito opens the dialogue with a request to Socrates for information about the meeting with the Sophists, only to admit at the end that he has already heard a report of the dispute and has decided as a result that the Sophists' wisdom was a useless one. Crito ends the *Euthydemus* at the beginning. Narcy is correct in suggesting that "l'ordre chronologique du recit va à rebours de la logique du dialogue, la lecture se trouvant de la sorte sollicitée sans cesse à des trajets inverses . . ."[88]

Plato's mise-en-scène mirrors his linguistic and narrative structure. The placing of the interlocutors is extremely precise. Plato places the pupil Clinias between Socrates and Euthydemus. On Socrates's other side is Euthydemus's brother Dionysodorus (*Euthydemus*, 273b). Initially, Clinias's lover, Ctesippus had stood on Euthydemus's right, a position that would have placed Clinias at the center of the conversants. But Euthydemus blocked Ctesippus's view of his beloved, so he moved to a position directly in front, joining a group of spectators who form a wall around the conversants so effectively that Crito, late on the scene, could not hear what was going on. No one is more effectively surrounded than Socrates and Clinias, with a Sophist on each side and the crowd in front. Quite literally, they are walled in by their interlocutors.

The physical structure matches precisely the eristic technique: if the Sophists can show that language denies the possibility of an intermediary position between extremes, then Socrates and Clinias will be rendered equals and will be, symbolically at least, eliminated. Plato brings home this brooding threat grammatically. Although as two individuals the Sophists surround Socrates and Clinias, they speak in the dual voice—in other words as one. More precisely, they are, as the eristic art would suggest, indifferently either single or double, as circumstances require. Victory is more important than individual identity.

The dialogue is replete with images of force.[89] The Sophists are described as masters of pancratic competitions, the toughest of all Greek sports. The brothers are titled as *pammacho*, "all in fighters" (271c), whose technique of educating Clinias is to throw the boy for falls (277d). Socrates, in his moment of greatest apparent defeat, compares himself to a sailor about to be drowned by the "third wave" (traditionally, the fiercest and deadly one).[90] Yet more striking is the fact that many of the violent images combine the suggestion of destruction with that of being surrounded and trapped. Socrates accuses the Sophists of wanting to "surround me with words and so hunt me down" (295d). At the start of the dialogue Socrates asks Crito to offer his sons as bait by which to lure the Sophists into giving the two older men lessons, but the fishing metaphor is subsequently inverted. It is Socrates who is forced "to make a desperate effort to escape, twisting about as if already caught in a net" (302b).

The historical identity of the student Clinias reinforces the suggestion that the two educational strategies have direct political implications: Clinias is a scion of one of Athens' most famous families, being the first cousin of Alcibiades. The identity of the Sophists is less clear: Dionysodorus is probably the same person as the general referred to by Xenophon (*Memorabilia* 3.1.1), while the existence of a real Euthydemus is suggested by Aristotle who attributes to him sophisms not extant in Plato's work.[91] More important is what Plato writes about the two: he stresses their enforced mobility, their transient state.[92] Their trade appears to have sent them first to the Athenian colony of Thurii, which subsequently exiled Dionysodorus and Euthydemus to a life of wandering (271c). Their skills are correspondingly extraterritorial. No matter what the location, their skills of fighting and legal advocacy are potent (271d–72a). Their acumen in "fighting in arguments and refuting what may be said, no matter whether true or false" is in universal demand (272a–b). This is the skill they claim to "teach better than anybody else and more quickly" (277d). (Their art thus makes a virtue of necessity—tailored to those who cannot stay long in one place). Moreover, the dialogue reinforces the claim that the politics of the eristic strategy are potentially egalitarian. The Sophists stress that they can teach their skills to everybody: in the *Euthydemus* they handle Socrates, Clinias, and Ctesippus in identical fashion. The fact that Ctesippus learns the technique during the course of the *Euthydemus* reinforces the Sophists' claim. (By contrast, Socrates implicitly suggests that his own protreptic is too sophisticated for slower students, such as Crito's sons [275b–c]).

The Sophists' eristic art rests on certain linguistic assumptions that become vivid in the *Euthydemus*. Most essentially, they break up any permanent relationship between language and its objects. The relationship between signifier and signified is continuously contingent. What defines the use of any word is the strategic context in which it appears. In the first sophism, for example, *manthanein* is taken to mean either "learning the unfamiliar" or "understanding better what is known" (275d–76e). The eristic art takes every advantage of the ambiguities and rules of grammar: the verb *einai* becomes the victim of equivocation on its existential and copulative senses (283bd). Moreover, the sense of a word has no necessary temporal duration. Each use can be discrete, and the interlocutors may discount any appeal to prior understandings, as Socrates discovers (278b). The sense of a word stands only so long as that sense remains unrefuted. The speaker achieves victory either by forcing on the opponent the simultaneous affirmations of opposites in a single proposition or by the abandonment of his own initial claim.

As befits a dialogue whose subject is education, the theme of learning and knowing links together the exchanges between the protagonists. The Sophists force the unfortunate Clinias to admit that it is both the learned and the ignorant who "learn" and, simultaneously, that one learns neither what one knows already nor what one is entirely ignorant of (275d3–77c4). The result of this passage, if it is taken seriously, is to suggest that learning, as a developing journey from a state of ignorance to a position of knowledge, is impossible: there is simply no coherent account of the time or space in which it could take place.[93]

But *Euthydemus*, with matching sophistic logic, also suggests that every participant in the dialogue knows everything if they know anything. The dialogue reaches this claim through a number of steps. Initially, the Sophists offer either to teach or to prove to Socrates that he possesses the knowledge of how to act according to virtue. Socrates responds by asking only that they prove it. (293b). Such a request has echoes in a famous passage in Plato's *Meno*.: "the soul, since it is immortal . . . has learned everything that is . . . When [a man] has remembered only one thing . . . which is what men call learning, there is nothing to prevent him from discovering every-thing else" (81d2f). If one puts the two passages together, a successful outcome to Socrates's request to the Sophists, that they help him remember the nature of virtue, presupposes that he, Socrates, has remembered, and thus knows, how to learn. The *Euthydemus* con-tinues with an eristic display in which the brothers produce the following "concession" from Socrates: "If I know one thing, I know all, for I cannot be a knower and a not-knower at the same time" (293d5). Dionysodorus applauds the concession and generalizes it: "everyone . . . knows everything, if he really knows something" (294a10).

Socrates naturally finds this same claim "unbelievable" and at-tempts to resist the Sophists' demonstration of the same by breaking the rules of eristic argument (295a). Rather than answering Dionysodorus's question directly, Socrates introduces the "soul" as the entity by which he knows that, and only that, which he knows (295e). Following the same line of reasoning employed in the *Meno*, Socrates interposes the soul between the antinomies they offer: all-knowing or knowing nothing. The drama of the moment is high-lighted by Plato's use of neologisms to stress the fact that Socrates is distancing himself from the Sophists' position.[94]

What Socrates has to show the Sophists is that, in some sense, he can avoid a condition they find contradictory, namely, of being "both knowing and not knowing at the same time" (293d), while preserving the thought of the *Meno* that the soul is the repository of all knowl-edge. Socrates defends the position: he knows certain things and not others at any particular time. If Socrates is successful, he will dem-onstrate both that he does know something, that he can remember and learn more, but that he does not know everything about the knowledge of his soul.

We are now in a position to examine the passage immediately prior to this, in which Socrates has tried to persuade Clinias to pursue a virtuous life. In his protreptic Socrates starts with a basic premise. A man who means to be happy must possess a list of goods—riches, nobility, power, and honor, and a series of attributes: self-control, justice, bravery, and wisdom (279bc). Socrates goes on to argue that creating or owning possessions is useless without the knowledge of how to use what is possessed (289a). Therefore the pursuit of knowledge is indispensable. Renewing his argument after the Sophists' interruptions, Socrates lists pairs of skills: lyre makers and lyre players involve two separate, equal arts, those of making and using (289bc). As he proceeds, however, a hierarchy begins to emerge. Fishermen are ranked below cooks who know how to use the fish (290b). The knowledge of use is privileged over the knowledge of manufacture. Clinias, grasping the principle governing his lesson, searches for the ultimate "use" principle. His search ends with a pair of knowledges, those of dialecticians and those of statesmen. The former know what to do with the products of geometers, astronomers, and calculators, the latter with those of generals (such as Dionysodorus).

Socrates, approving of Clinias's list, takes up the art of statesmanship, of ruling, and runs into trouble: "When we got to the kingly art and were giving it a thorough inspection to see whether it might be the one which both provided for and created happiness, just then we got into a sort of labyrinth: when we thought we had come to the end, we turned around again and appeared practically at the beginning of the search"(291b). The causes of Socrates's failure, and the infinite regress that his search for the kingly art produces, have been exhaustively analyzed by Sprague.[95] The crux of the matter is Socrates's demand that the royal art both produce something unique and provide the skill to use it, and no such art can be found. Identifying the required art "as that which will make men good" leaves unanswered the question: "good at what? At flute playing? and so on."[96] Socrates's attempt to locate social and political hierarchy in the process of learning results, here at least, in failure.[97] His attempt to isolate degrees of learning, precisely the effort that the Sophists are about to decry, has been primarily responsible for the collapse of Socrates's position.

The crucial point is this: the royal art, if it is to satisfy the conditions Socrates demands, must exactly "know and not know" everything. It must know what is good in carpentry, for example, although it clearly lacks a knowledge of carpentry. In short, if Socrates could describe the royal art, he would indeed be embracing a claim—to know and not to know at the same time, the impossibility of which Socrates had "conceded" at 293d5. Only his teaching of the wisdom of the soul can explain why Socrates need accept neither the conclusion of 293d5 nor the absurdity of 294a10.

What is striking, however, is that in the *Euthydemus* Socrates declines to teach Clinias the nature of the royal art, thus leaving empty his defense of oligarchic politics and suggesting that there is a limit to Clinias's capacity to know the soul.

By contrast, the Sophists' claim about knowledge is fundamentally egalitarian. Clinias and Socrates are treated as what they are: equal citizens. The Sophists can teach the eristic art of argument to everyone, a justification, perhaps, of the Sophists' claim that everybody knows everything about what they can know, namely the use of language.[98] Equipped with the eristic art, the "knowledge" of the carpenter can prove equal to that of Socrates. One need not inhabit a city to exercise power—the Sophists are bound to no polis—for there is no escape from the ambiguities of language, which serves them as their weapons.[99] Their political education of Ctesippus teaches him to perceive of power as the master of the space between linguistic absolutes: how to handle language as a measuring rod that is internally transparent, reflecting its own shape and denying any internal opacity. In each use of language its equal and opposite image appears. Exposed to such language, Ctesippus will learn to judge the possibilities it opens up and to measure his own desires accordingly. Dionysodorus and Euthydemus offer no substantive instruction in history or morals, mathematics or science. Indeed, their teaching is devoid of normative content. But while Plato may have intended the reader to conclude that sophistry represents a false, because empty, teaching, I want to conclude the reverse. The aggressive word play of the brothers offers a foundation for democratic education, a teaching about the forms of language and the devices of rhetoric. Without prejudging the use to which citizens will put their understanding of public utterance, the Sophists have laid bare the instrumentality of judgment. They have made visible the magic of words.

The *Euthymedus* closes with Crito's report of his encounter with a stranger who had attended the discussion that Socrates has just finished relating.[100] This stranger, a "composer of clever speeches," who was highly critical of Socrates for wasting his time with the Sophists, now becomes the focus of Socratic abuse. Socrates describes him as inhabiting *methoria*, a "border country" (Hawtrey) or "no man's land"

(Sprague), somewhere between the philosopher and the statesman (305c7). What makes the criticism interesting for our purposes is that Socrates, in his search for the royal art, had sought a resting place at precisely this untenable point: "It was in this connection (the composing of speeches) that I expected to find the very knowledge we have been seeking all this time would put in an appearance" (289d–e). Perhaps Plato is suggesting that between the pedagogics, epistemology, and politics of oligarchy, and that of the democratic polis there is no shared ground, no compromise.

Democracy, Epistemology, and Education

I have detailed and substantiated the triadic relationship to which Protagoras gestures in the Great Speech through an analysis of the *Theaetetus*, the *Euthydemus*, and the context of historical Athens. The epistemological standard of the "man as measure" doctrine grounds and justifies the democratic structure of Athenian politics. Rejecting "authority," or "foundations," in areas of political judgment and values, the Sophists argue that political justification has to involve what humans have chosen to struggle for or died to preserve. The polis educates its citizens, those men who are the measure of all things, by means of tradition, political memory, and the vested hopes within the polis, the "convenantal values that are vital to its identity."[101]

This education insures the coherence of the otherwise dangerously relativistic doctrine of man as measure. Speeches in the law courts and assemblies by an elite trained in sophistic rhetoric form a critical component of that education. Public speech operates in an agonistic context that forces the elite to make accessible their linguistic techniques at the very moment when the citizens must assess public language to resolve the fate of their polis.

Tying the triadic relationship of education, democracy, and understanding together is a model of the citizen himself. Consistent with the Protagorian doctrine that man is the measure, whatever a citizen thinks he knows represents the sum total of his belief and education. At the same time, as the citizen is moved by political rhetoric, civic ceremony, and political fortune to remeasure himself, the content of his opinion is constantly changing. In this sense it is (as the *Euthydemus* suggests) the educated who learn, since there is no formal start to the process of socialization or linguistic mastery. Rather, as Protagoras suggests, the capacity to acquire a public language appears to be innate, and the conditions that enable its articulation are inseparable from the maintenance of a political arena to which it can refer.

This model of democratic education poses a stark contrast to Plato's vision of aristocratic education. Plato's effort to uncover a self-sustaining knowledge, the promise of a cognitive telos that would generate on behalf of its bearer an oligarchic political power or a disdain for politics altogether, delegitimates the voice of those who cannot attain the requisite wisdom. On the contrary, as Protagoras's arguments logically imply, it is the doctrine that "man is the measure of all things" which is the standard of value, or required reference, uniquely consistent with the premise of mass participation. Everything follows from that standard: for Protagoras language is not Plato's window onto the eternal but, instead, a prism whereby the citizen can view and judge himself; being is not an ideal form but a growth in self-conscious awareness made possible through the encounter with one's own shifting political horizons. For its part the demos permits the elite to provide exemplars for the citizen, and it does so through verbal agon in which words are beaten into measuring rods. Put another way, public speech, through which an oligarchy might manipulate a demos, becomes a prime tool for their clarification of policies and goals.

In the *Euthydemus* this rendering is displayed for us. That dialogue represents an ideal: a debate that lays out its own forms, invites judgment, and instructs the listener in the practice it demonstrates. Through the speeches of the rhetors, themselves trained or influenced by the Sophists, and the public ceremonials and histories from which the words take their reference points, the polis instructs the citizens in the constraints and possibilities of their civic lives. At their best, the experiences of collective self-judgment are cumulative; the understanding of connections between self and polis, between its history and projected future, deepen. As self-awareness thickens, the freedom to act as individual and citizen is more fully realized: the polis has educated its democratic citizens.

This completes my reconstruction of the Greek *Paideia*. Its strangeness to modern ears is to be found in almost every aspect. As Plato's *Protagoras* makes clear, the central focus is on judgment, as opposed to the mastery of technical—or, as we would say today, vocational—skills. Public activities equip the citizens, so far as possible, with the skills necessary to judge between the competing claims of elites or, should fortune smile, to present such claims before the people. Historically, citizens who argued before their peers in that assembly were not always the recipients of a training in sophistic rhetoric. But the influence of that training, and the agonistic structure of the assembly, had a profound effect: those in positions of power in Athens had not only to submit their decisions to citizens but also provide them with the vital tools of sophistical analysis by which they could evaluate such policies.

It is strange to encounter a model of democratic education which is premised on the idea that an education in grammar and the right to political participation are inseparable, a model in which the belief that "the truth is out of reach" centrally shapes the education of a polis.[102] The limits of language to measure the world represent the limits of the political itself and thus the boundary points of an education, which enables the citizen to place himself in that world. But the experiences that lie beyond the memory and walls of the polis, the languages that it cannot speak, and the knowledges that it cannot measure, these too exert a pressure on a democratic politics:

> For everything which is generated has some beginning, but the eternal, being ungenerated, did not have a beginning. And not having a beginning it is without limit. And if it is without limit it is nowhere. For if it is somewhere, that in which it is, is something other than it, and thus if the existent is contained in something it will no longer be without limit. For the container is greater than the contained, but nothing is greater than the unlimited, so that the unlimited cannot exist anywhere.[103]

The Sophists, perennial travelers and outsiders, are always the paradoxical educators of the citizens in a particular polis. The Sophists are carriers of language itself, of the meanings that the limits of grammar afford. They do not themselves interpret language for the polis; rather, they teach an elite to translate political choices into competing verbal messages. The Sophists are both inside and outside the space of Athens, their mastery of linguistic form is both a universal resource for education and a medium, which each community must transpose into the temporal and spatial contexts of a specific polis.

3

Rousseau and the
Education of Restraint

THE GREEK POLIS is no more: language is still the medium of democratic decisions, but time has splintered that frame of reference which once provided the subject matter of the rhetors' speeches. Historical memory and cultural practices continue to shape public vocabulary, but what can replace the walls of the ancient city as the means by which citizens might measure the wisdom of public words?

To this question Jean-Jacques Rousseau devoted considerable thought. Like Protagoras, Rousseau had no fixed place of abode, and, in common with all the Sophists, he was continually involved with questions of political education. Still, the leap from Protagoras to a consideration of Rousseau is not a small one. The shift in historical period transforms the problems of interpretation out of all recognition. Protagoras and his fellow Sophists exist in the grain of Platonic texts and in those few original fragments still extant. "Rousseau," by contrast, is a literary creation of massive proportions, both in terms of primary and secondary sources.[1]

The present chapter offers a reading of Rousseau which has a strong element of deliberate interpretive naïveté. In other words, I transcribe quite directly the ringing assertions of Rousseau's text, far more common than the rare passages of immediate opaqueness, and relegate to the footnotes controversial issues of more arcane interpretation. My broad principle of selection has simply been to survey those texts in which Rousseau is most directly treating the problem of education and to investigate their interconnection.[2] But my interpretation also moves at a second level. I focus on Rousseau's multiple uses of certain "spatial" metaphors and tropes, with particular emphasis on the ways in which these emerge in his images and stories. Rousseau situates his investigations of psychology, politics, and education around spatial axes: he creates characters in carefully limited environments, constructs fantasies around the possibility of solitary locations, and builds a science of politics upon the conceit of a state isolated from the psychological, material, and sexual influences of the outside world.

As so interpreted, Rousseau's educational treatises offers us a somewhat opaque but powerful image of democratic education which builds on the Protagorian model of the prior chapter. Rousseau exemplifies in forceful ways Protagoras's dictum to become the man of measure. At the most immediate level the relationship between the metaphors of measuring rod, on the one hand, and Rousseau's depiction of spatiality, on the other, is suggestive of a link between the two conceptions of human education. Recall the idea in Plato's *Euthydemus* that Clinias must master the grammatical "space" between syntactic absolutes or Pericles's famous fusion of the image of virtue and the topography of the Athenian polis, a city "open to the world." Acutely aware of the classical exemplar, Rousseau takes the concern with measurement and space to a plethora of new sites. Rousseau's multiple examinations of psychological, erotic, political, and historical spatialities offer a pedagogic context, an environment, a grammar for the measurement of an open world.

Rousseau agrees with Protagoras on a critical issue: the measurer, the unit of measure, and the field of experience one measures are in dynamic interrelation. But as a result of extending the field of measurement out of all recognition to reflect the conditions of modernity, Rousseau transforms our understanding of each element of the triadic relationship. Not incidentally, that transformation puts pressure on Protagoras's pedagogic optimism. While Protagoras could argue that education is the process of growth in capacity to measure, Rousseau will suggest how problematic such an apparently optimistic vision has become. Rousseau confronts us with the suspicion that the enterprise may be finally incoherent, a suspicion that John Dewey will try to allay.

We will shortly turn to the investigation of Rousseau's spaces. But my reading of Rousseau implicitly takes issue with prior readings that have in part shaped the modern understanding of education and politics. To make clear one's debt to these readings may seem a distraction to certain contemporary scholars, whose interest lies in plundering Rousseau for pearls or poison. My own approach to the task is burdened by the assumption that the method of a book about education must reflect the model it advocates. I do not believe that Rousseau's texts can be isolated from the refraction that occurred as they were read by generations of readers; in themselves they become a theme of the history of interpretation and education. To place the encounter with such ideas within their interpretive horizons is, for reasons that will later become clear, one exemplar of an educated measurement.

The very volume of contemporary scholarship on Rousseau is almost comical, reflecting the arcane histories of academic dispute, fashion, and happenstance. Very roughly, one can divide Anglo-American and French research into two schools. The largest school seeks to account for the overarching core of Rousseau's teachings; these treatments either regard his work as largely self-explanatory or stress the interplay between Rousseau and his intellectual context. Those who are concerned more exclusively with what Rousseau himself wrote (or meant)[3] proclaim Rousseau to be a consummate pessimist, a brilliant political scientist, or an optimistic forefather of participatory democracy. The contextualists, by contrast, read Rousseau as heir to the natural law or contractarian tradition or a republican with Roman and Machiavellian roots, or all three. The second school focuses on specific topics within Rousseau's corpus. Within this group are to be found studies of Rousseau's texts on sexuality, on education, on the Social Contract, and on himself. Here Rousseau is read as a Socrates *manque,* as a source of deepest wisdom, or an exemplar of autodeconstruction. Indeed, in this last case Rousseau has become the focus of a full-fledged debate over the status of textuality, language, writing, and interpretation.

Within this double mass of erudition there is, however, a kind of unannounced hierarchy, a shorter list of texts to which the great majority of scholars refer. At the very top, unsurprisingly, is a work that fits poorly into any camp, the treatment by Jean Starobinski. The work of a fellow Genevese, Starobinski's treatment of "Transparency and Obstruction" in Rousseau has struck a generation of scholars as the most profound treatment of his thought. Starobinski is fully conscious of Rousseau's intellectual and social context, but his text is not encumbered by the need for defensive footnotes "proving" that Rousseau meant what Starobinski takes him to mean. Few if any scholars have thought more about the interrelationship, both chronological and thematic, of Rousseau's extraordinarily diverse and massive writings, and few are so ready to make suggestive and daring juxtapositions.[4] Starobinski's mode of interpretation, while eschewing the idioms of postmodernism, is one of the most powerful examples of what Hans-Georg Gadamer has termed the "historicality of understanding." Starobinski's reading is an effort to place reader and text within a single tradition marked by the prejudices of modernity, on the one hand, and the singularity of the text, on the other.[5]

The work of Starobinski leads us to the question that must inevitably be faced by the author of yet another study of Rousseau, namely, why it is necessary. Traditionally, the response was obvious: Rousseau's notorious embrace of antinomies—be they individual and collective, solitude and community, natural and artificial freedom, or Sparta and the *haute-bourgeoisie* household—cried out for explanation and, if possible, synthesis. It is more than possible, however, that Starobinski has solved the puzzle. Robert J. Morrissey summarizes:

> In Starobinski's view, Jean-Jacques does not see the world, he sees only himself, and in so doing looses the freedom to see. What Rousseau is looking for, and will never find, is a state of universal Sameness—whence his desire for transparency, unity, freedom, and a moral and ontological absolute. But since Sameness can only be defined in terms of self, freedom for Rousseau is above all freedom from Otherness. The only escape is *either* to make one's own Sameness function as a transcendental absolute . . . by making the world a transparent extension of the self, *or* to refuse any encounter with the Other . . . and withdrawing in alienation from the world.[6]

Even those post-Starobinski scholars who find this reading overly psychological have replicated his synthesis in parallel, if more "political," terms. Thus, to take a recent example, Arthur Melzer bases his account of Rousseau's political theory on the latter's conviction about the selfishness of man—but the result is remarkably similar: "If . . . selfish selflessness is what divides man against himself and others, then he can be restored to unity and justice by inducing him to embrace totally either side of the contradiction: complete selfishness or complete sociability."[7]

From a multiplicity of critical viewpoints scholars have neutralized Rousseau's antinomies: whether it is in the synthesis of natural law and republican virtue, a message for the few juxtaposed with one for the many, or the extension to its opposite extremes of a single logic of freedom, critics have repetitively solved the "problem" of Jean-Jacques Rousseau. Since Starobinski's work only Jacques Derrida has taken "Rousseau" in a fully new direction, but he too takes important and acknowledged cues from Starobinski.[8]

Inevitably, my treatment is indebted to Starobinski's readings of "transparency" in Rousseau and Derrida's considerations of supplementarity. But Starobinski's analysis always leads back to the enigma of Rousseau himself, in whose persona existence "pierces the clouds for one brief but timeless moment."[9] My interest is on the ground beneath, and in what may have been illuminated with regards to the education of human beings. For his part Derrida is fascinated by the task of displaying syntactical deferments in Rousseau's "text." Passionately seeking harmony, Rousseau constantly evokes replacements or supplements by which to recover the lost peace of an already destroyed innocence. Derrida follows the traces of such supplements to the act of writing. I place "Rousseau" in the cross-currents of longings and deferments which his writings articulate and argue that, in so doing, one learns something about the role of a teacher.

I am not the first to distill a pedagogic message from Rousseau. One group of scholars focuses on Rousseau's psychological model of humanity; while they applaud his acumen, they have been reluctant to draw any general practical consequences from his work. In an extreme interpretation, Rousseau's psychology is so purely a product of his idiosyncrasy that it cannot contribute to a general social theory. In the opening passage of his *Confessions* Rousseau writes: "I know my own heart, and have studied mankind." Critics have often suggested that Rousseau's heart, his "innate perversity," made an "objective" study of mankind quite impossible.[10] J. M. Cohen finds it "strange that a cluster of beliefs . . . which have so deeply affected educational and political practice . . . should be naively shown to owe their inspiration merely to the over-stimulated infancy of a motherless child in eighteenth century Geneva, and to its rough interruption by a premature encounter with the rough ways of the world."[11]

Scholars have linked Rousseau's repeatedly expressed desire for security, stability, and protection with the familiar biographical details to the advantage of neither. Rousseau's birth cost his mother her life; the laws of his native Geneva had provoked his father's exile. The "beaten apprentice, the thieving lackey, the vagabond of the roads," longed for a home.[12] It is easy to suggest that Rousseau's appeal to his readers to "learn how to stay in [their] place" and to "measure the radius of [their] sphere and stay in the center like an insect in the middle of his web" was the product of a wandering soul. One can read Rousseau's interpretation of sexual desire, his ambiguous view of family structure, directly out of his life story. In his *Confessions* Rousseau even does the work for us (*E*, 81; *OC*, 1:536).[13]

The vagabond of the roads watched his opera (*The Village Soothsayer*) performed before the king of France and was to receive a pension from George III of England. The lives of diplomatic secretary, composer, botanist, Paris socialite, political refugee, and paranoid were all his. His pessimistic judgment of humanity was the pronouncement of one who had occupied, always uncomfortably, a multitude of its social strata. These facts are familiar, but the conclusion to be drawn from them is disputed. Everywhere Rousseau looked he found reasons for pessimism: do we conclude that his view was in extremis or *sub specie aeternitatis*? Many commentators choose the first: they do not dispute Rousseau's genius nor its essential marginality. His is the gaze from and about the limits of human existence, and one should not mistake it for an account of its core.

Scholars who focus more directly on Rousseau's political theory of education—those who might be said to regard themselves as his theoretical disciples—denigrate his psychology. In the view of critics such as Alexander Meiklejohn, Carole Pateman, and Benjamin Barber, Rousseau had a profound political insight. Perhaps Meiklejohn puts it best: "For [Rousseau], the political state is not a secondary institution. It does not merely 'secure' rights which men have received. . . . Government is primary. It creates 'rights' and 'wrongs.' They are meaningless without it. The state is the creator of mankind. It makes civilization, makes culture, makes human beings."[14] When Rousseau writes that "men are as government makes them," Meiklejohn, Pateman, and Barber think he is right. They further agree with Rousseau that, "if morality and intelligence are fundamentally political, then political institutions may be trusted to teach them."[15] If men are to be free, political institutions will have to educate them to rule. Finally, these writers applaud Rousseau's insistence that, if citizens are to preserve their freedom, it is they who must constitute the ruling political authority. Educated democratic citizens rule over themselves because they will "perceive in the common force the workings of their own wills."[16]

The difficulty of such accounts is that problems that Rousseau regarded as fundamental simply get wished away. Two examples will suggest the general tendency. In a footnote Barber remarks that Rousseau tried to "give the procedural devices of the General Will the support of customs and mores, but these customs and mores suggest a form of unitary consensus that is inimical to genuine democratic politics."[17] Barber would like a little more dissent and rather more differentiation in his politics. The problem is that Rousseau regards unitary consensus as the necessary goal of certain forms of democratic politics: "The more harmony there is in the assemblies, that is the closer opinions come to obtaining unanimous support, the more dominant as well is the general will. But long debates, dissensions, and tumult indicate the ascendance of private interests and the decline of the state" (*SC*, 109). This is not just a marginal observation by Rousseau. The freedom that can belong to citizens is theirs only so long as they can find themselves in a public realm marked by the harmony of public and private interests. Once differentiation begins the psychological association starts to collapse, the citizen experiences the commands of the sovereign as external to the self, and freedom has disappeared.

Pateman's brief treatment of Rousseau offers a second example of wishful thinking. Pateman argues that the citizen of the *Social Contract* learns to be a "public as well as private citizen." She goes on to remark that "Rousseau also believes that through this educative process the individual will eventually come to feel little or no conflict between the demands of public and private spheres. Once the participatory system is established . . . it becomes self-sustaining."[18] Rousseau explicitly stated the contrary: his model state is not self-sustaining, nor can it survive very long.[19] The reasons go to the heart of Rousseau's idiosyncratic project: the citizen of the Social Contract is an artificial creation, a being who suppresses the universal, natural, private instinct under the force of historical necessity. This suppression is sustained by the logic of the contract (as Pateman suggests) and by the Lawgiver. But the suppression will inevitably fail: the natural instincts are too strong. Notwithstanding Pateman and Barber's optimism, Rousseau believed that being a "public as well as a private citizen" was not a sustainable psychological condition. To experience and accept the simultaneous claims of private and public wills was virtuous, certainly—but also painful and beyond the strength of modern humans.

When Barber writes that "the danger is that the nurturing of affective ties will impede genuine cognitive debate" or goes on to worry that "the enhancement of empathetic imagination will corrupt the capacity for moral autonomy," he chooses to circumvent the complexity of Rousseau's teaching.[20] It is true that there are moments when Rousseau suggests that a citizen can retain autonomy and engage in debate without thereby ceasing to be a citizen. Rousseau's imaginary reconstruction of his native Geneva in the *Letter to D'Alembert* does imply some such possibility. But the extraordinary fragility of this enterprise underlines its theatricalism and its irony. Rousseau regarded two other possibilities as more psychologically sustainable: the complete withdrawal from society or the utter loss of our natural individualism in the collective will. His pessimism emerges in the demonstration that neither choice is fully satisfactory, because each represents the renunciation of a struggle that is the foundation of self-knowledge and thus of the capacity of self-conscious evaluation or measure. As idealized tableau, the extremes of self, as isolated or conflated into a common will, shine only by comparison to man's actual condition of enslavement to vanity.

In sum, scholars who find Rousseau's account of democratic sovereignty persuasive will not accept Rousseau's insistence that the terms of the Social Contract could occur, if at all, only in the Corsica of his day. I analyze below Rousseau's argument that "men are as government makes them" and his conviction that citizens must receive a political education if they are to become their own rulers, but in the light of Rousseau's conviction that the creation of virtuous, as opposed to docile, citizens is the most difficult of all political tasks.

The Space of Democratic Education

I suggested above a spatial interpretation of Rousseau's understanding of education. At its most reductive the most basic message is the following: the capacity of human beings to discipline their desires is minimal. Absent such self-discipline, they become the slaves of social fashion. Citizens therefore need help. Small, egalitarian communities isolated from the rest of the world can provide the means of achieving self-discipline. Therefore, political geography and psychological training are inseparably related. Ergo, education takes place most effectively in isolated communities.

Rousseau's writings on Geneva suggest a working example of this relationship. According to the *Letter to D'Alembert*, Rousseau was convinced that what virtue there was among the citizen body would be lost if entertainment diverted the public imagination from communally regulated self-congratulatory images and focused it instead on images taken from the world beyond the city walls. The introduction of a theater in Geneva would do just this. It would destroy the city by privatizing the public imagination. The theater audience would learn to disdain civic attachments and would discover how mundane were the civic symbols that it had once celebrated. Therefore, the coexistence of a secure political identity and a city open to the world of drama was impossible. The walls of Geneva quite literally contained and made possible a virtuous life in which citizens brought into balance their desires and capacities.

Rousseau professed little confidence that his fellow citizens would understand these consequences of drama. They would, he proclaimed, respond to the seductive charms of the theater, motivated by the desire to look sophisticated in the eyes of Europe. Vanity would lead to psychological enslavement. When they pursued the phantom of international approval, Genevese would become discontent with the delicate, stable civic balance they had built within their walls. In an effort to save Geneva from a fate he had predicted Rousseau intervened with his own strategy of psychological manipulation: he made a drama of Geneva's exceptionalism and treated the theater as an assault on the proud self-image of the Genevese citizen.

What we learn from a rapid overview of Rousseau's treatment of Geneva finds resonance throughout his other texts. Where there are no physical walls, Rousseau suggested, education must construct them in the mind. Sexual desire, suitably managed, can constrain behavior and promote virtuous self-discipline. Unmanaged, it leads to boredom then restlessness and, finally, enslavement to unquenchable desire. In a corrupt society, in which sexual mores are no longer a concern of the state, Rousseau believed that the novel remained a potent source of political education. One can channel pity, which accompanies the experience of watching another human being suffer, into social altruism; unmanaged, it degenerates into hubristic privatizing indifference. Instruction can redirect the search for individual glory so that its achievement is inseparable from public ends.

In the company of others our imagination will always construct dreams of manipulation, of private advantage. We want society to admire us as individuals, which means we long for inequality and hunger for the envy of our peers. They own the capital of our self-esteem; in seeking to draw continuously on the account, we become another's slave. This, in Rousseau's view, was the identity of the contemporary bourgeois. Only a thoroughgoing political education could teach people to see themselves as the public and thus gain a modicum of stability rather than constantly imagining themselves happier elsewhere.

Pessimistic about the human capacity to sustain conflicting psychological drives, Rousseau defined each historical period by the strategies it adopted to avoid such conflict. In his age (as in ours) the preferred strategy was servitude to public opinion. What especially troubled Rousseau was that this process created elites who manipulate opinion for their own private ends. If citizens are to preserve their identity and freedom, public opinion must become the self-conscious, critical concern of all. Such opinion must represent a shared accord on the limits of legitimate behavior, on the parameters of social inclusion and exclusion. Rousseau designs democratic education to promote this goal. Properly educated citizens will be willing to shape public preferences around certain constraints inside of which they are prepared to organize their own lives. In other words, democratic education permits citizens to create and rule themselves and recognize themselves in their own creations.

Rousseau was ambivalent about the human capacity for communal self-rule. Convinced that individuals would strive for private ends, Rousseau introduced into his models the figure of lawgiver-tutor, a flesh-and-blood deus ex machina, to prod, shape, and direct the citizen toward the maintenance of social homogeneity. Manipulated, but content to pursue goals that the state has arranged so as to be within reach, political education could teach citizens to forget temporarily the fact that their common identity is an artificial myth. At its most utopian Rousseau's conception of communal education contains the model of a citizen who can learn through the logic of the contract "to consult his reason before heeding his inclinations" (*SC*, 56). Conscious of the instincts that individuate them, committed to the family structures that surround them, and loyal to the state that defines and embodies their public aspirations, citizens could attain that "elevation of soul" which comes from achieving virtuous self-discipline.

These brief remarks introduce one element of Rousseau's conception of political space—his reinterpretation of the ancient polis. But Rousseau's spatial vocabulary embraced many more dimensions than the city-state alone. He sought to explore the psychological terrain evoked in the struggle to maintain self-generated limits on behavior, a terrain that necessarily broadens the scope of Rousseau's inquiry. Once again we can state his thesis in its starkest form and then suggest its density. Rousseau's basic claim is that, whether the actors are citizens or isolated individuals, efforts at self-discipline which alone make freedom possible simultaneously produce the onset of pathological disturbances.

Freely willed self-discipline, or virtue, as Rousseau often termed it, "is a state of war" which one cannot sustain for long (*NH*, 2:682). Every text hammers home the message. Despite Rousseau's efforts to manipulate their preferences, the citizens of Geneva would succumb to the temptations of their private longing for cosmopolitan respect. They would come to regard their city walls as prison walls and would dream of escape. Since the citizens of the Social Contract would find virtue too great a psychological burden, the lawgiver must deprive them of every vestige of individuality, and even that strategy (which makes truly virtuous behavior impossible because it is no longer consciously willed at all) will eventually collapse. Julie, the heroine of Rousseau's novel of that name, finds the weight of virtue an intolerable one. Unaided, she attempts to construct her own closely circumscribed world, in which she holds her passions and duties in balance. But that world of Clarence, like the city of Geneva, is ultimately stultifying. Julie feels the artificiality of it all and chooses suicide.

Rousseau infinitely complicated this portrait of the psychological topography of self-discipline by writing himself into it. Exhausted by his own voyages, both intellectual and physical, Rousseau sought a life in which:

> Nothing [is] external to us, nothing apart from ourselves and our own existence; as long as this state lasts we are self-sufficient like God. This feeling of existence unmixed by any other emotion is itself a precious feeling of peace and contentment which would be enough to make this mode of being loved and cherished by anyone who could guard against all the earthly and sensual influences that are constantly distracting us from it in this life and troubling the joy it could give us. (*Reveries*, 89)

But Rousseau could not trust himself to exercise the necessary mental or emotional discipline that would preserve the dimensions of solitude. In his darkest moment he was forced to conclude that he might only be happy in the most impenetrable enclosure of all, in the Bastille.[21] Within its most closely circumscribed space, Rousseau speculated, he might find again the possibility of harmony within the self.

So much for a summary of two dimensions of Rousseau's conception of the spatial. Already, in this rapid transposition of Rousseau's texts, the images of containment, exteriority, and interiority occupy center stage. Moreover, such a reading introduces critical strands of Rousseau's thought on the relationship between education and politics: the notorious pessimism, the acute analysis of vanity and social envy, are in view. At the periphery of his thought lies the conviction that the achievement of freedom is inconsistent with the limitless, that learning the art of self-containment is the prerequisite of our freedom and, thus, of all other learning.

But this is only the beginning. While Rousseau is at pains to locate, and with exhaustive precision, the geopolitics of his imagined citizens, or the modern Eden of Julie's Clarence, the human capacities he seeks to secure appear to have no clear location. When we come to analyze the psychological elements of Rousseau's education, in particular the concepts of pity and virtue, we will discover that their status is ambiguous all the way through. As Derrida points out, Rousseau's texts are strewn with chains of supplementarities—replacements for the lost Eden of immediate presence that his writing evoked in terms of nature and speech. Such substitutions, however, mark that Eden as already unstable, always requiring the intermediate of its substitutes, writing and lost innocence, in order to reengage it. Direct encounter with the transparency of speech, of love, of nature, would, Rousseau writes in the *Confessions,* be fatal. [22]

Rousseau designed communities and psychological conditions to produce social equilibrium, homogeneity, and trust between citizens and between individual possibilities and longings. But these very spaces are substitutions for lost immediacy, and the spaces themselves are marked, as we see, by the longing to substitute for what they must deny, the presence of that which would destroy them. Thus, Julie longs to consummate her love with Saint-Preux, but his arrival presages her death: the space of his absence made possible the presence of herself and her love.

Interwoven with the unstable dynamics of transparency and substitution are the complexities Rousseau creates between himself as author, as subject, and as reader. In the novel *La nouvelle Héloise* Rousseau makes references to epistles he does not provide and footnotes for an author whom he asks us to imagine as other than the creator of the texts on which "he" is commenting. The wrenching apart of identities, at the level of grammar, syntax, and narrative voice, is pervasive and introduces a new dimension to the concept of spatiality. The Jean-Jacques who judges Rousseau, the characters (the Lawgiver, Wolmer, the Tutor) who embody roles variously ascribed by their creator to himself, these too resonate across the more immediate readings of the text and challenge the reader. This is why no adequate treatment of Rousseau's text can ignore his style or structure of writing.

The Education of a Human Being

Education is the indispensable link between Rousseau's political theory and his moral psychology. Proper education alone can prepare human beings for the onerous task of self-government. Rousseau outlines a number of suitable educational strategies and offers a sustained reflection on the paradoxes implicit in each. Rousseau brings his educational models to life through a variety of imagined stories: readers who encounter that variety, and can transcend the limits of each particular story, are subject to an idiosyncratic and remarkable education.

Rousseau's pedagogy is built around the communities he invokes, the individual characters he construes, and the textual tropes through which he locates his subjects in imagined time. In *Emile,* Rousseau's most sustained analysis of the problem of education, he creates a masterpiece of apparent lucidity. But from the reading of Immanuel Kant down to the present, perspicacious readers have struggled to ascertain a consistent message. The style of *Emile* is anything but uniform: Rousseau's fiction seduces readers into identification with the protagonist then wrenches them from such daydreams. Rousseau composes his characters through a shifting montage of traits. He constantly interrupts established temporal sequences and redefines the goals of his works in midstream.

In *Emile* Rousseau constructs a bitter image of his age through the portrait of the children he saw around him. Simultaneously, he juxtaposes this portrait with the perfection of the story's protagonist, Emile himself. Underpinning the juxtaposition is Rousseau's understanding of natural psychology: in particular, he identifies those unstable elements in human behavior which education will have to manage. The paradox Rousseau emphasizes in *Emile* is that the education of a naturally virtuous child depends on the teacher's employment of sophisticated artifice. Thus, Emile's tutor shapes the "natural" dispositions to virtuous ends through an education focused on the artful restriction of the child's experience. Rousseau is aware that the highly limited degree of autonomy permitted Emile, and the emphasis placed on manipulating his habits, is destined to trouble the reader. The continual comparison of Emile to the first image of the "contemporary" child only partly deflects the discomfort. Moreover, Rousseau's Emile is from the start an opaque creation. Rousseau's use of the concept "natural" as a simile for Emile is always an uncomfortable one; the fit is poor. Rousseau calls Emile "everyman" but suggests that he is equally an impossible fiction, the animation of theoretical exercises Rousseau wants to undertake. In contrast to his contemporary rival, the elements of Emile's character may appear stable and the result felicitous, but further consideration undermines this oversimplified comparison.

The challenge of reading Rousseau is that it is not always possible to keep in mind the double play of overt content and stylistically or structurally generated instabilities. Exegesis must hold each aspect constant before synthesizing can occur. Take the example of *Emile* once again. If there is a continuous conceit at work in the text, it is the idea that modernity has reduced adults to the condition of childhood. This suggests why Rousseau's analysis of child psychology and its education is directly relevant to an understanding of politics. The techniques of public education, Rousseau goes on to suggest, must reflect the fact that modernity has destroyed classical patterns of civic self-discipline and returned citizens to childhood. Or, rather, to the condition that is both that of childhood and adolescence—for modern man has the discipline of a child but the erotic appetites of neurotic pubescents. In books 4 and 5 of *Emile* and in *La nouvelle Héloise* Rousseau reconstructs this "development" and once again contrasts the consequence of its improper and proper management. Here, too, the link with Rousseau's political theory is direct: a political system that fails to manage the erotic instincts of its citizens will only magnify their inability to exercise self-control.

Rousseau reinforced this message in his more overtly political texts. Why are public discipline and public education politically indispensable? Because the amalgamation of self-rule and unbridled pursuit of individualism produces an intolerable tension in the citizen, just as in a child. In *Letter to D'Alembert* Rousseau suggests how a city republic can reduce this tension by the management of sexual behavior and the control of the public imagination. Rousseau argued that, if democratic government is possible at all, the polity must be so designed as to perpetuate habits of collective self-restraint and self-celebration.

In the *Social Contract* Rousseau explores the consequences of the collapse of such habits. In such circumstances a successful public education would have to enable citizens to transcend their sense of particularism. Social practice would educate citizens to recognize in the collective will a public authority with which they are ready to identify. Once taken on, this identity erodes the psychological experience of privacy and dissolves the tensions endemic in democratic politics.

But this model of the perfect citizen, like all of Rousseau's portraits, is built from unstable elements: the private and public wills in each member of the community are never perfectly fused. In *Emile* Rousseau closes a work about an ideal education in self-reliance by having Emile call for lifelong assistance. Rousseau wrote an unpublished sequel to the work ("Emile and Sophie"), with a variety of endings he could not choose between. In the "political" texts Rousseau starts by designing an egalitarian, democratic political structure that promotes and legitimizes psychological identification with fellow citizens. In this structure each citizen possesses an equal part of supreme

political power, and each is equally its subject. But the structure itself is never enough; private interests are summoned, like Glendower's spirits of the deep, to unsettle the harmonies Rousseau has so lovingly created. Moreover, the relationship between *Emile* and the political works is itself problematic: Emile is taught a version of the Social Contract but is never viewed as a citizen.

Rousseau might at this point have abandoned the idea of illustrating an education in self-constraint. Instead, he multiplied the experiment of imagination, creating of his life an *agathon* of virtue found and lost, of self-containment forged and simultaneously subverted by the forces of memory, of the erotic, of dreams. In a variety of confessional texts and a voluminous correspondence Rousseau revised those instabilities that are present in works such as *the Letter to D'Alembert, Emile,* and *The Social Contract.* Rousseau weaves images of displacement, of the horror of the unrealized and the unalterable, the absent, and the foreboding predictions of the future, into the portrait of a single life, which is itself in unstable relation with the known "facts" of Rousseau's own.

While many scholars of Rousseau's works try to bind his thinking onto a single branch, my intent is to find a path into the unstable locations that Rousseau continually closes around himself and his readers. Paradoxically, his experiments with the concept of limit are multiple: in basic structure they span histories, autobiographies, political treatises, letters, operas, and novels, to name but some. In rhetorical form they are subversive of any static position of interpretation, making of the reader's own location, as well as that of Rousseau, a series of interpretive problems.

Protagoras invites sovereign citizens to be the measure of all things. The spaces they will measure are defined largely by the polis and its history; the measuring rod is the language of Attic Greek, through which playwrights, generals, and orators offered the assembled citizens interpretations of their civic identities. Rousseau breaks the rod into pieces. Examining the fluid social conditions of his age, Rousseau knew that people would measure through their longings, their hubris, their loneliness, and their imagination. Rousseau's readers inhabit not one polis but many, and the language of their measurements are those of Babel.

Does Rousseau provide any assurance that we can reassemble the rod of measurement? Is it possible that to measure freely we must learn that for each of us there have to be self-sustained limits on the potentially infinite scope of our measurings? If so, how might we come to know the frontiers that enable self-creation?

Emile

My reading begins with *Emile,* since that work provides Rousseau's most sustained discussion of education. It is a treatise for "the study of the wise," a self-proclaimed successor to (and supplement for) Plato's *Republic* and an alternative to Locke's program for "raising a gentleman" (*Mountain,* 3:783; *E,* 40, 357). Rousseau wrote that the portrait of Emile embodies "the true principles of the just, the true models of the beautiful, all the moral relations of beings, all the ideas of order" (*E,* 253). The ambivalent genre of the work—part novel, part educational manual, and part theological treatise—is largely a consequence of the texts Rousseau was responding to. He continually makes reference to both Plato and Locke and is constantly distancing himself from the utopian quality of the former and the overly prosaic style of the latter. Rousseau thus insists on the possibility that Emile's education is not a philosophical fantasy—"wherever men are born, what I propose can be done with them" (35)—but at the same time Rousseau denies that *Emile* represents a blueprint for the education of an actual child. Rousseau records an encounter in Strasbourg in 1765 with a certain M. Angar, to whom he remarked, "I had no wish to prescribe a method."[23] On a second occasion Rousseau had to remind an overly exuberant admirer of his work that it was "impossible to make an Emile" (*CC,* 11:248). By structuring Emile's education in the form of an engrossing, often erotic novel, Rousseau reduced but never overcame the immediate tension between conceivability and practical impossibility.[24]

Emile tracks a child's development in a reconstructed and artificial environment. Rousseau isolates the "original dispositions" in man, the "habits conformable to nature," and projects their development toward a virtuous outcome. Ambiguity surrounds the task from the start, since the end sought is neither exactly natural nor artificial (*E,* 39). Throughout the work Rousseau implies that conventional society had made the task of educating for virtue extraordinarily difficult. The central conceit of *Emile* is that the corrosive effects of his age have forced on Rousseau the most disturbing features of Emile's education—the isolation of the young boy, his limited freedom, and the extraordinary authority of his tutor. (Rousseau would later claim that the purpose of *Emile* was "to show how vice and error, foreign to man's constitution, invade it from the outside, and deteriorate it progressively" [*Dialogues,* 1:934]). At each point of Emile's "natural" psychological development, external social threats mandate the Tutor's intervention. The work is a sustained defense of a series of walls that Emile's tutor must construct and maintain, lest the world beyond invade the delicate Eden within which Emile will grow up.

An additional feature of *Emile* shapes Rousseau's procedure. If he had created Emile to represent presocial man, the result would have been the production of a savage, a being whose integration into society would be inconceivable. But "Emile is not a savage to be relegated to the desert. He is a savage made to inhabit cities" (*E*, 205). Rousseau attempts to depict the development and education of natural habits that can survive social integration. To the extent that Emile's introduction to society fails Rousseau will blame society, not his educational method. Emile's eventual isolation only confirms the suspicion with which Rousseau opens his account: "Forced to combat nature or the social institutions, one must choose between making a man or a citizen, for one cannot make both at the same time" (39). The work hangs uneasily between the extremes of this antinomy: Emile is neither man nor citizen. The question is what the reader might learn from this impossible construction.

Rousseau employs the chronology of a maturing boy to investigate successively three critical elements of human psychology: dependence, socialization, and love. From those elements he produces an educational theory aimed squarely at undermining the confidence of the philosophes.

Rousseau's examination of human dependency begins with his identification of our first sensations. We are, in his view, equipped with natural powers of adaptability: "We are born with the use of our senses. . . . As soon as we have, so to speak, consciousness of our sensations, we are disposed to seek or avoid the objects which produce them . . . according to whether they are pleasant or unpleasant to us" (*E*, 39). Ambiguities abound here: in the *Second Discourse* Rousseau denied that men in prehistoric times were self-conscious—thus perhaps the "so to speak." Note, too, Rousseau's insistence on dichotomy: "seek or avoid" rather than "consider," "employ," or any other possible act that contains elements of both contact and rejection.

In his anthropological reconstruction Rousseau ties attraction and repulsion to strength. Nature grants humans the force to endure inescapable hardships. In the *Second Discourse* Rousseau had imagined men "accustomed from infancy to inclemencies of the weather and the rigor of the seasons, trained in fatigue" (106). In an effort to remain true to this model Rousseau insures that Emile's education reproduces the uncertainty of the savage's condition. The Tutor continually disrupts Emile's routines so as to strengthen the child against the threat of more malignant disruptions yet to come. "The only habit that a child should be allowed is to contract none." A proper education will provide Emile with the natural strengths of primitive man, readying him to confront the beast of human society. Lest modern conditions prove too comfortable, the Tutor must select what the child experiences. Emile must be "habituated to seeing new objects, ugly, disgusting . . ." (*E*, 63). Already the effort to preserve natural dispositions evokes careful manipulation of Emile's environment.

The first critical moment occurs when the child attempts to exert his will, using the primitive language of screams to effectuate control. Rousseau denied that this effort was innately evil: "If he seems to have more of an inclination to destroy, it is not from wickedness but because the action which gives shape is always slow and the action which destroys . . . more rapid" (*E*, 67). In Rousseau's imagined state of nature the first stirrings of the will to self-esteem, what Rousseau will term *amour de soi*, are harmless. In the *Second Discourse* Rousseau in fact says very little about the child of nature or his or her developing will power. In the absence of any family life and material security Rousseau imagined that mothers alone were likely to have raised their children and that such children would have rapidly developed self-sufficiency (*SD*, 218f). Rousseau conceived of young savages "capable of walking, acting and providing for their needs themselves," at which time they were presumably abandoned (218). The child's screams for help were likely to have elicited only the minimum of aid; those who were too weak to survive naturally perished. In *Emile* Rousseau attempts to duplicate this condition by having the Tutor ignore all but the most vital needs of the child. Rousseau asks rhetorically whether nature "has made [children] to be obeyed and feared" (*E*, 88). Even when giving help, the Tutor maintains the pretense that no connection exists between the child's demand and the Tutor's aid: "Experience and impotence alone ought to take the place of law for him. Grant him nothing to his desires because he asks for it but because he needs it. Let him not know what obedience is when he acts nor what dominion is when one acts for him" (85).

The replication of nature has necessitated a full-fledged drama of substitution, of artifice, and of strategic concealment. Rousseau justifies his reconstruction of the natural psychological history of a growing child by a comparison with the parenting going on around him. Rousseau offers a savagely sardonic portrait of a child whose wishes are scrupulously respected, whose demands are instantly met. The child develops a fixed pattern of expectation and models its behavior accordingly. Unfortunately, request succeeds request until the point at which even the wealthiest family cannot provide what the child demands: "Sooner or later politeness will force you, in spite of yourself, to end up with a refusal." But by the time this point has been reached, Rousseau contended, the child's psychology has already changed irrevocably. The child will regard the area within which his will rules as infinitely elastic. He will be "accustomed to seeing everything give way before [him]."

Even for this early stage in the corruption of man's natural psychology Rousseau suggests a link between a mismanaged upbringing, expanded space for maneuver, and a tyrannical politics. The spoiled child regards his family "as his slaves," considers refusal "an act of rebellion," and has become "a despot" (*E*, 87). The life of those who must endure his demands for "impossible things" becomes a misery, but the child himself becomes equally miserable (88). Reacting with rage and frustration when his will is thwarted, the child rapidly becomes a slave to his own brief psychological history. His experience never encompasses the notion of a limit until another human being appears to construct one at an utterly arbitrary point. In short, the absence of limits undermines the child's capacity to measure his environment: all that remains is a set of desires that prompt a debilitating because limitless search for satisfaction.

Since family generosity has appeared limitless, the sudden and apparently arbitrary occurrence of denial produces rage against all fixed boundaries. "One [child] beats the table and the other has the sea whipped"; a third spends the day screaming at his family. If by chance these children grow up believing that enough beating or screaming will expand the domain of their will, their subsequent deliverance from delusion will only be the more painful: they will find themselves "crushed by the weight of the universe," and, instead of finding themselves omnipotent, they will come to "believe they are impotent." But the parents bare the blame; by giving complete freedom to the will of their child, by treating its natural weakness as strength, they engendered "only folly and misery" (*E*, 88).

Rousseau, in the persona of the Tutor, permits himself the role of deceiver. The deception allows Emile a modicum of freedom— but only to the degree that the weak could be free. Childhood is, by definition, a condition of dependency: whether in the state of nature or in society, the child's "needs surpass his strength." In this condition he can enjoy only an "imperfect freedom" (*E*, 85). To insure such enjoyment the Tutor must adopt a double strategy. First, he engineers his own disappearance as a willing entity. He becomes, instead, part of a seamless continuum in the boundary wall of natural limits, a wall that Emile has long been accustomed to accept. The point is to insure that Emile will never encounter the prohibitions of another human will, an encounter that would result in an endless effort to manipulate or emulate other people. Instead, Emile will see only "necessity in things, never in the caprice of men" (89, 91).

The second stratagem calls on the Tutor to construct the enclosure around the child so that the resulting room for maneuver, far from appearing to be elastic, will represent an unalterable limit to what can be done. The result will be the "well-regulated freedom" that the youthful Emile enjoys. Emile will believe himself to confront the "laws of the impossible and the possible alone." This belief, of course, is false: "[The] sphere of both [the impossible and the possible] being equally unknown to him, they can be expanded and contracted around him as one wants. One enchains, pushes, and restrains him with the bond of necessity alone without his letting out a peep." The strategy rests on the theatrical assumption that the young Emile will remain unable to compare himself to others. If his *amour de soi* is to mimic its once natural condition, the Tutor will have to manage Emile's interactions with other people. He will enjoy "no necessary relation to others" (*E*, 92). Until his fifteenth year Emile "knows no other human being than himself alone, and he is even far from knowing himself" (187).[25] The unnatural tutor supplants the natural instincts of the parent in an effort to recover the unrecoverable innocence of an imagined age.

The psychological consequences of this unnatural space are felicitous for Emile. Thanks to the artifice of the Tutor, Emile will find the arena of activity granted to him by nature (for so he considers it) sufficient for his well-being. Within this arena Emile is free to act. In consequence, he "believe[s] he is the master" of his fate, but this false belief will harm neither himself nor others (*E*, 120). (Unlike the conventional parents, who end up trying to obey their own child, the Tutor never obeys Emile [89]). Emile will discover that the only method through which he can augment his domain is that of his own physical effort. Exercise, not fruitless attempts at psychological manipulation, will win the fruits of his desires. Emile will learn to measure just when to invest his efforts, which in turn will lead him to an accurate assessment of his own strength. Within a few years he will "ha[ve] tested it well . . . rarely will he act without being assured of success" (161).

Emile's development gives him the illusion of a freedom psychologically equivalent to that which Rousseau's savage enjoys. Savages learn how to eke out survival by adapting their behavior to the absolute constraints of nature: "The truly free man wants only what he can do and does what he pleases" (*E*, 84). Emile's "freedom" approximates these conditions. Uncommanded, he does what he pleases. Finding no pleasure in beating his head against "walls of bronze," Emile will learn that he wants to do only what he can accomplish (91). The giddy child of society, briefly allowed absolute liberty, finds himself helpless when that liberty is curtailed. Emile, who enjoys the sentiment of freedom, understands from the start that the domain of his freedom is necessarily limited. The symmetry is elegant.

But Emile enjoys only the sentiment of freedom. Rousseau never claims that Emile *is* free.[26] He is a "captive," held in the most perfect "subjection." The Tutor always remains the master of the child's will (*E*, 120). Rousseau claims that a dependent human being cannot be given greater freedom than this: Emile "is free to the extent that his constitution permits him" (162). By contrast, children constantly forced to combat the apparently arbitrary and malleable will of their parents lack all semblance of freedom. Instead, they become the victims of their own enforced habits of manipulation. Such children rapidly realize that "what they do is right if their disobedience is unknown." This, in turn, forces them to become actors: "You teach them to become dissemblers, fakers and liars in order to extort rewards or escape punishment" (90–91). Now it is not the Tutor who practices benevolent concealment of his intentions with regard to the child but, rather, the child who engages in malevolent concealment in an attempt to undermine authority. The "secret motive" is now transposed in an inversion of the natural order of command (91). Not only does the malleable will of the family enslave both parent and child to unquenchable desires, it bifurcates the identity of the child by forcing him or her to take on multiple roles.

Rousseau regards this education in deception—as opposed to an education through deception—as the most damaging perversion of the child's natural psychology. Only the examination of Rousseau's overtly political texts makes fully clear why this is so, but in his critique of modernity in the *First Discourse* we can find early evidence of his views. Rousseau's word choice suggests that his portrait of the psychology of the spoiled child in *Emile* represented his understanding of contemporary adults. In the *First Discourse* Rousseau concentrated on social habits of frenetic and open-ended activity: just as the spoiled children of *Emile* seek either to gain dominance over an ever-expanding universe or to conceal their disobedient behavior, so scientific "uncertainty" beckons the eighteenth-century bourgeoisie into a hopeless quest for solutions, and the fashionable arts offer a thousand disguises for dissemblers (*FD*, 38).

Science, in Rousseau's estimation, must have been invented by "a god who was hostile to the *tranquility* of mankind" (*FD*, 47; emphasis added).[27] For its part the cultivation of the arts produces a deep desire for "ornamentation," which promotes an obsession with becoming that which one is not (37; *SD*, 155). "Veil[s] of politeness" conceal from one another the citizen who "no longer dares to appear as he is" (*FD*, 38). Rousseau implies that men of arts and science only served to legitimize strategies of concealment. By either removing themselves from politics or developing seductive diversions for the common people, men such as Voltaire "spread garlands of flowers over the iron chains with which men are burdened" (36).[28] If the stars of the Enlightenment were not fruitlessly seeking scientific certainty, they were busy "chas[ing] after a reputation" with which they would never be content (64).

This habit of perpetual striving for the unobtainable and the will toward deception are the two behavioral patterns that Rousseau has identified in the psychological behavior of the miseducated child. Emile, on the other hand, who "has not purchased his perfection at the expense of his happiness," remains content within the finite arena of action shaped by the Tutor (*E*, 162).[29] Emile's freedom is curtailed, but this was no more than his dependent status naturally demanded. The portrait of the spoiled child demonstrates that "weakness and domination joined engender only folly and misery" (88).

Rousseau looked about him and found citizen-children populating the capitals of Europe, citizens educated by parents through a haphazard mélange of favors granted and others arbitrarily denied. Rousseau argued that this fluid condition, with its boundaries forever the subject of debate, had produced psychologically devastating results: "the worst education is to leave him floating between his will and yours and to dispute endlessly between you and him as to which of the two will be master" (*E*, 91). Rousseau's metaphor captures psychological uncertainty in spatial terms: to find oneself between two wills, in Rousseau's view, was to be subject to debilitating pressure.

It had to be one or the other: If education could not artfully place limits on a child's will, then parents would have to crush that will altogether. "Nothing must be demanded from him at all, or he must be bent from the outset to the most perfect obedience" (*E*, 91). "In such a system it must be all or nothing," Rousseau reminded Abbe M. (*MEW*, 91). This uncompromising antinomy will be of considerable consequence in Rousseau's design of the *Social Contract*.

Childhood, it appears, offers Rousseau a doubly suggestive theme. First, he could remind the (guilty) reader that every generation has been offered a hypothetical opportunity to preserve the good that the divine will had invested in all things (*E*, 37). Second, Rousseau's description of the spoiled child has certain affinities with his portrait of the Enlightenment. But such echoes are not sufficient in themselves to suggest why Rousseau's account of a child's psychological growth should be of more general interest. What needs to be added is the strong evidence that suggests that Rousseau does indeed conceive of contemporary society as composed of adults reduced to a psychological condition of infancy. As Pierre Burgelin remarks in his introduction to the Pleiade edition of *Emile,* in Rousseau's view "adults did not exist, but Children *are*" (*OC,* 4:xci).

When Rousseau wrote that "men in the civil state" have engineered a mutual helplessness that has "plunged . . . [them] once more into childhood," he was not simply indulging in hyperbole (*E,* 85). Rather, Rousseau interprets the condition of men through his psychology of willful desire; in this regard the child and the modern citizen are synonymous, for they are both weak and dependent. In *Emile* Rousseau made the obvious point that "we are born weak, we need strength" (38). But this is the same condition he ascribed to those desperate individuals who are the subjects of the *Social Contract:* they "would perish" if some means were not found to supplement their weakness (*SC,* 52).

Emile develops a theory of freedom designed for the psychologically helpless. Rousseau argued that bestowing unlicensed freedom on the weak enslaves both bestower and recipient. The spoiled infant is "child, slave and tyrant" (*E,* 48). By contrast, Emile's Tutor creates the psychological experience of well-regulated freedom in which the helpless can pursue their chosen ends without harm to themselves or others (92). By means of artful constraints, the Tutor attempts to forestall the vicious cycle of servitude which would otherwise arise when the weak attempt to command.

Significantly, the language in which Rousseau chose to depict the drama of childhood reverberates with political terminology. Human "progress" has reversed the natural order, inverting development back toward helplessness. This is why *Emile,* although ostensibly concerned with the education of a child, can be understood as a general analysis of the human condition. The fact that *Emile* offers a portrait of psychological dependency links it directly to the *Social Contract,* whose political structure depends on a general public experience of weakness and dependency.[30]

Emile, as we have seen, contains two portraits, Emile and the spoiled child. To grasp the full import of the text for Rousseau's political thinking one needs to trace the ways in which each model is relevant to Rousseau's conception of modernity. It is too simple to suggest that the spoiled child of *Emile* represents a complete psychological portrait of the adult; as so often, Rousseau's apparent identities partially dissolve on deeper examination. The crucial difference between the weakened adult and the spoiled child has to do with patience: the spoiled child "whips the sea" and screams at his parents; modern citizens by contrast, live in a condition that is permeated by "an air of *apparent* concord" (emphasis added). The vast majority experience "peace and repose," an instinctive readiness to embrace patterns of life which are seductively "tranquil" (*SD*, 176, 165, 164). The philosophers of the Enlightenment had been so captivated by this image of contentment that "they attribute to men a natural inclination to servitude due to the patience with which those who are before their eyes bear their servitude" (164). Rousseau undertook his portrait of the spoiled child in part to shame the reader, who will find him- or herself reproduced in the description. But Rousseau drew an important principle from the analysis: if an environment can summon and absorb the total energies of the individual, it can induce passivity even as it erodes the possibility of self-awareness.

Rousseau did not mean to suggest that such individuals were physically passive: "On the contrary, the citizen, always active, sweats, agitates himself [and] torments himself" (*SD*, 179). But in so doing, Rousseau makes clear, such men think themselves the happiest of mortals. Men who "ran to meet their chains" believed themselves to be enjoying "peace and repose" (165). The contemporary citizen "proudly boasts of his baseness" (179). Self-awareness had vanished to the point at which people are "seen to massacre each other by the thousands without knowing why" (161). This is not the psychological condition of the spoiled child, but it is exactly that of Emile.[31] The issue is one of self-perception: the condition of contemporary citizens appears to them much as Emile's appears to him; they think they are doing as they wish when, in fact, they are only perpetuating the regime of those who are molding their wills. These citizens are effectively "regulated." It is as improbable that they would struggle with their chains as it would be for Emile to dispute the Tutor's will. Rousseau's contemporaries understand their condition no better than the young Emile understands his. But they measure nothing; their servitude is not preparatory—as is Emile's.

Just as the modern adult is not exactly Rousseau's spoiled child, so there is the crucial difference between that adult and Emile. Emile is confined—there is "an enclosure around . . . [his] soul"; he is content to remain within it (*E*, 38). Contemporary adults found themselves in an open environment, constrained not by the presence of immovable "walls of bronze" but, rather, by their endless efforts to manipulate other wills to their own advantage. Their appetite for social praise is inexhaustible. In this sense they are so many spoiled children, ceaselessly striving for more. The frenetic, all-consuming nature of their efforts leaves no time for introspection: since it can imagine no alternative strategy of satisfaction, humanity thinks itself content to compete incessantly for rewards that are forever just beyond the grasp. Ignorant of the sources of their motivation, exhausted by the pursuit of the ungraspable, adults measure nothing but the infinite distance between themselves and an imagined moment of stasis, which forever recedes before them.

Because contemporary humanity represented a macabre and unstable synthesis of the mentality of Emile and circumstances of the spoiled child, Rousseau's complex investigation of childhood as a model of psychological dependency can reemerge in overtly political texts. Rousseau imagined constrained and inflexible environments within which the weak might experience the sensation of self-rule and thus recover a modicum of emotional peace. But these environments, which must be designed by one not himself a citizen, are only the politicization of the enclosure within which the Tutor situates Emile. Without the felicitous pedagogic space of that environment citizens will measure only their servitude.

Psychology of Socialization

Rousseau's reconstruction of a natural human psychology in the portrait of the young Emile depended on separating the child from any social interaction.[32] But if Emile was to enter society, this separation could not continue indefinitely. Recall that "Emile is not a savage man to be relegated to the desert. He is a savage man made to inhabit cities. He has to know how . . . to take advantage of their inhabitants, and to live, if not like them, at least with them" (E, 205).[33] The purpose for creating Emile depends on bringing him into society, but Rousseau had to justify this transposition in terms of the internal logic of Emile's own development, and this posed a problem. In the Second Discourse Rousseau had suggested that the man of nature had been content with solitude; Emile must be different to the extent that no such condition could bring him felicity—but to that degree he can no longer represent natural man. It has been convincingly argued that Rousseau has no good solution to the difficulty. Instead, he simply asserts that "God alone enjoys an absolute happiness" while claiming that our "attachments" provide for mortals whatever "frail happiness" can be ours (221). Matching Emile to the company of others was already to substitute forever the dream of original innocence. But without that substitution Emile's education would be impossible: no measurement could take place in a solipsistic world.

Is the psychological need for human company even somewhat natural and, if so, to what extent? Putting the same question another way, Rousseau asked what human disposition might draw us toward society. He locates that disposition in the capacity to feel pity, to experience an "innate repugnance" at watching another person suffer (*SD*, 130). But as one might expect, Rousseau is uncomfortable handling an emotion that is at once dynamic, interpersonal, and fickle. It is unclear how the man of nature, who can barely recognize another individual, can feel pity. Rousseau's assertion that the sentiment "precedes . . . the use of all reflection" is as opaque as his claim that the savage experiences a pity at once "obscure and strong" (132).[34]

In *Emile,* moreover, Rousseau revises this account of pity. As the Tutor permits Emile to mingle with others, the parallelism between his psychological development and that of natural man begins to dissolve. Pity is now described as "the first relative sentiment which touches the human heart according to the order of nature"—neither exactly artificial nor entirely natural. Pity is the product of Emile's first conscious judgments of other people, and the vehicle of actualization is his imagination: "At sixteen the adolescent knows what it is to suffer . . . [b]ut he hardly knows that other beings suffer too. To see it without feeling it is not to know it. . . . But when the first development of his senses lights the fire of imagination, he begins to feel himself in his fellows, to be moved by their complaints and to suffer from their pains" (*E*, 222). This is perhaps the decisive moment in Rousseau's psychological account. Imagination draws Emile out of his own sphere and into society because, in "putting ourselves in the place of the one who suffers, we nevertheless feel the pleasure of not suffering as he does." Rousseau argues that our imagination can draw us to pity the less fortunate even more powerfully than it attracts us to the better off. Pity is sweet, envy bitter, "because the sight of a happy man, far from putting the envious man in his place, makes the envious regret not being there" (221). Pity is mildly sadistic, and sadism can be attractive. As Rousseau later demonstrates in the "autobiographical works," self-pity can be so seductive as to be overwhelming.

The Tutor's excitation of the disposition of pity represents a crucial step in the management of Emile's education. But the operation is exceedingly delicate, as a glance at the *Second Discourse* makes clear. The difficulty is that the sentiment of pity for another being is psychologically extremely close to a sense of self-glorification. Absent constant supervision, the first inevitably dissolves into the second. In the *Second Discourse* Rousseau gives an example of just this consequence, which he traces to the division of labor. With the development of agriculture and metallurgy those with greater skills in these pursuits achieved a higher social status than their peers. Once the concept of "rank" becomes established the qualities that insured its attainment become the sole passport to prestige: "it was soon necessary to have them or affect them . . . [t]o be and to seem to be became two altogether different things" (*SD*, 155). Humans strove to win the admiration of their peers, through subterfuge, for egotistical reasons. Man came to "have a greater esteem for himself than for anyone else" because he became dependent on the belief that others held him in high esteem (222). The very possibility of self-love depended on a conviction of superiority.

Rousseau, naming this feel *amour-propre,* stressed the irreversibility of its poisonous effect. He calls it a "relative sentiment" because the judgment it rests on has no grounds beyond the "artificial" whims of socialized men (*SD*, 222). Emile is at risk: "The first glance he casts on his fellows leads him to compare himself with them. And the first sentiment aroused in him by this comparison is the desire to be in first position. This is the point where love of self turns into *amour-propre*" (*E*, 235).[35] Emile's psychological difficulties are augmented by the very perspicacity of his judgments—for, as he condemns his "fellows," Emile will be tempted not so much to succumb to their seductions as to flatter himself for having escaped them. On the one hand, Rousseau stresses Emile's superiority: the world of cosmopolitan Paris will shock him, as it would any "young man soberly raised . . . in the country" (330). Emile will see that "society depraves and perverts men" and will feel satisfying pity for them (237). "Emile is right" Rousseau affirmed, when he "prefers his way of being, of seeing and of feeling to that of other men." "Nurtured in the most absolute liberty . . . [Emile] conceives of no greater ill than servitude. He pities these miserable kings, slaves of all who obey them. He pities . . . false wise men . . . [and] conspicuous voluptuaries." If Emile "judges . . . well he will not want to be in the place of any of them" (245, 244). While other citizens need to believe themselves superior to their peers, Emile alone can honestly entertain that conviction and will hold firm to his station as a result.

On the other hand, Rousseau underlines the risks that Emile's immersion in society represents. In the process of "congratulating himself," Emile will "esteem himself more, and in feeling himself to be happier than them, he will believe himself worthier to be so" (*E*, 245). Earlier in the text Rousseau had contrasted the vanity that "gnaws" at the heart of the common man and the pity that Emile finds "sweet" as he first views such unfortunates (229, 221). But further analysis indicates that the pity Emile feels for those around him is always wedded to the vanity that follows on its heels. Somehow Rousseau must transform Emile's pity into a pride based on altruism lest it collapse into a self-enslaving narcissicism.[36]

This complex goal is precisely the task of Emile's remaining education.[37] Emile not only encounters men sick in body and spirit whom he will pity but also studies history books and then fables so that he might grasp the precarious nature of his elevated status. In this way "the human heart [is put] in his reach without the risk of spoiling his own" (*E*, 237). In his introduction to *Emile* Allan Bloom summarizes the strategy through which Rousseau preserves the psychology of moderation: "The first stage of Emile's introduction to the human condition shows him that most men are sufferers; the second, that the great, too, are sufferers and hence equal to the small; and the third that he is potentially a sufferer, saved only by his education" (20). Emile's pity for his fellow man is necessarily nonspecific. "It is of little importance to him who gets a greater share of happiness provided that it contributes to the greatest happiness of all" (252–53). The "less the object of our care is immediately involved with us, the less the illusion of a particular interest is to be feared" (252). The point is that Emile must not become overly involved with the individual characters he helps. If he becomes too committed, his judgment will blur, and his pity will "degenerat[e] into weakness" "it must, therefore, be generalized and extended to the whole of mankind. Then one yields to it only insofar as it accords with justice, because of all the virtues justice is the one that contributes most to the common good of men. For the sake of reason, for the sake of love of ourselves, we must have pity for our species still more than for our neighbor" (253).

The threat of *amour-propre* demands a wholesale revision of the Christian command to love one's neighbor as oneself. Rousseau regards this latter requirement as psychologically disastrous. In his view one's ability to love oneself in moderation rests on dissociation from the particular other and, still more radically, dissociation from oneself. As the Tutor closes the gap that had separated Emile from other men, he must insure that Emile be kept "at a distance from himself" (*E*, 252). As he closes one space, the Tutor must open another. His strategies are numerous: for example, by insuring that Emile's energies are constantly channeled toward the relief of others' miseries, the Tutor prevents Emile from becoming self-absorbed. But Rousseau justifies almost any tactic, including such nonaltruistic sports as hunting, so long as Emile's sense of personal identity remains indistinct.

Emile's sensation of superiority toward others evokes pity. Suitably managed, such pity can induce the onset of judgment between Emile and his peers. Emile, whose moral superiority to the majority has been preserved by containing his desires within inflexible bounds, can measure the lives of those whose dislocation has robbed them of self-awareness. Knowing them to be as they are, slaves to social fashion, he will pity them in general and thus use his judgment toward altruistic purposes. Education has virtuously socialized Emile's *amour-propre*.

Given such an account, it is not surprising to rediscover Emile's sense of generalized social altruism, pitched uneasily between envy, pride, and weakness, in Rousseau's political works. Here, in the form of civic sensibility, it will represent both the essential and impossible goal of Rousseau's conception of civic education—impossible in part because Rousseau's account of pity has something of a Byzantine structure. There are just too many poisoned possible outcomes. To transform an emotion that emerges from personal comparison to a particular other toward one that must emerge from a generalized, even abstract sense of self and other requires ornate theoretical acrobatics. But the harsh message remains the same; if the sentiment of comparison remains individuated, the virtuous will become corrupted by pride, and the weak will be enslaved by the unquenchable desire to be applauded by the crowd.

The Psychology of Love: Eros

One giant obstacle lies in the path of Emile's apparent readiness not to identify too closely with a particular other: the possibility that he might fall in love, that the space between him and another person would collapse. The experience of love, Rousseau knew, was the most dramatic case of obsession with a particular other. This is, in part, because the coherence of the concept of love depends exactly on the ascription of uniqueness to the beloved. For his part Rousseau was quite prepared to deny that love had any natural foundation: it is well known that in the *Second Discourse* Rousseau denies that sexual desire is experienced as focused on any particular other (135). In *Emile* he goes further, denying that sex is a need at all: "If no indecent idea had ever entered our minds, perhaps this alleged need would never have made itself felt to us" (*E, 333*).

But Rousseau cannot let Emile remain celibate, nor permit him a variety of sexual partners, because Emile must enter and thus judge society, and Rousseau regards a stable marriage as a powerful introduction to the commitments of citizenship (*E*, 327).[38] (One scholar of Rousseau argues that Rousseau sees the desire to attach oneself to another person as "the most natural indication of our need to regard ourselves not as wholes, but as part of a larger social whole").[39] In *The Social Contract*, of course, citizenship is a matter of being bound by "legitimate" chains. Emile claims to "glory" in the fact that his marriage to Sophie has put at least "one chain" around him (472).

The problem Rousseau faced was that of inducing Emile to fall in love and marry without making him obsessed or permanently absorbed with the identity of his beloved. Rousseau's strategy is based on the conviction that the psychological sensation of being in love need bear no true relationship to the actual character of the beloved: "In love, everything is only illusion. I admit it. But what is real are the sentiments for the truly beautiful with which love animates us and which it makes us love. This beauty is *not* in the object one loves" (*E*, 391; emphasis added). Emile is in love with Sophie before he knows her: "At the first sound of . . . [her] voice, Emile surrenders." Simultaneously, Sophie concludes that "her Telemachus has been found." Both Emile and Sophie have been taught to love an image of perfection in their imaginations; when they meet the merest echo of this image is enough to evoke the Pavlovian reaction, now transferred to each other (415).

It is easy to miss the radical nature of Rousseau's account. Sentimentality is an extension of self-love; the beauty it seeks results in a fantasy with which one identifies and for which one then seeks a location. Once again Rousseau offers us a synthesis that on close examination lacks the very stability for which he proffered it. Unlike Plato's search for *sophia*, there must always be a difference, a mismatch, between the attributes of the ideal and the irreducible, obdurate facticity of the object one chooses as the repository of that ideal. Rousseau's Sophie is a replacement for the ideal form, which Emile must take her to be. In the gap between her and her Greek namesake lies pain, humility, and the education of Emile's judgment.

In *Emile* Rousseau does what he can to narrow the gap. In constructing the perfect couple, Rousseau makes no pretense that he is portraying people with individual idiosyncrasies or complex characteristics. Emile's skills as athlete and carpenter are chosen to suggest the essence of masculinity: "this is man," insists Rousseau. Sophie cannot handle his carpenter's tools nor match his speed of foot, but she can bring succor to the ill with a delicacy he can only admire: "this is woman" (*E*, 437, 441–42). Emile and Sophie "see each other as perfect" because they are in love with an ideal portrait, which the other appears to embody (426). The abstract idealization holds in check the potentially enervating discovery that the particular other is blemished and thus keeps at bay the thought that one could endlessly substitute in the search for a more perfect spouse.

Such a construction cannot be stable. The individual idiosyncrasies of the particular other will destroy the harmonized space of idealized union. The troubling question is why Rousseau insists on such an improbable foundation for love. I have suggested one explanation: Rousseau's concern that the overidentification with a particular other induces a pity that too easily becomes arrogance. But why should Emile pity Sophie? Surely love and pity are not synonymous. Rousseau's response was that an overidentification with the particular beloved can produce yet another poison—not arrogance this time but hopeless weakness.

This becomes clear in the text when the Tutor calls on Emile to postpone the consummation of his marriage. The strength of Emile's sexual desire threatens to reduce him once again to the role of the frenetic, spoiled child: "As a result of having wanted to follow only your passions, you will never be able to satisfy them. You will always seek repose, but it will always flee before you" (*E*, 444). The Tutor confronts Emile with the consequences of his own desire and demands that he not succumb. Reminding Emile of Sophie's perfection, the Tutor reflects on the weakness, the imperfection, of a man who cannot control his desires. In other words, Emile, seeking to become as perfect as he imagines Sophie to be, is shamed into finding the strength to leave Sophie. It is at this moment of psychological torment that Emile first exercises virtuous behavior. The Tutor informs Emile that "there is no virtue without struggle," that the path to his perfection lies in the pain he experiences in denying his desires. Emile must create in himself the space for self-denial.

The purpose of the courtship in *Emile* is twofold. The idealization of love leaves Emile free to love any particular other without compromising his independence. But it offers, too, a psychological profile of virtuous behavior. The Tutor's strategy is to generate, by means of seductive imagery, the possibility of willed self-denial. It is this strategy that Rousseau will return to in his political writings: the image of the state replaces the image of the beloved; otherwise, the technique is identical. But in each case the reader is inevitably the voyeur: the invitation to willed self-denial is made seductive by eroticizing it or by ennobling it, or both. At a level of multiple fiction Rousseau sought to contain the reader within a structure whose harmony that reader wishes both to interrupt and to preserve. One wills that the marriage of Sophie and Emile be consecrated but submits to the textual authority that denies one that satisfaction. In return, the reader enjoys the privilege of knowing the characters better than they can know themselves, of sharing with Rousseau the creation and measurement of their identities and the growth of their knowledge. Rousseau invents a form of textual romanticism to teach the reader to reflect on the very limits of the will and its relationship to desire.

The Psychology of Love:
Family Happiness

In *Emile* Rousseau's separation of Sophie and her lover appears to have another, more political purpose. The two-year preparation for marriage is supposed to pave the way for an interest in citizenship: "In aspiring to the status of husband and father, have you meditated enough upon its duties? When you become the head of a family, you are going to become a member of the state, and do you know what it is to be a member of the state?" (*E*, 448).

But the union of Emile and Sophie, grounded on mutual illusion, is an unstable base for the development of social responsibilities. As the closing passages of the text make clear, Emile will have precious little to do with public politics. Rather, he will live in "simple retreat" and is "not the man who will be sought out to serve the state" (*E*, 474–75). The innate fragility of the marriage between Emile and Sophie is further reinforced by Rousseau's (unpublished) sequel to the work, in which Sophie commits adultery in Paris and Emile seeks refuge in solitary travel.[40]

Emile was not Rousseau's only excursion into the moral psychology of marriage and passion. In his best-selling novel, *Julie, ou la nouvelle Héloise*, Rousseau tried once again to portray "morality and conjugal fidelity, which are radically connected with all social order" (*Conf.*, 405).[41] In dramatic contrast to the relationship of Emile and Sophie, Rousseau abandoned the attempt to harmonize the sentiment of love with the institution of marriage and no longer tried to create the image of an idealized artificial union. Instead, Rousseau appeared to offer a less idealistic account of human relationships through which he intended to educate the reader: "If novels offered their readers only portraits of objects that surrounded them, only duties that they can perform, only the pleasures of their condition; novels would not make people foolish but wise" (second preface to *NH*, in *OC*, 2:21–22).

Rousseau announced that he himself has composed such a novel. *La nouvelle Héloïse* is divided into two substantive parts: the first an account of a passionate relationship between Julie and Saint-Preux, the second the story of Julie's marriage and family life. The passion that develops between Julie and her tutor has little in common with the relationship between Sophie and Emile. Rousseau persisted in describing the love between the protagonists as an illusion, but the sense in which he used the phrase is completely altered. The love between Julie and Saint-Preux is an illusion because it provokes Saint-Preux to prefer the imperfections he perceives in his beloved to the more perfect individual she might have been. This is why Saint-Preux is able to report to Julie that "love *does not blind me to your faults,* but it makes them dear to me, and such is its illusion that I would have loved you less if you had been more perfect" (*NH*, 2:436; emphasis added).[42]

In stark contrast to the relationship between Emile and Sophie, the passion that holds Saint-Preux and Julie in its sway affords each the possibility of the sharpest insight into the character of the other. Saint-Preux grasps with considerable acumen the struggles that Julie encounters as she attempts to forget her love for him. Indeed, he is not above using the knowledge to embarrass her (*NH*, 2:485). He sees immediately how Julie manipulates those around her at Clarence: "You carry out, in the simplicity of private life, a despotic empire," he remarks to his old mistress (2:607).[43] Moreover, Saint-Preux is under no illusions about Julie's power over him. The "strange empire" that Julie's passion constitutes and rules can render "privations as sweet as pleasures" and thus hold him helplessly in its grip (2:122).

For her part Julie is under no illusions about the strengths and weaknesses of her lover. She finds Saint-Preux on occasion "sublime and servile, full of farce and puerilities." She asks him despairingly when he will "cease to be a child" (*NH*, 2:687). At the same time she knows full well the power of his love: despite her marriage to Wolmar, Saint-Preux remains a "dangerous man," the more so because his travels have finally endowed him with an impressive maturity (2:634). (It is true that Julie claims that her love for Saint-Preux is based on illusion, but she does so in an effort to persuade him to accept her marriage with Wolmar, a context that suggests a strong degree of disingenuousness [2:372]).[44]

In short, unlike Sophie and Emile, the lovers in *Julie* see each other as particular, unique individuals with whom the reader is supposed to identify.[45] So strong is the lovers' mutual passion that they proclaim it impossible to exist without seeing themselves as constituted by the other. Saint-Preux longs to "reconstruct my soul in you [Julie] alone," and Julie, who believes she herself is "no longer anything," calls on him to become her "only existence" (*NH*, 2:83, 335). Separated from Julie, Saint-Preux tries to live an independent existence in Paris, only to experience shame and humiliation.[46] Utterly dependent on each other, it appears to the impartial observer that the lovers make a perfect couple. As Bromston remarks, "in sweet and happy union . . . they might have enlightened the world with their example" (2:193).[47]

Was it possible that, having "reunite[d] the two halves" of their being, the lovers would have become in time sober and responsible parents, the foundation of a stable order? (*NH*, 2:93). It was not. Rousseau was convinced that the love that brought Julie and Saint-Preux together was necessarily antagonistic to the development of domestic tranquility. His reasons were several. The first we have encountered in *Emilé*; a passion as strong as that between the two lovers in *La nouvelle Héloise* would exhaust itself if permitted to feed on overexposure. Sexual desire is a "fire that nothing can hold back," but it is of short duration (2:64). As Wolmar remarks, "if they had stayed together for longer they would again have become gradually colder" (2:509). In passionate affairs of the heart, Rousseau argued, separation was inseparable from preservation.

Rousseau's second argument is practical. The preservation of the domestic order that the novel celebrates required that men and women love each other in a way that left sufficient space for their domestic duties. Lovers who sought to ignore their domestic responsibilities by losing themselves in each other threatened to destroy that space through hedonistic irresponsibility: "Lovers never see anyone but themselves, are occupied incessantly only with themselves, and the only thing that they know how to do is to love one another. This is not enough for spouses who have many cares to look after" (*NH*, 2:372). "Man and wife" Rousseau argues through the voice of Julie (who is echoing Wolmar), "should not be thinking always of each other but jointly [should] discharge the duties of civil life" (2:372).

One can now make sense of the fact that the love between Julie and Saint-Preux could not represent a portrait of domestic harmony. Marriage, according to Julie, must be built on a "very gentle bond, which . . . is more durable than love" (*NH*, 2:372). Marriage involves devotion to pure duty, general and perfect. The love of Saint-Preux and Julie, on the other hand, celebrates the individual, the less than perfect. Saint-Preux, we recall, would "have loved [her] less if she had been more perfect." Yet Julie experiences "continual anxiety" when she reflects on the real failings of Saint-Preux (2:372).

In Rousseau's sequel to *Emile* the marriage of Emile and Sophie, based on an illusion of perfection, shatters when confronted with the reality of Paris. The passion between Julie and Saint-Preux, based on mutual knowledge and dependency, is incapable of making room for the responsibilities of the social order. This does not mean, of course, that the passion between Julie and Saint-Preux must simply be extinguished. The couple has to find a way to preserve a love threatened by internal instability, social pressures, and the transient heat of passion, because that love, while incompatible with marriage, can still become for them a passport to virtue and self-awareness. Saint-Preux and Julie must wage a continual struggle, often alone, to meet the demands of duty on the one hand and passion on the other. Their story is the edifying tale of the manner in which the passion that lies at the foundation of love may be controlled for the purposes of engendering virtue and preserving the love on which that virtue feeds. As Wolmar puts it, "Your mutual attachment related to so many praiseworthy things, that it was necessary to *regulate* it rather than annihilate it" (*NH*, 2:495; emphasis added). Just as the skill of the Tutor had provided for Emile a well-regulated freedom, so Julie and Saint-Preux must regulate each other's behavior for their mutual benefit.

One might argue that it is Wolmar who plays the role of tutor for the lovers. Himself capable of only "feeble passion," Wolmar reunites Julie and Saint-Preux at Clarence while insuring that his own presence as husband and father keeps them psychologically separated (*NH*, 2:493). Wolmar insures that the lovers "burn more strongly than ever for each other" in a way that can never transgress the bounds of "an honorable attachment" (2:508). But his success is less than complete, for Wolmar seeks to force Saint-Preux "always to see the wife of an honest man and the mother of [Wolmar's] children" (2:511). If he succeeded, Saint-Preux would no longer have to struggle with the memories of Julie and would be able to retire from the struggle that virtue demanded. Therefore, Wolmar cannot and does not succeed.

Nor does he succeed in creating a structure at Clarence in which Julie will forget her love for Saint-Preux. Although she suggests that there were moments when she experienced "the illusion" of having done so, she was deluded by the domestic tranquility of her household, and she dies knowing it (*NH*, 2:740). For her, as for Saint-Preux, "virtue is a state of war," not of victory (2:682).[48] Wolmar is the servant of passionate love rather than its master. He provides for Julie and Saint-Preux a separation, first physical and then mental, which permits them to maintain their love and grow in virtue.

The strategy is similar to that undertaken by the Tutor in *Emile*. He too separates Emile and Sophie, forcing Emile to experience the tension between desire and principle. But there is an important difference: Emile accepts the command of his tutor because he is captivated by the ideal image of husband and wife which the Tutor presents; Wolmar, on the other hand, separates Julie and Saint-Preux only because Julie has commanded him to do so. She has understood the psychological implications of her own passion and has willed the means of its restraint.

In each case the fruits of psychological struggle are habits of virtue and insight. As we shall discover, this idea of inculcating ethical judgment by the enforced separation of the sexes plays a principal role in Rousseau's conception of Geneva, while the induced sense of internal conflict between desire and inclination is the product of the general will. Rousseau politicizes but does not transform the role of Wolmar in the first case and Emile's tutor in the second. Moreover, the ambiguous relationship that Wolmar and the Tutor exhibit toward those in their charge reappears in the figure of Rousseau himself (in the *Letter to D'Alembert*) and the Lawgiver (in *The Social Contract*). Wolmar and the Tutor are both part of and yet essentially marginal to the emotions they engender; both are characters whose ghostly, improbable identities make possible their idealized roles.

The reader of *Emile* and *La nouvelle Héloïse* is given access to fictional spaces situated within boundaries both physical (as in the case of the child Emile) and psychological (as in the case of the separation of Emile and Sophie or Julie and Saint-Preux). The reader's desire to overcome the antimonies of these separations, to bring Emile to society or Julie and Saint-Preux to the physical passion one long anticipates, itself constitutes an education. Rousseau forges from the language of eroticism a syntactical space for learning: the illuminating self-discipline of chastity is made possible by the permanence and the absence of what is desired, the sexual consummation that would melt self into other. Forced to confront paradox after paradox of liberating constraint, Rousseau's readers can learn to measure their own desires by thinking through their reactions to his textual strategies. Emile's "perfect freedom" is grounded on artifice—but must sources external to the infant not take full responsibility for the education of one so helpless? His introduction to society collapses the boundaries within which Emile had once spontaneously enjoyed his childhood—but how else to enable him to take over the task of self-judgment and the measure of society? In what form but the preservation of desire from attachment to the particular other could Rousseau have preserved the discipline required so that Emile might develop acute judgment? Who, finally, is the author of these inescapable paradoxes, which represent the falling away, the substitutions for that impossible unity of knowing innocence—Rousseau, the Tutor, Wolmar, or ourselves? Reading these texts of Rousseau introduces us to the most critical tool of pedagogy, to its construction of managed separation. Between longing and fulfillment, between the self and the other, between the language of a particular community and the ideals through which that community might be measured, the pupil learns. But such learning can only occur if we, the citizens who will authorize our teachers to teach, can be brought to accept the same lesson.

4

The Education of
the Sovereign

ROUSSEAU asks questions that no educator can neglect, simply because those questions reach to the heart of the educational challenge. Childhood is not Blake's "age of experience"—thus, teacher and child together must manage the transition between helpless instinct and social awareness. This implies, however, that the teacher's practices embody a judgment about social mores and the perspective that the child will be led to adopt toward those mores. Rousseau was convinced that society around him had lost its capacity for self-governance and self-awareness through an infatuation with the pursuit of the limitless. His task, the successful outcome of which he was never persuaded of, was to educate future educators. Rousseau tried to teach the critical importance of self-imposed separations, limits, and denials. Children, Rousseau suggested, will only develop into adults capable of measuring the sphere, the language, and the social psychology of their culture, if their education has brought them to a familiarity and habituation with constraint.

Contemporary critics of Rousseau's influence on education fail to grasp that his romanticism and his celebration of the innocence of the child are both forms of immanent critique. The eroticism of separation is a commentary on and in part a replacement for Neoplatonism; it schools the judgment. The conceit of the innocence of newborn nature enables Rousseau to project his own conception of educated freedom, Emile's, against the "freedom" of modernity. The distance between the two conceptions is once again pedagogic. As readers, Rousseau asks that we judge between the two.

In the texts considered so far Rousseau has not pushed that comparison into the realm of the political itself. It is as yet unclear how an education grounded on self-separation, on the internalization of suspended consummation, might enable the ideal citizen to recreate the capacities taught to Emile. Nor is it clear what form of freedom and judgment such a citizen could enjoy. More critically, since Rousseau once again will insist that his imaginative constructions of political spaces are heuristic, we have yet to suggest what Rousseau's readers, the teacher-citizens, are to learn from his political treatises.

Certainly, there is no break of imagery or intent between the works considered in the previous chapter and those in which Rousseau speaks directly of politics. The three concepts already isolated— managed freedom, managed socialization, and managed love—are also the focus of Rousseau's political imagination. In each instance the tension between self-management and external control, or put differently, the problem of authority which underpinned Rousseau's efforts to redirect psychological development, will reemerge in political terms.

The building blocks for my analysis can be briefly summarized. Through the device of a reconstructed natural history Rousseau describes the psychological consequences of socialization in contemporary society. Modernity, in Rousseau's view, is the consequence of *amour-propre* run wild. Self-love has put humans at the mercy of their neighbors. Everyone strives to be envied by the less fortunate, who in turn must feel themselves pitied and thus humiliated. Rousseau condemns the resulting society principally because it rewards the successful use of deception: citizens begin to worship the material signs through which society identifies its icons. All sense of self-worth depends on differentiating oneself from another person for the sake of social praise. Success depends on persuading everyone else that our egotistically motivated activities are in their interests. (Rousseau did not greatly distinguish between private and public conditions because *amour-propre* socializes men from the start).

In Rousseau's view the philosophy, technology, and politics of his age infinitely exacerbated the difficulty of sustaining the self-willed and self-managed constraints of the type his model of education was designed to promote. Cultural developments have produced a form of adult dependency which undermines will power. The link is already clear in one of Rousseau's earliest works, the preface to *Narcisse:*

All our writers regard the crowning achievement of our century's politics to be the sciences, the arts, luxury, commerce, laws, and all the other bonds which, by tightening the knots of society among men through self-interest, place them all in a position of mutual dependence, impose on them mutual needs and common interests, and oblige everyone to contribute to everyone else's happiness in order to secure his own. . . . It is a wonderful thing, then, to have placed men in a position where they cannot possibly live together without obstructing, supplanting, deceiving, betraying, destroying one another! From now on we must take care never to let ourselves be seen as we are: because for every two men whose interests coincide, perhaps a hundred thousand oppose them. . . . That is the fatal source of the violence, the betrayals, the deceits and all the horrors necessarily required by a state of affairs in which everyone pretends to be working for the others' profit or reputation, while only seeking to raise his own above them at their expense. (104–5)

The general welfare and common interest of contemporary society is an operating myth that is generated by the psychological needs of its members. The bifurcation of man—private egotist and public actor—isolates him in the midst of society. But this is not a bifurcation the bourgeoisie is aware of. Rousseau's analogy of the spoiled child is apposite: ceaseless social competition has exhausted human energies and rendered people unable to conceive of alternative ways of life. The result is not a "natural man behind a mask" but, rather, a creature who has become wholly artificial under its concealment: "Almost never being in himself, he is always . . . ill at ease when forced to go back there" (*Emile* [Manuscript Favre], in *OC*, 4:57; *E*, 230). My analysis of Rousseau's overtly political texts concentrates on this problematic of openness and concealment and its relationship to self-knowledge, self-constraint, and freedom.

To Love the State: Educating the Weak

How might education redirect those who were blindly prepared to celebrate the conditions of their own exhaustion? Rousseau, profoundly pessimistic about the possibilities, concluded that "the blindest obedience . . . [was] the sole virtue which remains for slaves" (*SD*, 177). He sought an educative strategy to transform this virtue so as to "raise men above themselves."[1] Regarding adults as sick children in need of drastic medicine, Rousseau would risk deliberate manipulation in a bid to transform their political and psychological habits.

At first glance Rousseau's medicine appears draconian: "What is useful for the public," he wrote, "is hardly ever introduced except by force" (*OC*, 3:599). Citizens must be "made to feel happiness in order to make them love it," if necessary by "forcing them" to feel the happiness they had to love (*Heros*, 3:1263–64). But Rousseau was never content to equate happiness with violence. He knew that any state could employ force to suppress the populace under the pretext of educating and enriching them, "but this represents an illegitimate exercise of power" (*Corsica*, 281). "There was no art," Rousseau reminded his readers (and perhaps himself), "in making everyone tremble" (*Political*, 215).[2]

The state had other means at its disposal for the reeducation of its citizens. In the earlier passage from the *Narcisse* Rousseau had identified the consequences of socialized *amour-propre* on a population. It had "place[d] them all in a position of mutual dependence, impose[d] on them mutual needs and common interests, and oblige[d] everyone to contribute to everyone else's happiness in order to secure his own" (*Narcisse*, 105). Rather than combating this condition, Rousseau's method was to uncover strategies to render it benign. Policymakers could use the condition of mutual dependency to turn the lust for private gain back toward the disciplining constraints of community interest.

The first requirement for revitalizing a community was economic. The state had to offer its citizens material and psychological preconditions of peaceful coexistence. This implied an egalitarian civic existence: within the frontiers of the state a rough equality of material circumstance would reduce social suspicions and nurture public confidence. Only in these conditions could the state ask its citizens to give themselves to the service of one another. Citizens would learn that public "attachments" were worthy of the energy they would have to invest in their maintenance: "Do we want peoples to be virtuous? Let us then start by making them love their homeland. But how are they to love it if . . . they did not even enjoy civil safety there, and if their goods, life or freedom were at the discretion of powerful men, without its being either possible or permitted for them to dare invoke the laws" (*Political*, 219). If the state is to create a legitimate political education around the core concept of civic-minded virtue, it must bring aspiration and experience into alignment. The state can only ask citizens to love an entity of which they are a coequal part.

Rousseau's specific recommendations are therefore geared, whenever possible, to the end of material egalitarianism. He argued that "all fortunes" should be brought "closer to the moderation that creates the true force of the State" (*Political,* 235). Inequalities between citizens gave the strong both the interest and the means through which to make others miserable. Even the law becomes "equally powerless against the treasures of the rich and against the indigence of the poor" (221).

In Rousseau's incomplete designs for a constitution for Corsica we find the most developed form of his political economy. Rousseau's recommendations embrace economic egalitarianism, but only as a first step in political reconstruction. Rousseau reminded his reader of certain principles drawn from his psychology: "the great springs of human conduct come down, on close examination, to two, pleasure and vanity," adding as an afterthought that "in the last analysis everything comes down to practically pure vanity" (*Corsica,* 325). Citizens will more readily obey community law if within the life it circumscribes there is a space for vanity.

In a geographically self-contained and small island such as Corsica it might be possible for the state to monopolize and, through psychological manipulation, create the demand for and the supply of this most sought-after commodity. In Rousseau's blueprint for the island "all the means of acquiring social recognition" would belong to the state (*Corsica,* 310). It would award property ownership "only in proportion to . . . [the] services" of the citizen (317). "Naturally lazy" men would be kept busy in their fields providing food for the community or in the state militia protecting it (329). Vanity, on account of which humans gave "value to that which is valueless," would thus be transformed into virtuous pride. Citizens would derive "self-esteem from truly estimable goods"—namely, those goods that were of common benefit (326).

Corsica's geography, climate, and history were uniquely suited to plans that relied, quite literally, on closing off the space of political life from external influences. Economic and psychological transformation could perhaps prepare the Corsicans for self-rule: in the *Social Contract* Rousseau had famously described the island as the last remaining candidate for genuine political reform (*SC,* 75). But the geopolitics of Corsica were sui generis. Restructuring the political and psychological world of contented, deluded, and socially stratified mass society was a very different business. An egalitarian society grounded on the rule of law would not appear overly attractive to citizens whose minds were infused with the habits of an open-ended pursuit of self-glorification. Asked to propose a fresh constitution for the Polish state, Rousseau had first to overcome this obstacle: "Oh proud and holy liberty! . . . if [the people] realized at what price thou art won and preserved, if they felt how much more austere are thy laws than the yoke of tyrants is heavy: their feeble souls, enslaved by passions that would have to be suppressed, would fear them a hundred times more than slavery: they would flee from thee in terror as a burden threatening to crush them." Liberty was a food "hard to digest," and those who were in desperate need of its sustenance were weak stomached (*Poland*, 186). In the case of Poland, Rousseau despairs of success. He offered proposals by means of which the state could educate its citizens to love an idealized vision of Poland which would lie inchoate within their collective imagination and hopes. Rousseau took the artificially contained space within which the Tutor had invisibly constrained Emile and nationalized it. The task was all but impossible: evoking the geometric metaphors of which he was so fond, Rousseau equated the task of reordering the citizen's psychological orientation with that of "squaring of the circle in geometry" (161).[3]

The capacity of large, corrupt states to redirect the preferences of their mature citizens without terrifying them was considerably more limited than was the case in Corsica. Rousseau's habit of undermining a project as he outlines it resurfaces. It was simply "too late to draw us out of our ourselves once the human self . . . had acquired that contemptible activity that absorbs all virtue" (*Political*, 222–23). The redirecting had to take place at an earlier stage, before other preferences had a chance to take root. If education was to "move" "the hearts of men" it must operate before they become corrupt (*Poland*, 162). Thus, the education of the young reemerged inevitably at the heart of Rousseau's political thought: "To have . . . [citizens] as men they must be educated as children" (*Political*, 222). As so often, Rousseau turned the project for reform into a project of refounding the state through a pedagogic rebirth.

Carefully regulated public schools would teach children to love only what it was in their interest to love. "Public education" would represent "one of the fundamental maxims of popular or legitimate government" (*Political*, 223). Children would learn to ground their own self-respect on the pursuit of publicly chosen and supervised objects. "Trained early enough," they would "never . . . consider their persons except as related to the body of the State" (222).[4] In a country such as Poland, land-locked and continuously subject to the most violent external interference, education would replace the oceans that surrounded Corsica and build emotional "ramparts" behind which the Polish nation would survive (*Poland*, 168). Only education could produce citizens "patriotic by inclination, by passion [and] by necessity" (176n).

To love the Polish state was to love that which denied the possibility of privately defined ends. "Constantly occupied" from first to last with the pursuit of publicly constituted goals, the children of the state will be "accustom[ed] . . . at an early age to rules, to equality, to fraternity, to competition, to living under the eyes of their fellow citizens, and to deserving public approbation" (*Poland*, 179). So educated, the Polish child would never experience the path that would lead him to virtue as an onerous one. "Educated together and in the same fashion" as his fellow citizens, the young Pole would be relieved of the burden of having to resolve the competing claims of private and public spheres: the former would simply disappear (177).

In the *Second Discourse* Rousseau imagined the necessary moment at which mankind had finally thrown away its freedom: "The first person who, having fenced off a plot of ground, took it into his head to say *this is mine* and found people simple enough to believe him, was the true founder of civil society" (*SD*, 141). Since the concept of possession was now too powerfully enshrined to be ignored, Rousseau sought to generalize it to the state level. In Corsica the state would literally "own everything"; in Poland it would control access to all positions of prestige (*Corsica*, 317; *Poland*, 170). Citizens would become appendages to the state without which neither it nor they could survive: in order to liberate men from the crippling servitude to which they had succumbed individually, political education would have to relocate individualism into a single Leviathan: "The body politic, taken individually, can be considered to be like a body that is organized, living, and similar to that of a man . . . the citizens are the body and members that make the machine move, live and work" (*Political*, 211–12). Outside the machine there would exist no alternative locus, no competing possibility. If the education of the young Pole were successful, he would be prepared to emulate the example of Cato, who "takes leave of the earth when he no longer sees any homeland to serve" (*Political*, 219).

Rousseau's determination to leave the young citizen with a singular point of focus leaves him highly ambivalent about the family. When Rousseau speaks in the *Political Economy* of "the tender mother" who nourishes her children, and the "inestimable benefits they receive from her," he is speaking of the state—that same "common mother" who (or so he claims) would nurse his own siblings (*Political*, 223; *Conf.*, 221). "Even in the family" Rousseau remarks, "the Republic commands in preference to the father." It will "prescribe common laws to all the families and provide in a uniform manner for the authority of the father, the obedience of the servants, and the education of the children" (*Fragments*, 3:488).

Citizens would obey the laws of the state, which in turn would grant them "civil safety" and psychological tranquility (*Political,* 219). A reconstructed political economy would protect the citizens from the "multitude of relationships lacking order, regulation and stability" threatened by the modern age (*Geneva,* 158). Citizens who "love their duty" would conform their will to state laws; the laws, in turn, are designed to make nonconformity inconceivable: they have "plucked from [the] heart the passions which lead to the evasion of [the] laws" (*Political,* 218).

Rousseau's blueprint for economic and legal reconstruction is a conscious effort to recreate a political and psychological framework in which public education could motivate the weak to behave virtuously. In the *First Discourse* Rousseau eulogized virtue as an ancient achievement now glorious only in memory. There had been a time when the Persians had absorbed virtue with ease, when it had been the birthright of every Spartan, when Rome had embodied its temple (*FD,* 41, 43, 40).[5] It was the "sublime science of simple souls" which philosophers had long since "annihilat[ed]" (64, 50).[6] Those who had once respected the dignity of the "old fashioned words of fatherland and religion," who understood the claims of duty and "ought," were no more (50, 57).

Rousseau's recommendations to Poland and Corsica represented the recreation of the conditions of Sparta. Rousseau believes that, in an egalitarian economic and social structure, "sincere friendships" and "real esteem" might reemerge between the inhabitants of the community (*FD,* 38). The presence of an unbreakable cord that linked each citizen to the collective whole would insure tranquility within and without the city walls. Virtuous citizens with nothing to hide would find "security in the ease of seeing through each other" (37). Transparency within the city fused with the manliness of its male citizens was the best guarantee of destroying psychological and political anxiety.

Virtuous citizens would find themselves contained in an enclosure both physical and mental. The restricted space of the community would maintain those energies vital to its preservation: "Interest and commiseration must be confined and compressed to be activated," Rousseau concludes (*Political,* 219). Placed constantly before the gaze of their peers, and largely denied the example of the arts, no citizen would be able to develop the skills of dissemblance, which could only breed distrust. Those born into such a regime could no more think of questioning the legitimacy of its constraints than Emile could conceive of disputing the boundaries within which he found himself.

Rousseau's celebration of patriotic identification appears to leave little room for freedom—beyond the freedom from invasion. His emphasis on the need for "the most absolute authority" on the part of the government offers no scope for the exercise of spontaneously generated activity (*Political,* 216). Notwithstanding his claim that "liberty is better" than discipline, Rousseau seemed ready to sacrifice the former on the altar of order in the state (198). Even the Corsicans are to be reeducated to the point at which they are "incapable even of imagining a better or nobler way of life" (*Corsica,* 310).

What Rousseau tries to provide for the ever unfortunate Poles is the psychological condition of the savage, "whose heart is at peace and whose body is healthy." The Poles are "free" only in the sense that the savage can also be called a "free being" (*SD,* 127). But that which separated man from beast is precisely the capacity of the former to "realize[ ] that he is free to acquiesce or resist." It was "above all in the consciousness of this freedom that the spirituality of . . . [man's] soul is shown" (114). Rousseau was fully aware of the limitations that accompanied the kind of freedom which the Polish citizen, for one, could actually enjoy. If a self-conscious awareness of alternatives was not a luxury that the Poles could afford, Rousseau was aware of the cost. Inequality, cultural incoherence, and a constantly shifting geographical frontier had reduced the Poles to misery: their reeducation represents the kindergarten of Rousseau's pedagogic schema.

Taken out of context, these passages are naturally unattractive to the liberal reader and are no longer much discussed, but they have an importance nonetheless. Rousseau pinpoints the critical relationship between the geopolitics, social culture, and economics of education. A community can redirect the energies of its future citizens to the pursuit of collective goods by harnessing the ego to communal goals, but not when the effort is damned by a society in which the law is a servant of the few. Rousseau also suggests that the idea of a defined space within which the state can reanimate the loyalties, and thus the energies, of the disoriented young need not be simply geographic. The education of the Poles would occur through an exposure to patriotism that Rousseau defined in a historical, even a mythical, vocabulary. Rousseau acknowledged that such a vocabulary would enable only the most rudimentary self-awareness, but, while lacking sophistication, the energies that such an education could unleash would allow the citizen to measure the performance of the political elite against an ideal of communal destiny. Rousseau was comfortably certain that such judgment would be harsh enough to provoke reform. It was a start.

Geneva: The Education of
Sovereign Citizens

Rousseau's political experiments went far beyond Corsica or Poland. His debates with the city republic of Geneva constitute a fresh drama, a vision of the way political action might persuade a mature and free citizenry to maintain its collective identity and educate its children. Building on the model of *Emile*, Rousseau suggested how to seduce human beings, in full consciousness, to pity what they are not and thus to love the community through which they would define themselves. *The Letter to D'Alembert*, in which this dynamic of self-seduction is played out, is Rousseau's most direct and developed statement about the powers of democratic education.

Rousseau's relationship with Geneva, the city of his birth and occasional citizenship, was extremely opaque. In his *Confessions* Rousseau suggested something of the complexity:

> I passed through Geneva without going to see anyone, but I almost felt faint as I crossed the bridges. Never have I seen the walls of that happy city, never have I entered it, without feeling a certain sinking of the heart, the product of an excess of emotion. The noble ideal of liberty exalted my spirit, while at the same time the thought of equality, unity, and gentleness of manners moved me to tears, and inspired me with a keen regret that I had lost all those blessings. How wrong I was, and yet how natural was my mistake! I imagined that I saw all this in my native land, because I carried it in my own heart. (*Conf.*, 141)

The erotic attraction to the geography of the enclosed city; the attachment to the concept of a people, but not a single individual; the celebration of liberty; and the confession that the image owed more to internally generated fantasy than to the political reality—all these sentiments are in the text. Geneva unquestionably serves Rousseau as a metaphor for an imagined civic utopia. He anthropomorphized Geneva in terms that remind us of the mother Rousseau never knew, and he blamed his city for not corresponding to the perfection it ought to have possessed. The seductive urge to refound a community in Rousseau's imagination is as powerful as ever.

Nevertheless, Rousseau's conception of Geneva embodied more than such complex fictions. The city was also an irreducible political reality in his own life. It was Geneva that Rousseau's father chose to abandon when it failed to enforce its own laws. It was that city whose walls Rousseau's uncle helped to construct. It was Geneva that banned *The Social Contract* and *Emile*. Most important perhaps, Geneva, for all its faults, represented an ongoing political experiment in which citizen Rousseau felt himself inextricably involved and an experiment in which he saw much to applaud. To some degree the claims of the city were constitutive for Rousseau, self-proclaimed *citoyen de Genève*.

Rousseau's *Letter to D'Alembert* represents the occasion when a citizen sought to manage the behavior of his peers at a moment when they have been presented with an opportunity to pervert the nature of their civic existence. Rousseau argued that the dynamic of self-education (and self-flattery) on which Geneva depended was under threat, and he criticized his city for its refusal to take the threat seriously. The cause of Rousseau's consternation was D'Alembert's new proposal (contained in his article for *L'Encyclopedie* of 1757) that Geneva construct a public theater. D'Alembert argued that the absence of such an institution represented a lacuna in the town's otherwise impressive civic credentials. With the addition of a theater Geneva could "join to the prudence of Lacedaemon the urbanity of Athens." Since D'Alembert embedded this recommendation in a letter that otherwise consisted of unmitigated praise for the city, his advice appeared to offer Geneva an instant, single, and simple step to greatness. The city required only a theater to give itself that "fineness of tact" and "delicacy of sentiment" which it surely wanted (*L*, 4).

The theater would "form the taste of the citizens" to the point at which they could match "philosophy and liberty" to the social excitement that the theater would generate. For, unfortunately, D'Alembert confided to the Genevans, their virtue was considered "dull" by the French, and thus, by extension, by educated Europe (*L*, 4). Was it not slightly embarrassing, he suggested, that a city that "judges all the sovereigns of Europe," which was "rich in its liberty and its commerce," and which played host to Voltaire, insisted on boring itself and its visitors with "coarse and silly farces?" (142, 4).

Rousseau was fully aware of the fact that Geneva was not the utopia that D'Alembert had described. Three years before the publication of D'Alembert's article Rousseau had already reproached Geneva for its "indiscreet excess" (*SD*, 90). What made Rousseau's second intervention, in the form of the letter, inevitable was not D'Alembert's suggestion that perfection lay close at hand for the virtuous Genevese but, rather, that the path to such perfection lay in the direction opposite to that which Rousseau had urged. In D'Alembert's mind the city had only to realize that it could become a spectacle of the

Enlightenment, and it would discover itself to be perfectly suited to the role.

Only a challenge as elegant, persuasive, and poisonous as this could have demanded a response, for Rousseau was acutely aware of the risks raised by his own intervention.[7] The very fact of engaging in polemical debate would throw into high relief what might otherwise have been perceived as a modest episode in the life of Geneva. D'Alembert's letter could only be answered by directly revealing to the Genevese what Rousseau hoped from them.[8] But such a revelation was a crude and ineffective didactic tool; one of the principal criticisms Rousseau made of drama was that, "as a result of showing them that we want to instruct them, we no longer instruct them" (L, 28). Knowing that his letter represented just such a didactic episode, Rousseau confessed his "repugnance" at "putting [his] fellow citizens on the stage" and declared that he delayed doing so "as long as [he] could" (92).[9]

Despite these protestations, the precise form of Rousseau's intervention remains opaque. In one voice Rousseau identifies himself as a Genevese, but it will become evident that the substance of his warning depends on Rousseau's experience as a European wanderer. Rousseau makes of his self-imposed exile a resource for internal intervention in the city. The dilemma of location, of placement inside or outside the city, emerges again in Rousseau's strategy of (re)describing Geneva to its own inhabitants. He evoked a city that is recognizably the Geneva of 1754 but exaggerated the qualities of that city to the point of fiction. Furthermore, he did so in a vocabulary Rousseau knew to be as inaccurate as it was popular. Geneva is thus criticized by a critic whose life experience placed him neither fully inside nor outside the city and against a standard that both is and is not grounded in Geneva's own history. As in the case of the ancient *Epitaphios*, Rousseau asked his fellow citizens to judge themselves against an ideal and to consider the gap that separated them from its realization. In the cases of Corsica and Poland Rousseau serves as an external advisor called in for emergency reconstruction. In the case of Geneva he must authorize and legitimate his own intervention as a civic educator.

In the *Second Discourse* Rousseau had flattered Geneva before, but the tone was deliberately ironic. In the *Letter* he tried to persuade his fellow citizens that their lives must be judged by the standards he describes while suggesting to the more sensitive reader the very evil—namely, the theatricality of the letter—made necessary by any dramatic mode of political persuasion. Rousseau thus summons himself to political action through a form of intervention he then seeks to efface. Rousseau must use the weapon of literary theater to repel D'Alembert's yet more dangerous theater proper. Beyond this fragile double play Rousseau tried to strengthen the target of his critique—the weakened civic resolve of the Genevese. Only their internal weakness makes D'Alembert's attack dangerous.

To hold up a mirror before the Genevese was to put at risk patterns of behavior which could still evoke in Rousseau the image of a truly virtuous citizenry. In his description—part historical, part imaginative—Rousseau makes more specific those conditions for civic virtue which had been inchoate in the *Discourses*. In the virtuous Geneva of Rousseau's imagination the citizens enjoy a form of life which embodied a particular balance between self-understanding, energy, and spontaneously enacted tradition. The walls of the city (which he frequently evoked in the text) enclose the unique space within which this balance is played out. The material vocabulary of politics is egalitarian, all energies are dedicated toward communal survival. But the police force of the city is more than hunger; it was also tradition, eros, and shame.

Geneva was able to feed its citizens and afford them relatively "easy circumstances," only through dint of the hard work of its members. Within the city walls "everyone is busy, everyone is moving, everyone is about his work and his affairs" (*L*, 93). Only through the assistance of sumptuary laws and this constant industry was the city able to achieve its self-sufficiency. Departures from the city, which would result in the loss of productive activity, could occur only in the evening hours, when exhaustion would permit no greater distraction than a country walk (96).

If a high degree of material equality was the first binding feature of Rousseau's Geneva, the second was temporal stability. The unchanging civic experience of successive generations was both an enabling condition and a constraint on private freedom. In particular, Rousseau is concerned with the threat to stasis posed by sexuality. Unregulated sexual mores would undermine civic allegiance. It followed for Rousseau that the preferred locus of sexual activity had to be the family. In contrast to the *Political Economy*, there is no ambivalence or ambiguity in his endorsement. Geneva is not Sparta: the Genevan family complements rather than stands at odds with the state;[10] marriage is "the first and holiest of all bonds of society" (*L*, 128). Perhaps the single most essential role of the family was to supervise the education of the young. Rousseau depicts parents in constant interaction with their children: the fathers, taking their sons hunting, turn "scamps" into soldiers (112). At "solemn and periodic balls" mother and father together supervised their child's introduction to the opposite sex. The presence of grandparents at these functions served to cement the impression of the sanctity of the family unit in the eyes of the child (129). In a well-known letter to Dr. Tronchin, Rousseau summarizes the virtues of Geneva's education: "It is thus that the children ought to be educated, the girls by the mother, the boys by the father. This is exactly the education suited for us, midway between the public education of Greek Republics, and the domestic education of the monarchies in which all the people have to exercise in isolation with nothing in common save obedience" (*CC,* 5:242).[11] In addition to the family there was an alternative civic structure available for the cementing of sexual stability. These were the "circles," traditional institutions the role of which Rousseau totally transformed and eulogized in an imaginative reconstruction.[12] Circles were simply gatherings of citizens differentiated by sex. Men would meet to gamble and drink, women to gossip—but Rousseau believed that such apparently innocuous activities could cement virtuous family life and the safety of the city.

Understanding Rousseau's heavy reliance on the circles rests in turn on accepting at least one part of his teaching about the feminine sexual instinct. Rousseau attributed to women the biological desire to bind their mates ever more closely to themselves. This desire is facilitated by their modesty, a delicate but fearsome weapon. It is only "an apparent obstacle" that "seems" to keep men at a distance, but in fact it is the means by which men can be held most tightly in a woman's orbit: "The desires, veiled by shame, become only the more seductive" (*L,* 84). On the other hand, women do not, or more precisely should not, want a final victory. Too great a familiarity with men might encourage that sex to indulge women with "amorous speeches," but in the end familiarity would breed contempt (104).[13] Men tied too closely to women would become feminine: "[The] weaker sex, not in the position to take on our way of life . . . forces us to take on its way . . . and no longer wishing to tolerate separation . . . the women make us into women" (100).[14] Rousseau is convinced that Geneva could not survive if its women succeeded in feminizing men by allowing themselves to be the objects of possession, for the city must be defended by the strong, not the effeminate. But the city is likewise vulnerable to masculinity run rampant: the preservation of family life depends on sustaining and disciplining the male sex instinct. Even though the Genevan is "a steady sort" who "like[s] to live with his family," Rousseau wants to preserve the allure of sexual attraction by rendering it a scarce commodity (99).

The circles maintain, then, a politically crucial sexual balance:[15] by separating the sexes spatially and temporally, Rousseau sought to reproduce in political terms the enforced separation of Emile and Sophie, sublimating the desire for instant sexual gratification for the sake of the city. In their segregated gatherings male citizens would experience a camaraderie safe from the "fear of ridicule" that women would heap on their activities. Men learn in the circles to become "friends, citizens and soldiers" (*L,* 105). Women, in the safety of their own social gatherings hone the skills of their sex: through the trading of gossip they would learn the techniques of erotic management. In becoming "scandal mongers and satirists," they become the rulers of their husbands; gossip would censor male behavior (105–6). In Rousseau's view the circles should enable citizens to achieve the distance from one another that made public judgment possible and effective and thus sustained the homogeneity of the city.

Rousseau characterized a self-sufficient and harmonious city as one in which citizens had come to accept spatial constriction and unchanging temporal cycles. The reward for such acceptance was a psychological peace that came from the mastery of established social mores and public beliefs. Since public life freed citizens from any incentive to take advantage of one another (for the egalitarian, closed, and self-sufficient city has no benefits to bestow differentially), they could afford the luxury of public honesty. They would experience "the ease of seeing through one another" (*L,* xx), a civic transparency unavailable to the inhabitant of a more cosmopolitan, open, and inegalitarian community.

This is the virtuous image of Geneva which Rousseau saw as vulnerable to the introduction of a theater. What disturbed him was the manner in which the theater would misdirect Geneva by converting and then absorbing energies urgently required by the city. The audience that found itself admiring virtue on the stage would consider its dues to civic virtue fully paid up in the theater: "Has he not acquitted himself of all that he owes to virtue by the homage which he has just rendered it? What more could one want of him?" (*L,* 25). This argument is buttressed by Rousseau's analysis of the psychological reactions of the theatergoer. For the audience of Racine's *Berenice,* Rousseau admits, "the sacrifices made to duty and virtue always have a secret charm, even for corrupted hearts." But the play evokes a second and stronger emotion: the audience will feel pity for the queen, who must forgo her love for *raison d'état.* The spectator might overtly acknowledge the worthiness of Titus's departure yet privately hope that the act might have proved unnecessary. In the end the audience finds itself "secretly grumbling at the sacrifice . . . [Titus] is forced to make for the laws of his country" (53).

The experience of secretly pitying the costs of love will prove more seductive than the public celebration of civic virtue. This is enough to condemn it in Rousseau's eyes. For civic virtue embraces a network of affections and allegiances which tie family and city together, but the allure of theatric love threatens to remove "friends, neighbors and relatives" from the mind of the citizen (*L,* 17). Spectators who applaud Racine's Beatrice but write an alternative ending in their heads learn a damaging lesson. Such a citizen sees "people sacrificing everything to their duty while nothing is extracted from him." From here there is but the smallest leap to the idea that one might pursue private actions, sufficiently camouflaged, at the expense of public duties (24). As if these damaging consequences were not sufficient, the image of love on the stage, the image that so eclipses the virtue to which it has there succumbed, destroys the delicate sexual balance so crucial in Geneva. Rousseau makes several attempts to pin down the dynamics of this process: he suggests that putting love on stage will "increase the ascendancy of women" by affording them a fresh arena for the exercise of their powers. But he continues the argument by suggesting that the women of Geneva will in the end suffer a diminution in respect if their powers are made manifest on stage (47–49).

The theater would divert, undermine, and upset the loyalties on which Geneva depends. It could not do more. Rousseau stressed repeatedly that the character of the audience would remain independent of the example presented to its members onstage. Theater is not redemptive: "Let no one then attribute to the theater the power to change sentiments or morals, which it can only follow and embellish" (*L,* 19). Because, in the end, the playwrights have for their object "only applause," they cannot risk showing the audience a portrait too close to the bone. Nowhere were spectators to be found who would enjoy "see[ing] themselves in a light which made them despise themselves" (18).

Corrupted men may be entertained by the theater but cannot thereby be reformed. Virtuous men, such as the citizens of Geneva, are in no need of character reform, but their behavior patterns are vulnerable to the seductive alternatives the dramatist portrays on the stage. Paradoxically, within the closed space of the the theater the Genevese would discover only infinite sources of dissatisfaction with the civic spaces circumscribed by Geneva's walls. D'Alembert had suggested that a theater in Geneva would bring in foreign visitors; Rousseau is more concerned that it would lead to an exodus of the natives. Addressing D'Alembert directly, Rousseau wrote: "Do you know, Sir, whom we ought to try to attract and keep within our walls?

The Genevans themselves" (L, 132). This is precisely the task that D'Alembert's intervention has made more difficult.

Rousseau knew that the Genevese would need more than theoretical arguments to persuade them to go without the theater. With a mixture of flattery, and perhaps a touch of irony, Rousseau suggested to his fellow citizens that they make a spectacle of themselves. As a contemporary critic remarks, "public life as Rousseau imagines it is primarily a dynamic of self-seduction."[16] "Let the spectators become an entertainment to themselves, make them actors themselves, so that each sees and loves himself in the others so that all will be better united." No external portrait would distract the citizens from a display of collective narcissism: the citizens will see "nothing, if you please" (L, 126). Stage, pit, and city would become one again, self-love and virtue reunited, the balance of politics reestablished.

At least such was the image with which Rousseau both consoled and tortured himself. Excluded by politics from the real city of Geneva, Rousseau reconstructed it in his imagination and then sentimentalized his own exclusion. As citizen, he flattered his fellow citizens with an image of the perfect city; as solitary wanderer, he traced the origins of odyssey to his exclusion from the real city; as dreamer, he imagined himself welcomed back to a perfect republic. Above all, he sought in his testament to make citizens long for their city. The longing is already vivid in the *Confessions* at the moment when, as a young man, Rousseau found that the city guard had closed in his face the walls that hold virtue within: "It was too late. When I was twenty paces away I saw them raise the first bridge. I trembled as I watched its dreadful horns rising in the air, a sinister and fatal augury of the inevitable fate which from that moment awaited me. In the first access of my grief I threw myself down on the grass and bit the earth" (*Conf.*, 49). It is clear that Rousseau's self-conscious assignation of himself as "citizen of Geneva" is more than a rhetorical trope. Rather, it is an extension of naming, a performative self-identification that simultaneously assumes a citizen's liberating identity and shoulders constraining communal attachments. Rousseau's citizenship affords him yet another arena, both geographical and historical, both historical and projected, through which to measure his own identity. Rousseau put himself on the stage of his city—a city of public openness, continual celebration of the *moi commun,* and public education. Rousseau imagined a civic identity through which citizens would experience the rhythms, the achievements, the very existence of civic space as an extension of their own activity.

The cost of this ideal is correspondingly severe. The walls that enclose this civic Eden are absolute; citizens must condemn or pity the world beyond. As one exiled by the city, Rousseau consistently applies such judgments to himself. For the citizen there is no movement, but for Rousseau, always on the move, there can be no full citizenship and thus no home. Once again, in the course of measuring an existence for potential perfection, Rousseau reminds the reader that neither the Geneva of 1754 nor he himself can inhabit such a space. But the careful projections of the *Letter* may also have a wider message, which offers instruction for contemporary democratic citizens who must negotiate open-ended civic identities in communities with porous boundaries.

The Social Contract

The *Letter to D'Alembert* was not Rousseau's last word on political education in a city like Geneva. In the *Social Contract* he outlined the formal requirements of political organization which will educate citizens to the point at which they can become a self-governing sovereign body. Rousseau would later insist on the fact that the model for the *Social Contract* was Geneva itself, a claim not without foundation.[17] In any event, the opening books of that work suggest a political structure that would not be out of place in the Geneva Rousseau evoked in the Letter to D'Alembert. As in that earlier work, the sovereign citizens who would be parties to the social contract must make choices that will determine the shape of their material and moral world.

There is, however, a central difference between the intended audiences of the two works. The citizens of Geneva (in Rousseau's reconstruction) had long since achieved political socialization: social customs had to maintain the identification of self and city through civic self-flattery, but those customs were already in place. The *Social Contract* opens, so to speak, at an earlier and a later point: private desires are rampant. Rousseau recasts the creation of political virtue in more formal terms, shifting the temporal and spatial language from the specific to the abstract. In other words, following the example of the *Second Discourse* and the *Emile*, Rousseau imagines a moment of refounding.

Rousseau's exploration of the conditions of political order starts from a simple premise: humans who come together to "find a form of association that defends and protects the person and goods of each" must collectively agree to alter their behavior if that association is to survive (*SC*, 53). If the conditions of the association are correctly chosen, Rousseau argues, the citizen will be "forced to act upon other principles and to consult his reason before heeding his inclinations" (56). The source from which that force derives its legitimacy must be the citizen himself, such that, in heading those "other principles," he "obeys only himself and remains as free as before" (56, 53). In other words, the citizens of the *Social Contract* must be the architects of their own paths to virtue.

In the *Geneva Manuscript* (an earlier draft of the *Social Contract*) Rousseau had already indicated that the forging of self-sustaining structures that would harmonize the public and private interest was fraught with difficulties. "Where is the man" he asked, "who can thus separate himself from himself; and if concern for his self-preservation is nature's first precept, can he be forced to look in this manner at the species in general in order to impose on him duties whose connection with his particular constitution is not evident to him?" (*Geneva,* 161; altered translation).[18] Rousseau's concern is once again with the construction of a space for education and perception, for creating the psychological room for judgment. In the first two books of the *Social Contract* Rousseau suggests that the gap between private and public interests is likely to remain imperfectly bridged. Education can only make possible the negotiation of that chasm. For while it is "not impossible for a private will to agree with the general will on a given point," such an agreement would be the result of "chance" and its longevity "impossible" (*SC,* 59).

In the *Social Contract,* as in the *Letter to D'Alembert,* Rousseau investigates the construction of political identity, albeit this time at the level of universality. Rousseau asks how independent beings might come to think of themselves as owing a certain allegiance to the public interest and how such people might learn to reinterpret themselves through one another's needs. It is the same question that Protagoras had initiated in ancient Athens and shares a similar premise: "If there were not some point at which all the interests are in agreement, no society could exist" (*SC,* 59). In a Hobbesian vein it is fear and scarcity that persuade people that their selfish interests require collective solutions (52). The second assumption Rousseau relies on is at odds with Hobbes's teaching. Rousseau argues that those ready to relinquish independence for the sake of self-preservation would not surrender their freedom merely for peace and quiet: "It will be said that the despot guarantees civil tranquility to his subjects . . . but what have they gained if the wars that his ambition brings on them, if his insatiable greed, if the harassment of his ministers are a greater torment than their dissensions would be?

What have they gained if tranquility is one of their miseries? Life is tranquil in jails, too" (49).

Those who must embrace public help for the promotion of private desires will wish to remain in every degree the arbiters of their own fate. Again, Rousseau made the famous claim to have solved just this dilemma—of having found the "form of association . . . by means of which each one, uniting with all, nevertheless obeys only himself and remains as free as before" (*SC*, 53). But the nature of that freedom has inevitably changed from that which individuals had enjoyed in their prepolitical state. In the *Geneva Manuscript* Rousseau had acknowledged as much: there is a "great difference between being obligated to oneself, or to a whole of which one is a part" (164). In the *Social Contract* Rousseau is at pains to argue that the change is a positive one. The "civil freedom" that the Social Contract would provide the citizen was not synonymous with the "natural freedom" that it has replaced but, rather, a condition that promises to produce an "intelligent being" from a "stupid limited animal" (*SC*, 56).

To grasp the nature of this transformation is to understand the way in which an ideal political structure can provide an ethical and intelligent freedom. But this understanding depends in turn on making clear the precise nature of the contract to which these new citizens are to be subject: "The act of association includes a reciprocal engagement between public and private individuals, . . . each individual, contracting with himself *so to speak,* finds that he is doubly engaged, namely toward private individuals as a member of the sovereign and toward the sovereign as a member of the State" (*SC*, 54; emphasis added). How is one to understand this "so to speak?"[19] To give a full account of what Rousseau intends his later definition of the role of government must be added to this passage. "Government" is an "intermediate body established between the subjects and sovereign for their mutual communication, and charged with the execution of the laws" (78). This understood, one can grasp the manner in which the contract assists citizens as they learn to negotiate the terms of their private and public interests. Citizens learn to view themselves from a double perspective. The first is as members of the sovereign, the body from which "the government receives . . . the orders that it gives to the people" (79), the second as one of "the people," who must carry out the government's bidding. From this second perspective each citizen experiences a "private interest [that] can speak to him quite differently from the common interest" (55).[20] The fact that certain members of the sovereign will also find themselves serving as members of the government further complicates the picture.

The individual citizen has a natural interest in persuading the sovereign to maximize the advantages accruing to himself. But in what sense can his efforts to do so encompass an autonomously generated and yet public political education? Rousseau pinpointed a number of possibilities inherent in the structure of the contract which he was at pains to denounce. The most obvious was that the citizen could seek to build alliances within the sovereign body in order to promote group interests. In such a case the political education of the citizen would consist in the development of guile and opportunism. Rousseau somewhat blandly argued that the state should forbid such factions or, failing that, that "their number must be multiplied and their inequality prevented" (SC, 61).[21] The second possibility was that a citizen with the requisite skills might persuade the sovereign to grant him singular advantages that would benefit him alone. Thus, Rousseau's insistence that the enactments of the sovereign "be general in its object as well as in its essence; that it should come from all and apply to all" (62). In the absence of such a condition no citizen would have been prepared to enter into association with others.[22]

Rousseau designed these formal constraints to leave citizens with only one possibility; each can promote his own welfare only so far as he can persuade his fellow citizens that everyone will benefit from enactment of a law to that citizen's advantage. While the selfish instinct of the individual citizen "tends by its nature towards preferences," the structure of the contract to which one is a party educates those preferences. The Social Contract prompts citizens to realize that they would only find public support for their projects when they could tie those projects to a general interest (SC, 59). Political education takes the form of a lesson in respect for the equal claim of each citizen on the resources of the community.[23] This is the sense in which the contract incorporates "an admirable agreement between interest and justice which confers on common deliberations a quality of equity that vanishes in the discussion of private matters" (63).

Recall Rousseau's earlier assumption that there had to be a common ground between the preferences of potential citizens. In struggling first to influence the general will in a way that will advance their interests and then by abiding by its general dictates, the citizen would animate that common ground. In summation, Rousseau asked, "Why do all constantly want the happiness of each, if not because there is no one who does not apply this word *each* to himself, and does not think of himself as he votes for all?" (SC, 62). The citizen learns to promote his private interest even as he is forced to reinterpret it through the language of collective interest, that collective interest being itself a necessary condition for his survival.[24]

Despite the ingenuities of his subsequent defenders, Rousseau's intuitively powerful image of the sovereign citizen undoubtedly suffers when one reduces it to specifics. Deeply concerned to ease the path from singular to collective perspectives, Rousseau attempted unsuccessfully to shorten and guarantee its passage. His description of the mechanism of voting, which is supposed to reveal the general will, results in a rare moment of opacity (*SC*, 61).[25] Later in the *Social Contract* Rousseau abandoned the whole effort, commenting that "what generalizes the will is not so much the number of votes as the common interest that unites them" (63). But this offers no illumination about how that interest is to be discovered.[26]

If no voting method could serve to separate communal from selfish interests, Rousseau would have to find some other force to achieve the result. Rousseau cannot embrace the protagorian class of professional educators, for they would represent a faction who would split the state apart. But Rousseau's citizens are children who need help: "Does the body politic have an organ to enunciate its will? Who will give it the necessary foresight to formulate acts and publish them in advance, or how will it pronounce them in time of need?[27] How will a blind multitude, which often does not know what it wants because it rarely knows what is good for it, carry out for itself an undertaking as vast and difficult as a system of legislation?" (*SC*, 67). Citizens cannot simply rely on the wisdom of their compatriots, for this would be expecting the impossible: "men would have to be prior to laws what they ought to become by means of the law" (69). Rousseau's notorious solution to the problem is to reintroduce Emile's tutor, now in the form of the Lawgiver. Once they have completed the initial Social Contract, Rousseau consigns the task of preparing citizens for self-rule to the wisdom of a Moses, a Lycurgus, a Solon, or a Jean-Jacques.

To the Lawgiver alone belongs the task "of transforming each individual into a part of a larger whole from which this individual receives, in a sense, his life and his being (*SC*, 68). Private citizens "must be obligated to make their wills conform to their reason," but, since they cannot do so on their own, they must sacrifice their individuality and retain only enough reason to "bear with docility the yoke of public felicity" (67, 69). Granted the success of the Lawgiver, the process by which the community discovers the general will changes. It is no longer the consequence of a voting procedure but, instead, its precondition. Certainly, "the vote of the majority always obligates all the others," but the vote of the majority is only efficacious if "all the characteristics of the general will are still in the majority" (110–11). Most of Rousseau's readers fail to note that this proviso renders the vote politically redundant:[28] no vote count could ever determine whether the majority view that it revealed did or did not represent the general will—only the Lawgiver will be able to judge.

In book 1, Rousseau had emphasized the fact that the individual citizen would have "a private interest" that "can speak to him quite differently from the common interest." Indeed, such a citizen had a "naturally independent existence" that would pull him in the opposite direction of the common interest he was forced by circumstances to embrace. Rousseau had carefully distinguished the "public person" from the "private persons who compose it and whose life and freedom are naturally independent of it" (*SC*, 55, 62). The entire drama of these early passages consisted in the virtuous efforts of individual citizens to recognize the legitimate claims of the community in which they had a vested interest.[29] He must "consult his reason before heeding his inclinations." In the process of so doing, "his faculties are exercised and developed, his ideas broadened, his feelings ennobled and his whole soul elevated" (56). To travel the path toward virtuous citizenship was an achievement: to give "obedience to the law one ha[d] prescribed for oneself" required the acceptance of a fresh claim on one's privacy (56). The citizen who partakes of the Social Contract in such a manner is surely not the cardboard figure found in many commentaries.[30]

But Rousseau subsequently reclaimed, through the persona of the Lawgiver, the role of legislator, founder, and educator. Into the very text in which he explored most extensively the problem of self-willed socialization and sovereignty, Rousseau inserted himself most aggressively. The Lawgiver, in creating the "moral person of the state," engineers the collapse of any remaining natural instincts and replaces them with his own artificial constructions (*SC*, 55). Without the use of "either force or reasoning" this "genius" must insure that the majority of the citizen body approves of the laws that he proposes (69, 68).[31] Much of the remaining text of the *Social Contract* consists of an account of the skills and information pertinent to the achievement of this end; a flexibility with regard to the "constitution of government," caution toward the timing of the creation of the state, skill in preventing the "waning of patriotism, the activity of private interest, [and] the immenseness of States" (80, 102). The circle of Rousseau's political imagination has closed, and we are back in Corsica.

Scholars have exhaustively analyzed these passages, and they are not pertinent to our project.[32] It is important, however, to grasp what degree of freedom remains to the citizen subject to the art of the Lawgiver. In *Letters from the Mountain* Rousseau takes up the issue directly. The freedom of the party to the Social Contract, Rousseau argues, "does not consist as much in acting according to one's own will as in not being subjected to the will of anyone else; it also consists in not subjecting the will of another to our own" (*Mountain*, 3:841).

On this account the freedom of the citizen in the *Social Contract* is the mirror image of what Rousseau permits Emile. Emile "does what he pleases," but this is in fact also what the Tutor wants him to do (*E*, 84). In the assembly the citizen attempts to articulate a will that has already been forged by the Lawgiver; it is not his own will at all, except in the trivial sense that he happens to be one of a group of receptacles that contain the fruits of the Lawgiver's art.[33] The success of the Tutor/Lawgiver is precisely that both the child and the citizen believe themselves to be "acting according to" their own free will, when in fact awareness of alternatives has been psychologically obliterated. It is hard to take issue with the plethora of commentators who have found in the person of the Lawgiver evidence of Rousseau's ultimate pessimism about the capacity of men fully to govern themselves.[34] Only the announced failure of the Lawgiver's art, the inevitable moment of decay which is built into his project, constrains Rousseau's hubristic impulse to self-glorification.

Measuring the Sphere

Protagoras's fragmentary declaration suggests why self-measurement is the foundation stone of democratic politics. Jean-Jacques Rousseau, through thousands of pages on politics, education, botany, drama, autobiography, theology, music, fiction, and correspondence, gives us a (perhaps the) most powerful exemplar of a self-measured life. Beyond all else that life consisted in an open-ended investigation of the sentiments of existence, as they are forged in human history and as one might yet imagine them in the future. In *Emile* Rousseau wrote: "This is, then, the summary of the whole of human wisdom in the use of the passions: (1) To have a sense of the true relations of man with respect to the species as well as the individual. (2) To order the affections of the soul according to these relations" (219).

Everything is measurement. Rousseau pits the condition of the bourgeoisie, the priest, and the philosopher against their various pretensions. Rousseau assesses the experience of eroticism, of ideal community, of political marginality, solitude, and glory against their self-limiting conditions. Throughout Rousseau investigates his own experience as he constantly renegotiates his identity in the context of a public world. He finds no final answers, only multiple possibilities. Many relations and many orders compete in his imagination. His genius was to be open to those relations and orders, to measure their possibilities, and to understand that to each possibility of judgment belonged a sense of limit, both artificial and indispensable. In Rousseau's view modernity, too, is limited by its viscerating vocabulary of social competition. But the limits of modernity are not heuristic. In sanctioning the limitless pursuit of advantage, modernity presents itself as the transcendence of boundaries, as an invitation to endless transgression. But Rousseau teaches that the invitation is poisoned, for no measurement is possible against the constraint of the open-ended. The modern citizen is constituted by a language that denies itself a measure. The result is a deafening white noise.

Rousseau's constant use of multiple perspectival frameworks make it difficult for one to deduce from his books a conventional political or pedagogic theory. The central paradox of Rousseau's work on psychology and politics is that he strove to make men consciously unhappy with their condition, an unhappiness he regarded as inevitable and possibly permanent. Rousseau installs in his readers a longing to be elsewhere, in another age, in another political structure, surrounded by an eroticism induced by imagination, separation and restraint, in the fictional Clarence or a partially imagined Geneva, in a reverie or a reformed Corsica. Of his own life, too, Rousseau creates a plethora of fantasies in which the longings for another state of being constitute, in their endless intersections with lived experience, a fatalistic romance with alterity.

Always imagining alternatives, Rousseau simultaneously induced fear of movement. As we have seen, he called on his readers to "measure the radius of . . . [their] sphere and stay in the center like the insect in the middle of his web" (*E*, 81). The wise man, according to Rousseau, "knew how to stay in his place." So it is in the domestic empire of Clarence, in which "each member of the household is in their place" (*NH*, 2:536). Rousseau's advice to those attempting to reform the Polish constitution was underpinned by the command to "never shake the machine too brusquely" (*Poland*, 272).[35] Much of the venom that D'Alembert would attract from Rousseau was due simply to the fact that he advocated change: "all innovations are dangerous," Rousseau concluded (*L*, 123). An interference that too palpably signaled its dynamic intentions, or threatened actual social disorder, was anathema to him. Rousseau's reluctance to take an active role in the resistance to the patriciate in Geneva was the cause of frustration and later anger among his Genevese supporters.[36]

Rousseau's evocative political spaces thus share the double structure of the rest of his thought. The reader is invited into an alternative, legitimate space characterized by its fictionality, momentary stability, fragility, and, ultimately, impossibility. But those same readers are invited to applaud these imagined social structures and to become uncomfortable in their own. The result of the double invitation is to make stasis as uncomfortable as revolution. The *Social Contract*, despite its initial promise, confirms Rousseau's double teaching. For a people to voluntarily place themselves under their own collective authority, to embrace the structures of democratic self-rule, they would have to transcend their own particularity and welcome the constraints that made that transcendence possible. But the *Social Contract* makes clear how extraordinarily difficult this process of self-transformation is. Rousseau's ultimate conviction is that, like his Emile, his idealized citizens will need constant supervision if they are to undertake the task of self-rule. But the Lawgiver will pass away, and, eventually, the egalitarian, self-disciplining community that educated the citizens in virtue will pass too, leaving only an "illusory" and "ineffectual" state (*SC*, 108).

Checked by his own realization that the collective will, the *moi commun*, was essentially fragile, Rousseau's last years were occupied with the exploration of solitary self-mastery. He concluded that the happiest beings were those able to "draw . . . our existence up within [ourselves]" (*E*, 83), so recreating the life of the savage who lived "within himself," but this time with the addition of self-awareness (*SD*, 179).[37] The search for help in the process always risks dependency. It is an unhappy Julie who must turn to her cousin with the plea that Claire "restore me to myself!" (*NH*, 2:144). In order to secure the spaces of solitude Rousseau constantly strove for the attainment of inner peace within a stable and unitary structure.[38]

This fantasy of withdrawal parallels almost exactly the unconscious contentment of the savage, whose spirit "agitated by nothing, gives itself over to the sole sentiment of its present existence" (*SD*, 117). It was a matter of "put[ting] ourselves in harmony with ourselves" (*E*, 41). "How I would breath in overpowering joy," wrote Rousseau to Malesherbes, "when I felt certain that the whole day I would be my own master" (*Third Letter*, 1:1139). Savages might live in tranquility, but they would fight ferociously against "tranquil subjection" (*SD*, 164). On rare occasions Rousseau believed himself to have reached the point at which he could have been happy even in the Bastille, though he always fled before that real possibility (*Reveries*, 90).[39]

To be one's own master, either as solitary or as a *moi-commun*, was a reverie and an impossibility for the bourgeoisie, who chase forever the receding mirage of the admiration of others and refuse to limit their desires: "The truly free man wants only what he can do and does what he pleases. That is my fundamental maxim" (*E*, 84). Corrupt *amour-propre* makes this impossible: modern citizens are too weak to remain solitary, too selfish to celebrate communal attachments. So, Rousseau's thinking expands to embrace still a third possibility. Since he believed that "[a] being endowed with senses whose faculties equaled his desires would be an absolutely happy being," the self had to be reeducated to welcome constraint: "The real world has its limits, the imaginary world is infinite. Unable to enlarge the one, let us restrict the other" (80–81f). Rousseau's most considered theory of education centers on the creation of an environment in which the educator can transfer authority, self-awareness, and the capacity for judgment from himself to the pupil. In *La nouvelle Héloise, Emile,* and the *Letter to D'Alembert* Rousseau explored the possibilities of this transfer.

As he constructs the worlds of communal education, solitary revery, and the education of "everyman," Rousseau endlessly renegotiates his own role. He is always elsewhere, and elsewhere is rarely a somewhere in particular. In his *Confessions* Rousseau remarks: "Having an imagination sufficiently rich to adorn all stations with its chimeras, sufficiently powerful to transport me, so to speak, at my whim from one to another, it mattered little to me in which I might be in fact."[40] Temporal and spatial separation from imagined locations of rest, innocence, and delight induce a melancholy that Rousseau creates from loneliness, pain, and eroticism. Rousseau's "sentiments of existence" are haunted by forebodings, memories, reveries, and imagined intrusions, which displace their promise of stability but promise ever different possibilities.

Rousseau fuses time and space into fictional worlds that readers can neither fully recover nor forget. "In the heart of the forest," Rousseau recalls, he "sought and found the image of earliest time" (*Conf.*, 1:388). But neither forest nor time embody *the* authentic possibility of existence. Every form of experience is limited not only by its own frontiers—be they geographical, psychological, or biological—but also by the readers' simultaneous awareness of other unrealized forms of life. For all the acuity of Rousseau's social analysis this odyssey toward no place of rest induces a profound pessimism.[41] Rousseau leads himself and his readers into spirals of displacement and impossible return. The only constant is his unfolding self-awareness, remeasuring itself against his experience of self and society, his imagination, and his memory.

Readers often interpret Rousseau as the prophet of extremity: innocence or corruption, nature or artifice, solitude or community, proud Genevese or wretched Parisian. Thus, Starobinski concluded that "there is no middle between transparency and opacity."[42] But at every stage such a conclusion is also misleading. The extremes themselves are never stable; they are in decay or in the irrecoverable past or in the fragile medium of the imagination. Moreover, the extremes are maintained in each case by a figure, always partially autobiographical, who constitutes them and a project, always incomplete, which they circumscribe. Thus, Rousseau's pedagogic spaces are also constituted by chains of deferments, of substitutions for the original innocence and transparency they are supposed to recreate. Between the citizen and the formation of his will is the education of desires; between Emile and nature unfolds Emile's capacity to judge; between Julie and Saint-Preux lies the education of an unrealizable passion; between nature and bourgeoisie Europe lies the dream of Sparta and Geneva. Rousseau himself, in the person of the Tutor, of Wolmar, of the Lawgiver, interrupts the autonomous process of education. Ultimately, between Rousseau and Jean-Jacques there exists in the place of transparency the triumphs and opacities of the author's self-measurement—*Rousseau juge de Jean-Jacques*.

Rousseau is, rather, the thinker in extremity. In work after work he tried to seal within a limited world the freedoms those limits alone could afford. But he himself is never enclosed: even to his beloved Geneva he was an exile. Announcing in *The Social Contract* the very principles of political legitimacy, Rousseau declares their transient and utopian quality. He stands in what the Greeks termed *methoria,* the borderland between territories. Today we might call it no-person's-land: it marks the boundary around locations within which societies and individuals measure their ambitions and their worth. But it is itself without defined space, and thus Rousseau, the citizen of *methoria,* finds himself free but also condemned endlessly to imagine new lands.

This seems to me to lead us toward the critical lesson of Rousseau's thought and one that makes him the teacher of teachers for modern democracy—the natural successor to Protagoras. From the unstable location of authorship Rousseau maintained that the educator must represent an authority figure and must set out the parameters, physical and psychological, within which the pupil will begin to master the art of measurement. Rousseau argued that one learns such an art by measuring desire and performance against the limits of physical, material, and psychological possibilities. Teachers should assess for themselves the manner in which contemporary society undermines judgment with the false promise that the unlimited pursuit of untutored desire empowers the child. In response, the teacher can draw a boundary around the child. From the perspective of modern society that boundary must represent a denial, a form of social critique, but for the child the boundary enables the development of self-awareness.

This is why every teacher of democratic citizens stands with Rousseau in the *methoria*. The responsibility to teach places the teacher between the consensus of his or her age and the unknown future. The teacher makes a pedagogic promise that the student will judge that consensus with fresh eyes, as Emile does. But the teacher must also evoke, in the construction of the pedagogical space within which the child will learn, an idealized conception of the standard of measure which the educated children will one day employ for themselves. In his work on Geneva Rousseau gave a powerful example of how this is done. He drew on civic memory and myth, and on his own experience of its limits, to induce in his audience-citizens a desire for a community of reformed self-celebration and understanding. Thus, the teacher must construct the space of the pedagogic between the ideals and the vocabulary and self-understanding of the given society. If either is neglected, children will have neither the capacity to measure their society nor a place in that society from which to measure.

More challenges still confront the educator open to Rousseau's understanding. Just as the justification of Protagoras's instruction of an oratorical elite lies in the fact that such an elite will educate citizens to judge competing speeches, so Rousseau's education rests on the claim that the teacher must finally make his or her students aware of the stratagems of containment which have constituted that education. Thus, the pivotal moment in *Emile* when the Tutor hands over to the young man the responsibility for his own self-constraining and reveals precisely what he is doing. A teacher's journey intersects with the students, and the two move in a position constituted, respectively, by authority and innocence. Eventually, however, the task reaches its telos, and teachers, in revealing the techniques of pedagogy, make themselves redundant. The student, educated so far as possible to be the measure of all things, measures too the path of his or her own education.

One final task remains: the justification of the role of this teacher to the wider community. The community must be persuaded of the fallibility of its own judgment, of the responsibility of its educators to broker the difference between its self-understanding and the silences, the blindness, which that self-understanding has induced.

Rousseau can only suggest how this might be done in the structure of his works. Intoxicated with the topographies of Rousseau's communal and erotic Edens, we simultaneously recognize ourselves to be exiles from them. Or, rather, it is in the instability, the utopian nature, of those Edens that we read the diagnosis of our own incapacity for self-constraint. Rousseau's education of Emile, his (Rousseau's) standards of political justice, and his portrait of sustained erotic attachment hold up to us the freedoms and insights that such self-constraint alone would make possible. Displaced from mindless repose by the impossibility of such myths of transparency, Rousseau prepares us for renewed judgment on the power of myth, on the relationship between insight, desire, and self-constraint—about the conditions of political freedom. Subject to Rousseau's displacements, we become students once again and so remember what kind of teachers we need.

5

Dewey and the
Vocabulary of Growth

> It is an experiment, as all life is an experiment.
> —*Justice Holmes, dissenting,*
> *United States,* 250 U.S. 616, 630 (1919)

JEAN-JACQUES ROUSSEAU was a true disciple of Protagoras, a figure whose odyssey of judgment entranced or infuriated all who encountered its full impact. Rousseau forces us to remember that the task of a teacher is Herculean indeed, involving as it does a critical confrontation with contemporary practice, a grasp of psychology, and the construction of a pedagogic space. That space, in turn, must be constituted by an ideal forged from the historical, geographical, and constitutional material of the culture. The metaphor of unsullied nature against which Rousseau measures the blinded passions of modernity offers a powerful point of leverage for the development of the pedagogic perspective. But Rousseau's life and work cannot represent the whole answer to the riddle of democratic education. The pedagogic paths that he constructed between that heuristic ideal and contemporary norms of civil society are so hostile to the latter as to render those paths highly idiosyncratic. Modernity is Paris, in Rousseau's view, but he portrays Paris as a kind of unmitigated psychological disaster, beyond the reach of anything but the instruction of the romantic novel. He says little directly about the material out of which one might forge an education for modern urban populations. Moreover, Rousseau's intellectual wanderings, in which he explores the psychological and political possibilities and constraints of man as measure, fall short of offering a theoretically compelling foundation for those explorations. Although Rousseau flirted with philosophical conceptions, especially in *Emile* and the *Essay on the Origin of Languages,* he is never fully comfortable with them.[1]

The third architect of a theory of democratic education is the American philosopher John Dewey. Dewey's focus was rarely on himself, almost always on the possibilities of public reform. Balancing Rousseau's seductive enchantment with idealized educational environments, Dewey tested the limits of incrementalism, albeit an incrementalism shaped by idealism. Most important, Dewey offered a "naturalistic metaphysics," which, correctly interpreted, confers the highest possible legitimacy on democratic politics and offers an educational strategy for its realization. Dewey writes: "Any theory of activity in social and moral matters, liberal or otherwise, which is not grounded in a comprehensive philosophy seems to me to be only a projection of an arbitrary personal preference" (*LW,* 14:150).[2] In Dewey's view democratic education is legitimated, and its content properly delineated, by the very conditions of human experience.

Dewey argues that politics could and should enhance the natural potentiality of experience to be "meaningful." Dewey's justification for democratic politics, and for the education on which those politics depend, is found in his theory of knowledge. To put a complex matter simply, Dewey believes that of all political systems a certain form of democracy best realizes the capacity of life to embody "meaning." Rhetorically, Dewey asks, "Is democracy a comparatively superficial human expedient, a device of petty manipulation, or does nature itself, as that is uncovered and understood by our best contemporaneous knowledge, sustain and support our democratic hopes and aspirations?" (*MW,* 11:48).

Dewey's conviction that we can infer an account of politics from natural ontology marks his greatest intellectual debt. Throughout his work Dewey never escapes the influence of one of Rousseau's most profound readers, G. W. F. Hegel. From Dewey's days as a student at Johns Hopkins University through the period of his mature work in aesthetics, he is continually retranslating, reconstructing, and redirecting the Hegelian ontology. What was it in Hegel's thought which so entranced Dewey, which launched this most democratic of philosophers in a direction so different from that of Rousseau?

One answer is that in Dewey's reading Hegel's thought embodied a method of synthesis which became integral to Dewey's own intellectual project. At the age of seventy-one Dewey reaffirmed the liberating nature of this dynamic fusion: Hegel's "synthesis of subject and object, matter and spirit, the divine and the human . . . operate as an immense release, a liberation. Hegel's treatment of human culture, of institutions and the arts, involved the same dissolution of hard-and-fast dividing walls, and had a special attraction for me" (*LW*, 2:153). To break down barriers for the purpose of synthesizing (Dewey would use "integrating") human experience, to grasp the totality of culture as an interpenetrating whole, represented an irresistible vision that underpins all of Dewey's work. The Hegelian synthesis was the achievement of Geist, the termination of human history objectified in the Spirit coming to know itself. What Dewey does is to render indeterminate the Hegelian sensibility and see it as the provisory, transitory achievement of a reflective, organic interaction of the human-being-in-nature.[3] In the place of Hegel's history of Geist, Dewey offers an account of human experience. Nevertheless, that experience mirrors Hegel's model in a critical respect: the dialectical logic of *Aufhebung* is matched, perhaps mirrored, in Dewey's account of the "logic of experience." That "logic," correctly grasped, enables humanity to order its social structures by thinking through the commonsense impact of experience:

> The value of research for social progress, the bearing of psychology upon educational procedure; the material relations of fine and industrial art; the question of the extent and nature of specialization in science in comparison with the claims of applied science; the adjustment of religious aspirations to scientific statements . . . the relation of organization to individuality—such are a few of the many social questions whose answer depends upon the possession and use of a general logic of experience as a method of inquiry and interpretation. (*Studies*, 2:313–14).

Dewey retains from Hegel not only the scope of his synthesis but also something of its temporal structure. In Dewey's reconstruction Geist's moment of fulfillment becomes the present moment in human time: education duplicates and replaces the metaphysical voyage of the Spirit. In *The Philosophy of Right* Hegel writes: "The final purpose of education, therefore, is liberation and the struggle for higher liberation still. . . . In the individual subject, this liberation is the hard struggle against pure subjectivity of demeanor, against the immediacy of desire, against the empty subjectivity of feeling and the caprice of inclination."[4]

In Dewey's reformation of Hegel's ontological pedagogics, themselves clearly indebted to Rousseau, the educated citizen will grasp "the present . . . [as] complex, containing within itself a multitude of habits and impulses . . . a pressure forward, a glance backward and a look outward. It is a *moral* moment because it marks a transition in the direction of breadth and clarity of action or in that of triviality and confusion" (*HNC*, 14:195).

The break from Rousseau and the Hegelian telos is that "look outward." Dewey argues that human beings could learn to combine each effort of synthesis with the awareness that it was undertaken in a dynamic, ever-changing universe. At each moment there must be "an adjustment of our whole being with the conditions of existence" (*AAE*, 17). Dewey was fully sensitive to the burden of this uncertainty. "There are moments," he remarks, "when the responsibilities imposed by living in a moving universe seem intolerable" (*MW*, 4:141). In such moments Dewey turned to the "one citizen of the New World fit to have his name uttered in the same breadth with that of Plato." Although Dewey invokes his name quite rarely, and borrowed little directly from his work, it is Emerson whose tireless celebration of the open road most resonates in Dewey's hopes. Dewey is contemptuous of those who cannot see Emerson as a philosopher. It is to Emerson that we owe the thought "that each individual is at once the focus and the channel of mankind's long and wide endeavor, and that all nature exists for the education of the human soul" (3:191, 189).

Dewey's model of democratic education is, in one perspective, a synthesis of Hegel's organicism and Emerson's democratic sensibility. Dewey fuses Hegel's universalism with Emerson's celebration of the open road. Education, for Dewey, is about the preparation of citizens who will engage in the constant reconstruction of the public sphere. The material for that reconstruction will come in the form of imagining possible courses of future action. In these projections human beings can redirect their activities and reorder their environment in ways that reflect an understanding of human history and organic experience.[5] In this process, Dewey argues, we embody at the level of an educated behavior the structure of all existence: "There is in nature, even below the level of life, something more than mere flux and change. Form is arrived at whenever a stable, even though moving, equilibrium is reached. Changes interlock and sustain one another. . . . Order is not imposed from without but is made out of the relations of harmonious interactions that energies bear to one another" (*AAE*, 14).

When such order is the consequence of deliberate human action Dewey termed it artful. The achievement of order represents an "aesthetic, consummatory moment" in which one achieves the "complete interpenetration of self and world." Dewey echoed Emerson's belief that education could make such moments of fulfillment more secure. But Dewey was equally committed to Emerson's view that this possibility was uniquely generated by a democratic politics. The structure of a democratic state offers a "stable, though moving, equilibrium," an integrated political space in which humans could continually renegotiate the dimensions of social and individual practice in a considered response to a dynamic world.

Lacking Emerson's poetic and stylistic gifts, Dewey sought to give an account of experience which grounded Emerson's celebration of democracy in an empirical naturalism. In Dewey's view a democratic political order is the organic condition in which citizens can best promote a widely shared public language, an ethical science, and aesthetic experience, and it is the task of a democratic education to foster and celebrate this growth.

Dewey and Contemporary Thought

Dewey's interweaving of latent Hegelianism, aesthetics, democratic politics, and education has not always proved especially palatable to his readers. Any reconstruction of Dewey's thought must be cognizant of the fact that controversy surrounds Dewey's status in the contemporary pantheon of educational theorists. The most important recent work on democratic education plays down Dewey's contribution to the topic, largely through bypassing it.[6] Other critics of Dewey's work on education are scarcely more generous. Charles Frankel attributes Dewey's impact to fortunate circumstances and asks whether his work "should be put aside as the expression of an intellectually soft and politically innocent era."[7] More recently, E. D. Hirsch has blamed Dewey for recommending those policies that have left a large percentage of the American population illiterate.[8]

Nor are many examiners of Dewey's political theory as a whole more enthusiastic. C. Wright Mills faulted Dewey for his inability to see politics as an arena of unresolvable conflict. Michael Oakeshott makes a parallel claim regarding Dewey's view of decision making, arguing that he employed a never-attained future as the crucial but vacuous criteria of meaning.[9] Even A. H. Somjee, who gives Dewey credit for suggesting the need for "adequate tools of inquiry," complains that "his attempts in this direction have been both limited and unsatisfactory."[10] Dewey's plea for an articulate public has found a more sympathetic audience in the brief work of James Gouinlock,[11] but the single work devoted entirely to a defense of Dewey's political theory has been Alfonso Daminco's little-noticed volume of more than fifteen years ago.[12] References to Dewey's work in better-known texts of American political theory are few.

The response to Dewey's neglected philosophy, however, has recently undergone dramatic change, heralded, perhaps, by Richard Rorty's announcement elevating Dewey to the company of Ludwig Wittgenstein and Martin Heidegger. Rorty's claim that Dewey's attack on the philosophical tradition places him with other "deconstructive" voices has evoked considerable discussion.[13] The second development has been that an increasing number of philosophers have taken seriously Dewey's writings in metaphysics and aesthetics.[14]

H. L. Mencken called Dewey "the worst writer ever heard of in America"; Lewis Mumford termed his prose "as depressing as a subway ride."[15] Dewey frequently employs terms in his more political and educational writings which invite simplistic interpretation or dismissal precisely because their philosophical sense is not overtly present to even sympathetic readers. In turn, his use of an unadorned vocabulary to depict extremely developed ideas creates confusion, frustration, and careless reading. Take, for example, Dewey's understanding of growth; it is tempting to treat this concept as an empty generality and the arguments Dewey builds on it as harmless good advice. Dewey, Daminco informs us, wants a society that "measures moral progress by the continuing growth and development of individual personality."[16] This sounds unobjectionable—and vacuous. In fact, Dewey's analysis of growth is as difficult and suggestive as any concept he employed; an understanding of the philosophical foundations of growth is essential if one is to understand Dewey's faith in moral progress and individualism.

Following the example of William James, Dewey tried throughout his work to overcome the philosophical heritage of dualisms: body/soul, subject/object, idea/thing, meaning/existence. In Dewey's view, by contrast, the conditions of experience are continuous with one another: "The structure of human behavior within its natural setting grounds all levels of knowledge, and reflection on this grounding is at once epistemic and ontological."[17] Dewey believes that the traditional vocabulary of philosophy stands between us and the essential effort to celebrate the natural possibilities of experience as they might emerge in public, democratic life.

This belief suggests why Dewey's contrasting vocabulary, however imperfectly, represents a critical component of his pedagogic intent. It is through this vocabulary that Dewey attempts to habituate his readers to a new phenomenology. Efforts to "translate" Dewey's prose thus risk misreading him from the start, by forcing his sense into a semantic framework that his own work makes problematic. Nevertheless, Dewey's often opaque prose is not always necessary for his quite precise beliefs: he needs literary help to clarify his arguments. The reader must therefore reassemble, connect, interpret and critique Dewey's writings in a way that allows his teachings a greater chance of carrying us with them.

Dewey offers a single, unified philosophical conception: a view of human experience such that a revitalized democratic community might be seen to flow constitutively from the potentialities of that experience once it has been properly understood. Dewey shares with Rousseau the conviction that such an understanding must incorporate the totality of the human condition:

> The state of culture is a state of interaction of many factors, the chief of which are laws and politics, industry and commerce, science and technology, the arts of expression and communication, and of morals, or the values men prize and the ways in which they evaluate them; and finally, though indirectly, the system of general ideas used by men to justify and to criticize the fundamental conditions under which they live, their social philosophy. We are concerned with the problem of freedom rather than with solutions: in the conviction that solutions are idle until the problem has been placed in the context of elements that constitute culture as they intersect with elements of human nature. The fundamental postulate . . . is that isolation of any one factor, no matter how strong its workings at a given time, is fatal to understanding and to intelligent action. (*FC*, 23).

Knowing where we are is to know what we are and what we might create. To misunderstand the contexts that made up one's experience is to deprive oneself of the highest human possibilities—experiences of growth and consummations of meaning achieved through planning, goal setting, and artful doing, in a social system that allows full participation. Dewey was convinced, with Rousseau, that his readers lacked an accurate sense of what they might be precisely because they did not know where they were. The first task was to measure the practices of contemporary society.

The Lost Public

Dewey assumes that Human became such only in a social, linguistic context. He has little patience with speculative reconstructions of a presocial life. Individuals "exist and operate in association," a behavior that represents a "universal trait" of nature which is a condition of associations (*PP*, 23, 34). What needs to be understood, rather, is the emergence of a political public. Dewey spends much time on the transition from signals to signs, and thus on the origins of language itself. It is language that makes politics possible, for language enables humans to organize social activity and to react in a systematic fashion to its defects. In *The Public and Its Problems* Dewey defines the public as those people who can persuade society to take their interests into account in matters of public policy (15).

Dewey presupposes two human capacities in this definition. First, a capacity to act on the basis of the experience that one's private possibilities are intimately tied to the behavior of others: "notice of the effects of connected action forces men to reflect upon the connection itself . . . each [individual] acts, in so far as the connection is known, in view of the connection" (*PP*, 24). Second, the ability to realize that, through cooperative reflection and thought, people avail themselves of fresh "purposes, plans, measures and means" (34). Of course, each individual seeks so far as possible to secure those preferred future conditions, which he or she believes the group can bring about. But of equal concern is the fear of unpredicted consequences: "the characteristic of the public as a state springs from the fact that all modes of associated behavior may have extensive and enduring consequences . . . beyond those directly engaged in them" (27). For this reason, Dewey argues, the public establishes laws and institutions (53).

What motivates Dewey's political writings is his conviction that, in the modern period, those institutions had become ossified obstructions to the very source of their legitimacy—namely, the awareness of those effects of connected action which were in fact conditioning the lives of every citizen. Dewey cites the example of corporate manufacturing and new technology, which "radically alter" economic and thus social activity. These changes have occurred outside the scrutiny of political institutions established to meet earlier economic problems which now "persist of their own momentum": "The new public which is generated remains long inchoate, unorganized, because it cannot use the inherited agencies. . . . To form itself, the public has to break existing political forms" (*PP*, 31).

Dewey argues that the modern public, even that public organized in ostensibly democratic states, had lost a crucial ability to articulate its current interests within the historical forms that hold them hostage. Because the conditions of modernity had become so complex, people lost all sense of orientation: "the public is so bewildered," Dewey concludes, "that it cannot find itself" (*PP*, 122). What makes this loss fascinating to Dewey is the degree to which human action depends on a culture embodied in those historical forms. Dewey constantly repeats the claim that an individual is not a disembodied unit—"in his isolation possessed of fully fledged wants"—but, rather, a product of the established connections that constituted his practice and imagination (102).

How, then, to identify those new types of conduct which could result in a reorientation of modernity? We might expect Dewey to provide institutional solutions, blueprints of social reform which emerge from his account of blocked channels of political development. But he does not. In fact, the terms in which he envisages a successful reorientation of the public seem to emerge from a very different source and a very opaque vocabulary: "The work of conversion of the physical and organic phase of associated behavior into a community of action saturated and regulated by mutual interest in shared meanings, consequences which are translated into ideas and desired objects by means of symbols" (*PP*, 153). What has the organization of a modern public to do with "shared meanings" or symbolic translations? What has this language to do with bringing home to a public those revolutionary possibilities embodied in a modernity in which that same public finds itself disoriented and thus disempowered?

Answering these questions leads us inevitably toward an examination of Dewey's understanding of experience. It is this understanding that supports the possibility of an education that can help humans create meanings that extend beyond mere survival: education links organic possibilities to cultural growth and political reform. Readers impatient with the need to examine his phenomenology might recall Dewey's own claims that philosophy may be "defined *as the general theory of education*" (*DE*, 328) and that "the first object of a renascent liberalism is education."[18]

Dewey's understanding of preconceptualized human experiences reveals the possibilities for human fulfillment and the capacities and limits of language and science as tools in its achievement. The idea that such fulfillment is capable of liberation and growth will emerge as the central argument of Dewey's axiology. In that axiology, however, every important concept Dewey invokes in his political educational theory will already have surfaced. When I turn to that theory itself it will be clear that it represents "only" the direct extension of Dewey's philosophy. Through education, both formal (in schools) and informal (beyond the schoolroom), we can reach toward the ideal of a democratic community. In such a community the qualitative possibilities of experience, based on collective and artistic effort, can become the heritage of every citizen.

Dewey thus envisions a critical role for democratic politics and democratic education, meaning a process of goal selection and an identification of required means, which actively involves every citizen. Dewey grounds the possibilities of this type of democracy on his understanding of preconceptualized human experience. He realizes that a democratic education is a critical tool for securing the promise of democratic politics. In all of this he makes people, as citizens, the measure of all things.

The Meaningful World

In order to understand the world and our place within it we must first encounter it. Dewey claims that that encounter takes place primarily through forms of pure experience, which is often the experience of communication. Through language or concept the natural world is "liberated from local and accidental contexts" and is brought to consciousness, or invested with meaning (*EN,* 166). Dewey denies that this process rests on any division between world and human being. Human life in all its manifestations is thoroughly naturalistic. Nature itself contains the conditions for communicated meanings as developed by humans. The conceptual world is a human product, which individuals develop from pure experience.

Dewey's argument begins with an evocative portrait of human existence, in which he shows that the multiplicities of human experience are continuous with the natural world that constrains them. He places communication, or language, within that continuum. Eventually, Dewey wants to show "the extent to which the antecedent reality of the situation admits the possibility of transformation of the situation" through human judgment and activity.[19] But in order to support this position Dewey needs to affirm that reality and human inquiry are not two different ontological entities. It is, rather, the case that the process of inquiry redirects reality even as experience of reality enables (and constrains) inquiry. As R. W. Sleeper suggests, "The boldness of Dewey's ontological conjecture lies in regarding the object of knowledge as both real and transformed through the very process [human activity in the world] by means of which it becomes such an object."[20]

Dewey affirms a continuity between nature and human experience. In Dewey's description of the generic traits of nature we find an account of basic human behavior. Since Dewey's democratic faith and educational recommendations ultimately find their foundation in just such an account, it is worth quoting him in detail:

Existentially speaking, a human individual is distinctive opacity of bias and preference conjoined with plasticity and permeability of needs and likings. One trait tends to isolation, discrete; the other trait to connection, continuity. This ambivalent character is rooted in nature, whose events have their own distinct indifferences [sic], resistances, . . . and also their particular openness, warm responsiveness, greedy seekings and transforming unions. The conjunction in nature of whimsical contingency and lawful uniformity is the result of these two characters of events. They persist upon the human plane, and as ultimate characters are ineradicable. Boundaries, demarcations, abrupt, [sic] and expansive over-reachings of boundaries impartially and conjunctively mark every phase of human life. (EN, 242)[21]

Dewey's use of the word *traits* should not obscure the central point: nature, whether human or otherwise, is one—but we can perceive it from a double perspective, much as we can describe a single curve as convex or concave. From one perspective, "in every event there is something obdurate, self-sufficient, wholly immediate, neither a relation nor an element in a rational whole, but terminal and exclusive." From another, nature is, simultaneously, "a scene of incessant beginnings and endings," and all events are part of "sequences, coexistences, relations." The natural world is "a history which is a succession of histories and in which any event is at once both beginning of one course and close of another; is both transitive and static" (EN, 85, 98, 86, 100). Thomas Alexander offers a useful summary of the structure of these natural histories, which Dewey terms "affairs" or "situations": "All situations are marked by a 'stable' or formed and structured aspect and by a 'precarious' or dynamic aspect. Every structure in nature exists in relation to variability; in fact, structures emerge as means of coping, striving for homeostasis but having to undergo and adapt."[22] Human existence is a particular phenomenon, and a natural one. Human experience embodies and reflects the structure of all natural situations. What is particular are the qualities of that experience. Like animals, we experience and react to immediate stimuli, but, unlike other animals, our experience affords a consciousness of objects as meaningful, or, as Dewey put it, consciousness "is the perception of actual events . . . *in* their meanings, the having of actual ideas" (303).[23] Ideas, in Dewey's view, are the natural structures in which and through which human beings evaluate and reorder their environment.

This understanding of consciousness, or the having of ideas, is linked to his broader picture of human experience. For it turns out that the discrete "focal" moment of consciousness is only part of an adequate description of thought as a whole. In Dewey's words: "The greater part of mind is only implicit in any conscious act or state; the field of mind—of operative meanings—is enormously wider than that of consciousness" (*EN,* 303). Human experience embodies a greater sensibility: the intellect "is set in a context which is noncognitive," a "vast complex" of dynamic emotions, sensations, instincts, and past activities: " 'Consciousness,' in other words, is only a very small and shifting portion of experience. . . . *In* the experience, and in such a way as to *qualify* what is shiningly apparent, are all the physical features of the environment extending out into space . . . and all the habits and interests extending backward and forward in time of the organism . . . when the word 'experience' is employed . . . it means just such an immense and operative world of diverse and interacting elements" (*EEL,* 10:322–23). Consciousness focuses on the problematic aspects of an experience, or what is at the heart of problematic situations.[24] But it can only do so because we are, simultaneously, the product of this greater context of nature, of the "situation" as a whole, which generates for conscious thought the scene and the vocabulary of its activity.

Dewey insists that this sense of "an indefinite context of other consequences from . . . among which the aim is selected" is as much a part of the "*present* meaning of activity" as are immediate perceptions (*HNC,* 14:179). Just why Dewey wants to claim that our experience of events as meaningful must incorporate this sense of the wider context will be clarified below: for the present we need to say a little more about consciousness itself. Dewey argues that every time human beings become aware of their environments, tacitly accepted meanings become the focus of conscious attention as language or symbols. The carpenter who has been merrily hammering nails becomes conscious of the hammer when it shatters in his hand. He becomes aware of the object because a history of which it and he were a part has become problematic—and he seeks to restore its continuity. "The mediated and ongoing aspect of the situation which calls for acting and discrimination will exemplify itself in consciousness as cognitive relations."[25] To be conscious of an object is thus to come to the awareness of it as part of a problematic, ongoing, but interrupted, situation and to experience the episode in relational or associative terms.[26]

But consciousness is not the whole story, for alone it cannot account for our experience of life as meaningful. Dewey's task was to show, first, that human beings are conscious of objects as meaningful and, second, how our uncognized sense of a broader "situation" or "environment" enters into the meaning of our experience. These claims will be treated sequentially: a response to the first question involves the introduction of Dewey's linguistic model, while answering the second will lead us toward Dewey's understanding of a critical component of human behavior, the act of decision making.

What does Dewey mean by "meaning"? The answer is descriptively straightforward: "When we name an event," he remarks, "we invoke a meaning, namely, the potential consequences of the existence" (*EN*, 191). Dewey directly links the process of creating meaning with the existence of linguistic communication. Both the possibility of meaning and of its loss are effectuated by language. As suggested already, Dewey's account of linguistically created meaning begins by differentiating human beings from other species. Animals, Dewey argues, exhibit "psycho-physical" activity "but not 'mental,' that is, they are not aware of meanings." Dewey understands mind as "an added property assumed by a feeling creature, when it reaches that organized interaction with other living creatures which is language, communication." The naming through language of "qualities of organic action" makes possible "identification and discrimination of things to take place as means in a further course of inclusive action" (258). Such activity is suggested by our verb form *to mind:* we mind something only when we can discriminate it, when we can mark or measure it in relation to another event.

This is the crucial claim that links Dewey's linguistic model with his understanding of meaning; the naming of objects is always a relational statement in which a possibility of interaction between the human organism and the world is opened up: "To term a quality 'hunger,' to name it, is to refer to an object, to food, to that which will satisfy it, towards which the active situation moves" (*EN*, 259). Even if a hunger remains unsatisfied, it has meaning to the extent that it has been identified as resolvable, or resistible, in conceivable future contexts: "The qualities of situations in which organism and surrounding conditions interact, when discriminated, make sense" (260). Here Dewey intends the word *make* in both an existential and a phenomenological sense. Or, rather, he sees no distinction between those two senses: the organic situation is made sense, is "minded" and "meant," in language.

Dewey points out that many human reactions are prelinguistic, formed of immediate, inarticulate reaction to the objects around us—"things in their immediacy are unknown and unknowable. . . . Immediate things may be pointed to by words but not described" (*EN*, 87). But such experiences, if they are to form the basis for meaning, can be placed in a story: "knowledge is a memorandum of conditions of their appearance, concerned . . . with sequences, coexistences, relations" (86).

Language is the medium of this memorandum. It renders experience available for selected reproduction, repression, or prolongation.[27] Humans experience immediate sensation within a context in which they can discern its possible relations to other events; it forms the beginning of what Dewey calls a "series": "The result is nothing less than revolutionary. Organic activity is liberated from subjection to what is closest at hand in space and time. Man is led or drawn rather than pushed" (*EN*, 270). When we see an object that is white with lines drawn across it we most often see it as paper, but with sufficient information we might see it in other contexts or relationships, as a chemical compound, for example: "Since possibilities of conjunction are endless . . . its potential meanings are endless" (319). In a spirit that had profound implications for his political theory, Dewey embraces those consequences that Rousseau found so threatening, welcoming the fact that "an environment both extensive and enduring is immediately implicated in present behavior" (279). In Dewey's view sense makes space for itself.

When we have linguistically described an object-event, we can place it into ever fresh contexts. Initially, the meanings of events "may be infinitely combined and rearranged in imagination," but only if this "inner experimentation" can "issue forth in interaction with crude or raw events" can language occur. As the storehouse of such past interactions, it is naming that turns experiences into discrete objects, that gives those experiences a meaning: "As objects function in a variety of object contexts, their meaning is constantly enlarged, and when such objects are matters of direct experience, the funded meaning makes events remote in space and time consciously significant in present experience: an environment both extensive and enduring is implicated in present behavior" (*EN*, 279). Language frees events from their initial locality or closedness: "Brute efficiencies and inarticulate consummations as soon as they can be spoken of are liberated from local and accidental contexts, and are eager for naturalization in any non-insulated, communicating, part of the world" (166).

It is important to note that, in Dewey's model, meanings exist whether we are conscious of them or not; indeed, most of our behavior rests on "an antecedent stock of meanings . . . the ones which we take for granted and use: the ones of which we are not and do not need to be conscious." (*EN*, 309) The point is that, when we perceive events and then identify them as objects, we attempt to integrate that object into a complex, conceptualized world of meaning. Our language is simply the storehouse of previous efforts of the integration of events into meaningful objects. As our experience of fresh contextualizations grow, so will the language that records their history: "when an event has meaning, its potential consequences become its integral and funded feature . . . [to] *perceive* is to acknowledge unattained possibilities; it is to refer the present to consequences, apparition to issue, and thereby to behave in deference to the *connections* of events" (182). (Dewey might usefully have emphasized the word *behave* also.)[28]

Meaningful Behavior

It remains to show how our uncognized sense of a broader situation enters into the meaning of our experience. Recall that all human behavior, including those moments in which meanings are generated, will exhibit universal traits of nature—the discrete, or qualitative, and the dynamic, or relational. As Alexander rightly recalls: "As experience becomes more organized, the qualitative immediacy does not retreat before a spectral world of relations. Rather, both the immediate or qualitative side and the mediate or relational side become more articulate and interwoven. The present moment, by being *part* of a whole developing situation, becomes suffused with the apprehension of the significance of the event."[29] How does the situation of human behavior embody this interweaving of immediate conscious sense and the unresolved, broader portion of the situation in such a way as to make use of the capacities of language for generation of meaning? The answer lies in the interaction between two elements of behavior, which Dewey terms "impulse" and "habit." Dewey's understanding of impulses is relatively straightforward: they are the "instinctive activities" that "may become organized into almost any disposition according to the way it interacts with surroundings." As such, they are potentially "the organs of re-organization and re-adjustment" (*HNC*, 14:65, 69, 68).

Dewey's view of habits is more complex.[30] He rejects the view that habits are passive predispositions waiting to be stimulated. "All habits," he writes, "are demands for certain kinds of activity; and they constitute the self": "We may think of habits as means, waiting, like tools in a box, to be used by conscious resolve. But they are something more than that. They are active means [*sic*] that project themselves, energetic and dominating ways of acting" (*HNC*, 14:25). This would suggest that habits are somehow personal or private patterns of behavior, but Dewey stresses that "they are adjustments *of* the environment, not merely *to* it" (14:38). We are born into organic/social structures in which certain patterns of response to particular situations are already established as meaningful. But this is not to say that such patterns are permanently fixed; on the contrary, people confronted with novel situations modify habits even as they attempt to alter the new environment. Dewey usefully summarizes the events he wishes to characterize as "habitual": "[A] word to express that kind of human activity which is influenced by prior activity and in that sense acquired; which contains within itself a certain ordering or systematization of minor elements of action; which is projective, dynamic in quality, ready for overt manifestation; and which is operative in some subdued subordinate form even when not obviously dominating activity" (14:31).

Enough has been said to underline Dewey's view that habits are not merely a means toward the attainment of certain ends but also prepattern the ends themselves. The habits of a sailor, painter, or scientist—to use Dewey's examples—will insure that the same phenomena may actually become the occasion for a totally different response in which each person realizes different ends. (High waves will suggest a navigational challenge, a pictorial opportunity, a phenomenon for analysis). Preexisting habits actually predetermine how we will situate events in cognitive structures whenever we encounter them.

So long as our activities proceed unhindered, we may remain unaware of the role of habit. "Habits . . . perpetuate themselves, by acting unremittingly upon the native stock of activities." But an obstacle placed across the path of unconscious behavior throws into relief the direction in which our habits were leading us. In such instances the relation between impulse and habit become problematic, and deliberation becomes possible. There can occur "reflection upon the way in which to use impulse to renew disposition and reorganize habit" (*HNC*, 14:117). As we reassess that now unsatisfactory movement into the future, there takes place what Dewey terms a "dramatic rehearsal" of possible alternatives: "Each conflicting habit and impulse takes its turn in projecting itself upon the screen of the imagination. It unrolls a picture of its future history, of the career it would have if it were given head" (14:133).

Dramatic rehearsals link problematic situations with the possibility of meaning. Faced with the unknown, we attempt to select an action through which we can resolve the problematic situation. Dewey terms this action the "end in view." But the selection of such an action is not made ex nihilo: as Dewey goes on to explain, the fact that we are conscious of an object or action as possibly resolving the problematic depends in turn on our habits. First, he describes the relationship between habit and objects of perception: "The trinity of . . . forecasts, perceptions and remembrances form a subject-matter of discriminated and identified objects. These objects represent habits turned inside out. They exhibit both the onward tendency of habit and the objective conditions which have been incorporated within it. Sensations in immediate consciousness are elements of action dislocated through the shock of interruption" (*HNC*, 14:127). But such sensations, which represent the breaking of certain habitual patterns of behavior, "never monopolize the scene," for "there is a body of residual undisturbed habits which is reflected in remembered and perceived objects having a meaning." The very possibility of being uncertain about a course of behavior rests on the fact that not everything is doubted at once—that a particular episode emerges from that broader context of organic and social habits. Dewey thus sees the moment of doubt as a double one: the consequence of the fragmentation of certain habits and the maintenance of others. Taken as a whole, "the complexity of the figured scene in its scope and refinement of contents depends wholly upon prior habits and their organization" (14:128).

In our dramatic rehearsals, or thought, we confront a differentiated event presented to our consciousness through the disruption of a habit of which it was once an unremarked component. Then we attempt to reconstruct our situation, and thus our habits, by reorienting our activity to order or structure that event. It is this activity, Dewey thinks, that invests our current acts with meaning: "Imaginative forethought of the probable consequences of a proposed act keeps that act from sinking below consciousness into routine habit or whimsical brutality. It preserves the meaning of that act alive, and keeps it growing in depth and refinement of meaning" (*HNC*, 14:145). In so far as we are successful, we will have discovered that "end[ ]-in-view" which "constitutes the meaning and value of an activity as it comes under deliberation" (14:155). In other words, we will have found in the selected object the means of making sense out of a situation the unity of which had broken down.

In seeking a consequence sufficiently compelling to motivate present behavior and release our impulse to action, we are in fact "striving to unify our responses to achieve a consistent environment which will restore unity of conduct" (*HNC*, 14:128). The next step is to grasp Dewey's account of the significance, the meaning, of our activity. Recall again that the end-in-view, or consequence, which we select from those made available through habit, "is set in an indefinite context of other consequences just as real as it." Despite our best efforts, "the 'ends' that are foreseen and utilized mark out a little island in an infinite sea" (14:179). The world is both denser than we can perceive and more interrelated. Dewey's language is geometric: "The 'end' is the figured pattern at the center of the field through which runs the axis of conduct. About this central figuration extends infinitely a supporting background as a vague whole, undefined and undiscriminated. At most intelligence but throws a spotlight on that little part of the whole which marks out the axis of movement" (14:179). We have returned to that "vast complex" that constitutes the field of mind; the "vague whole" that Dewey invokes is central to his understanding of the total meaning of an act. While intelligence cannot encompass simultaneously the breadth of that field, it can come to the realization of its omnipresence. Such a realization will produce "the sense of an indefinite context of the consequences from among which the aim is selected" and awareness that this sense can "enter into the present meaning of activity" (14:179). What is this sense? It is a consciousness that "the little part of the scheme of affairs which is modifiable by our efforts is continuous with the rest of the world," or "an encompassing infinity of connections" (14:180).

Sensing how the successful selection of an end-in-view can reconstitute the situation, each of us can simultaneously sense that there is an "enveloping whole" that our own behavior is constantly altering. Dewey goes on to describe the sensibility he seeks to evoke: "When . . . a sense of the infinite reach of an act physically occurring in a small point of space and occupying a petty instant of time comes home to us, the *meaning* of a present act is seen to be vast, immeasurable, unthinkable. This ideal is not a goal to be attained. It is a significance to be felt, appreciated. Though consciousness of it cannot become intellectualized . . . yet emotional appreciation of it is won only by those willing to think" (*HNC,* 179).[31] This ideal sensibility of our mental topography lies at the heart of Dewey's theory of democratic education. There is no epistemic separation between self, others, and world. The "mindful" choice of a path of action must be based on an understanding of how one's own character ("the interpenetration of habits") is at once a product of the world that forged that character and the source of a set of possible futures through which we can transform that interconnected world (14:29).

Two points already made in the current subsection merit emphasis. First is the role that language and habit play in choice. It should now be clear that language, which allows us to identify the potential consequences of an event, is in fact an encoded storehouse of human activity or habits. It follows that language and habit are connected through group interaction. Habits held in isolation from the effects of communication will be slow to alter. But in an environment of communication our habits develop a plasticity based on an accumulation of experiences in which communication has been a precursor of altered behavior: "Communication not only increases the number and variety of habits, but tends to link them subtly together, and eventually to subject habit forming in a particular case to the habit of recognizing that new modes of association will exact a new use of it" (*EN*, 281).

Second, we have stressed Dewey's view that the caliber of decision making varies in proportion to the availability of a stock of habits which provide the meaningful contexts of our discrete perceptions, choices, and actions. To recall Dewey's description of our "dramatic rehearsals," or moments of deliberation, "The complexity of the figured scene in its scope and refinement of contents depends wholly upon prior habits and their organization" (*HNC*, 14:128). But this suggests that there may be a link between habits and the possibilities of education—or, rather, that habit formation is "a fact of learning." Recall that habits are dynamic in quality: "Each habit demands appropriate conditions for its exercise . . . to find these conditions involves search and experimentation; the organism is compelled to make variations, and is exposed to error and disappointment." But in making these variations, the organism learns; in a positive spiral knowledge feeds on itself: "an old habit . . . gets in the way of the process of forming a new habit while the tendency to form a new one cuts across some old habit. Hence instability, novelty, emergence of unexpected and unpredictable combinations. The more an organism learns—the more that is, the former terms of a historic process are retained and integrated in this present phase—the more it has to learn, in order to keep itself going; otherwise death and catastrophe" (*EN*, 281).

While the relationship between habit and decision is clearly paramount, it is less clear what Dewey is suggesting about the link between an educated or superior choice and the role of habitual behavior. Once again Dewey's focus is on the moment in which a situation becomes problematic, when "each conflicting habit and impulse takes its turn in projecting itself upon the screen of the imagination. It unrolls a picture of its future history, of the career it would have if it were given head" (*HNC*, 14:133). In such a situation what course of action should one choose?

The answer lies in this concept of a history. Habits with potential futures are habits with realized pasts, and moments of imaginative rehearsals are in fact projected recollections of our histories (*HNC*,

14:143). From the knowledge of our behavior afforded by such recollections, we attempt to select a "particular activity which operates as a coordinating factor of all other subactivities involved." As we have seen, Dewey calls the selection of such activity the end-in-view. In short, our own habit-histories provide the most vital clues about the probability that a particular end-in-view may successfully serve to orient current behavior toward the future: "The problem of deliberation is not to calculate future happenings but to appraise present proposed actions. We judge present desires and habits by their tendency to produce certain consequences. It is our business to watch the course of our actions so as to see what is the significance, the import of our habits and dispositions" (14:206). But what are our habit-histories histories of? They are the patterns of behavior that have emerged in response to novel stimuli, to immediate sensations or qualities, both pleasurable and otherwise. Old habit-histories demand revision when they cannot procure the realization of a desired result, or end-in-view. Recall that Dewey regards nature as composed of events which are, at the level of qualitative experience, finalities and as aspects of nature objectified or conceptualized, parts of natural series or histories. Our own unsatisfied desires—the occasion for thought—are just the desires for the possession of ends that are currently absent, desires "formed from objects taken in their immediate and terminal qualities; objects once having occurred as endings, but which are not now in existence and which are not likely to come into existence save by an action which modifies surroundings" (*EN*, 104).[32]

The core of Dewey's theory of intelligent action is in sight. In "imaginative rehearsals" we try to project various patterns of behavior into the future with the intention of picking a focus of action, or end-in-view, which will secure the enjoyment of an absent but desired object. Obviously, an awareness of one's own habits is indispensable in this process; the choice of end-in-view will only be successful if it can be integrated into our behavior. But such introspective awareness is not enough. Habit-histories, or patterns of adjustment to the environment, can themselves incorporate new information about natural histories, or the conditions of appearance of those now desired ends. The choice of an end-in-view can be infinitely enriched through such information or knowledge. It is this knowledge that is provided in part by science, that "memorandum of conditions" which describes the dynamic context within which a particular discrete event or end will or can be made to occur (*EN*, 98). Human beings, in Dewey's view, experience such discrete events, seek to recreate or alter those histories, and find that in so doing their previous habits of behavior must be reconstituted with fresh information about their environment. "The intimate coordination and even fusion of these qualities with the regularities that form the objects of knowledge . . . characterizes intelligently directed experience" (xii).

Of course, a human organism can remain passive in the face of obstruction or ignorant of the tools for amelioration. But such a life, devoid of the need to have knowledge of natural or human history, is for Dewey one that lacks meaning. Dewey understands the effort to grasp the possibilities of experience as synonymous with human growth: "If the gap between organism and environment is too wide, the creature dies. If its activity is not enhanced by the temporary alienation, it merely subsists. Life grows when a temporary falling out is a transition to a more extensive balance of the energies of the organism with those of the conditions under which it lives" (*AAE*, 14). Dewey conceives of experience as a dynamic process in which human beings are engaged in constant interaction with an ever-changing world, a world that will inevitably embody the consequences of past interactions. The individual "either surrenders, conforms, and for the sake of peace becomes a parasitical subordinate, indulges in egotistical solitude; or its activities set out to remake conditions in accord with desire" (*EN*, 245). It is striking that Dewey employs the same spatial imagery as Rousseau, only to draw very different conclusions. To be motionless at the center of one's sphere is to rehearse one's natural death:

> The individual, the self, centered in a settled world which owns and sponsors it, and which it in turn owns and enjoys, is finished, closed. Surrender of what is possessed, disowning of what supports one in secure ease, is involved in all inquiry and discovery; . . . For to arrive at a new truth and vision is to alter. The old self is put off and the new self is only forming, and the form it takes will depend upon the unforeseeable result of an adventure. No one discovers a new world without forsaking an old one. (245–46)

Dewey did not deny that pleasures might be passively experienced, through "chance contact and stimulation," but he insisted that "happiness and delight are a different sort of thing," It is the obstacle that brings us up short, which forces us to recognize that the absence of former pleasures is to be welcomed. Recall Rousseau's efforts to insure that the unbending will of Emile's Tutor not be recognized by the child and contrast it with Dewey's conception of the heuristic obstruction: "If there were nothing in the way, if there were no deviations and resistances, fulfillment would be all at once, and in so being would fulfill nothing, but merely be. . . . Moreover, when a fulfillment comes and is pronounced good, it is *judged* good, distinguished and asserted, simply because it is in jeopardy, because it occurs amid indifferent and divergent things" (*EN*, 62).

These remarks conclude our examination of Dewey's philosophy of deliberation. In his view the quality of a decision depends on our habits—those patterns of behavior which lead us to certain patterns of activity and adaptation to the novel experience. Our habits are histories of predispositions, histories that help make possible the selection of a particular act in the moment of deliberation. It is possible to "Know what is the tendency of malice, charity, conceit, patience. We know by observing their consequences, by recollecting what we have observed, by using that recollection in constructive imaginative forecasts of the future, by using the thought of future consequences to tell the quality of the act now proposed" (*HNC*, 14:143–44).

Habits represent the prestructuring of our futures, but they can themselves be reconstructed. This is the foundation of Dewey's optimism and of his educational teachings: "Every attempt to forecast the future is subject in the end to the auditing of present concrete impulse and habit. Therefore the important thing is the fostering of those habits and impulses which lead to a broad, just, sympathetic survey of situations" (*HNC*, 14:144).

But such a survey of situations rests on more than accurate introspection and a willingness to adapt historic behavior patterns. The discoveries of science and technology have provided a second set of histories, which themselves represent methods of structuring our habits in the future as they have structured them in the past. When we seek to "use the foresight of the future to refine and expand present activity" science, or habits and techniques of problem solving, will be indispensable (*HNC*, 14:215). To measure the potential possibilities of human experience without access to scientific understanding is to blind oneself from the start.

Science as Reconstruction

Dewey's views on science have attracted widespread skepticism.[33] To an audience that is familiar and sympathetic either with the work of the Frankfurt school or the more recent work of Thomas Kuhn and Paul Feyerabend, Dewey's confidence in scientific methods can too easily strike an awkward note. Certainly, his apologists can point to qualifying passages. Thus, Dewey remarks in *The Public and Its Problems:* "the assimilation of human science to physical science represents . . . only another form of absolutist logic" (*PP,* 125). "It is very easy," Dewey wrote elsewhere, "for science to be regarded as a guarantee that goes with the sale of goods" (*LW,* 5:7). Nevertheless, it would be churlish to suggest that his occasional undercutting of scientific claims ever approached the brooding concerns that were, during the same period, motivating social research across the Atlantic. The point, rather, is that Dewey argues that the logic of science had been denigrated because it had been misunderstood. When faced with critics who wished to reject the fruits of scientific discovery or the lessons of its methods, Dewey confessed himself bemused: "Since we must in any case approach nature in some fashion, and by some path—even if only that of death—I confess my total inability to understand those who object to an intelligently controlled approach—for that is what science is" (*ION,* 5:88).

What did Dewey mean by this definition? He began by rejecting the view that science led to a fixed understanding of an unchanging reality. He called such a view "a survival of the older metaphysics," arguing instead that what should be sought was "regulation of change" (*QC,* 4:83, 231). In his view a scientific experiment is precisely this. It seeks to discover a relationship between dynamic entities by means of constructing an environment in which such a relationship becomes manifest. "The scientific search . . . signifies a search for the relations upon which the occurrence of real qualities and values depends, by means of which we can regulate their occurrence" (83).[34] Science is the "instrumentality of control of any particular termination" (*EN,* 98).

A scientific "fact" can only be asserted if we understand the way in which that occurrence is produced, which in turn depends on being able to manipulate the conditions upon which the occurrence rests. This view allows Dewey to insist on the pragmatic nature of scientific discovery: we can only know a fact the occurrence of which we have produced. In this sense, controlled experimentation was simply one example of intelligence at work: all knowing was "itself a mode of practical action and is *the* way of interaction by which other natural interactions become subject to direction" (*QC,* 4:86).

This link between science and thinking in general has a surface plausibility: for *imaginative rehearsal* simply read *experimental hypothesis.* In Gouinlock's view Dewey thought all problems, even political problems, "could be formulated as hypotheses that predicted desired outcomes conditional upon a specified reconstruction of existing circumstances" (intro. to *PP,* 2:xxxiii). The parallelism, however, between the logic of scientific procedure and that of rational thought is more problematic. The natural scientist can create an environment sufficiently controlled to isolate, regulate, and if necessary reproduce a specific relation. But as we have seen, the environment of human decision making is very different; it represents the resolution of a distinctive complication of "competing habits and impulses" which can never repeat itself (*HNC*, 14:135).[35]

What is it, then, that links scientific endeavor and intelligent thought? Dewey has in mind a similarity of procedure: "When we say that thinking and beliefs should be experimental, not absolutistic, we have then in mind a certain logic of method, not, primarily, the carrying on of experimentation like that of laboratories" (*PP*, 202). Science proceeds by a fused process in which thought and practical engagement with the world result in courses of actions which, if successful, reconstruct the environment so as to actualize a desired consequence. The success of a scientific hypothesis in such reconstructions rests on the same imaginative and careful engagement with one's environment that Dewey has sought to delineate in the case of all thinking. Indeed, as Hickman rightly suggests, the "artifact" of science, namely a certain form of knowing, "exhibits the most general traits of all other successful artifacts."[36]

But this analogy by no means exhausts the significance of science in Dewey's philosophy. When Dewey speaks of a "logic of method" he introduces a striking claim about the lessons to be derived from scientific success—namely, that such success rests on the presence of a community that authenticates scientific discovery and allows it to build on its own insights. Long before Karl Popper was to make a similar argument famous, Dewey wrote:

> No scientific inquirer can keep what he finds to himself or turn it to merely private account without losing his scientific standing. Everything discovered belongs to the community of workers. Every new idea . . . [has] to be submitted to his community for confirmation and test. There is an expanding community of cooperative effort and truth. . . . Suppose that what now happens in limited circles were extended and generalized. Would the outcome be oppression or emancipation? Inquiry is a challenge, not a passive conformity; application is a means of growth, not of repression. (*ION*, 5:115)

The possibility for science to grow in meaning depends on the existence of a public with a shared set of authenticating standards. On the basis of an experiment whose success is generally accepted, fresh variations become possible; familiar objects and definitions acquire fresh meanings, and knowledge expands: "the aim and end is the securer, freer, and more widely shared embodiment of values in experience by means of that active control of objects which knowledge alone makes possible" (*QC*, 37). The logic of scientific process, if we could but realize it, points us toward political structures in which knowledge emerges from a collective enterprise of discovery and concludes with a collectively authorized reconstruction of public life. Hence, Dewey's insistence that the tools made possible by science are worthless unless they are incorporated within the life of a community that has considered how such tools will affect its history: "Not just instrumentalities, but instrumentalities at work in effecting modifications of existence in behalf of conclusions that are reflectively preferred. Thus conceived the characteristic subject-matter of knowledge consists of fulfilling objects, which as fulfillments are connected with a history to which they give character" (*EN*, 161).

To meet the challenge posed by scientific discovery is to accept and work for a set of institutions in which the benefits of regulating nature will be available to all as recipients, directors, and codiscoverers. But this in turn suggests to Dewey the prime importance of a particular personal disposition or character—"an attitude of interest in change instead of interest in isolated and complete fixities . . . every new question is an opportunity for further experimental inquiries." The fixed habit is to be regarded with suspicion, for science has shown us not only that the world is a dynamic set of relations but also that we can successfully adapt to such a world. What is needed, above all, is "an attitude of criticism, of inquiry," a character "sensitive to the brutalities and extravagancies of custom" (*HNC*, 14:56).

In Dewey's view the fruit of scientific method is a body of information, a collection of natural histories which may be employed to redirect future histories. But in this sense human history itself is "scientific"—a storehouse of humans' efforts to redirect their environments: "Human history is long. There is a long record of experimentation in conduct, and there are cumulative verifications which give many principles a well earned prestige" (*HNC*, 14:165). Science, in turn, is only a natural history whose dimensions have been rendered transparent by the scientist. Science "constitutes the scheme of constant relationships by means of which spare, scattered and casual events are bound together into a connected history" (*EN*, 140). Science is a form of behavior in which traits of nature are "selected and ordered with reference to their function in promoting and controlling extensive inference" (*LW*, 12, 269; *Logic*, 270). Science, in Dewey's view, is simply a form of "minding" which takes into account both the "physical features of the environment extending out into space" and the organic history of those features (*EEL*, 10:322).

As Dewey summarizes: "A meaning is a representative function of a physical existent that is a component in a language" (*LW*, 12, *PP*, 52; *Logic*, 46). Dewey wants to stress that knowledge is both noun and verb, that our modes of talking are the tools through which the mind operates. Science, language, and action are not independent entities but, rather, aspects of the single natural process he calls mind. A year before his death Dewey was still trying to make clear that "*knowing* [is] the way of behaving in which linguistic artifacts transact business with physical artifacts, tools, implements, apparatus, both kinds being planned for the purpose of rendering *inquiry* of necessity an *experimental* activity."[37]

Dewey insists that science alone, as a set of tools, is worthless unless it is integrated into a scheme in which man seeks to project his natural history into the future. "Only as science is seen to be fulfilled and brought to itself in intelligent management of historical processes in their continuity can man be envisaged as within nature, and not as a supernatural extrapolation" (*EN*, 163). In other words, to employ science intelligently people not only must already have grasped the material possibilities that science affords but also have reflected in particular on their life history in which such possibilities can make sense: "Thus conceived, the characteristic subject matter of knowledge consists of fulfilling objects, which as fulfillments are connected with a history to which they give character" (161).

Scientific thought, that record of repeatable histories or relative stabilities in nature, must be integrated into our imaginative rehearsals of the future, in which, as we have seen, our existing habits and impulses are so deeply implicated. The result of such integrations is the intelligent use of our intellectual freedom: it becomes "an actuality when the recognition of relations—the stable element, is combined with the uncertain element in the knowledge which makes foresight possible and secures intentional preparation for possible consequences." Our freedom is the ability to "resolve, under the guidance of thought, the indeterminateness of uncertain *situations*" (*QC*, 199).

This shouldering of the burden of free thinking would become Dewey's litmus test and challenge to the political system. Dewey agreed with Rousseau that men were more accustomed to "forming ideas and judgements of value on the basis of conformity to antecedent objects" and were reluctant to give up the "inert dependence on the past." But only an "intentional construction of the future" was worthy of the capacity of men for freedom of choice (*QC*, 217, 231). Education, as we will see, is the effort to inculcate in the future generation the disposition to deliberate in the sense here suggested. Dewey calls the disposition "reason, the rational attitude," and insists repeatedly that it "is not a ready made antecedent which can be invoked at will" but, rather, "an achievement: . . . the thing actually at stake in any serious deliberation is not a difference of quantity, but what kind of person one is to become, what sort of self is in the making, what kind of world is making" (*HNC*, 14:136, 30, 150).

In Dewey's understanding the goal of a decision is to reconstruct problematic situations so that objects now experienced as obstructions or as unattained desires can be attenuated or attained within new patterns of life or habit. Key to the success of the enterprise is a willingness to grasp the tendencies of our existing habits, for those tendencies constitute much of our space for maneuver. Language allows us to convey such information without the need for all of us to reproduce the histories of our past interactions. No less important is a willingness to act upon the possibilities that a knowledge of natural histories has placed at our disposal—scientific information that suggests how objects and sensations may be reordered, reconstituted, reproduced. In this process our experiences grow through the fresh meanings that they produce. The appearance of an eclipse once meant a mystical occurrence—for an anthropologist it can mean that still—but other meanings are available for scientists. This is the main analysis, but a second, underlying argument has also been suggested. Dewey's model of deliberation and meaning points us to the significance of the relation between thought and time and to the unique status of the present.

The Temporality of Thought

Despite his emphasis on finding meaning through projecting histories of habit and nature into the future, Dewey insists that such projections are not predictions but, rather, efforts to discover the significance of a present situation. As we have seen, Dewey also stressed the need for people to pay attention to the influence of their existing habits: such influences set the context for future actions. The relationship between thought and temporality comes into sharper focus in Dewey's stinging attack on a rival understanding of intelligent action, that of utilitarianism. A brief examination of his argument is doubly important, since Dewey's faith in the powers of deliberative planning and science might seem to link him with the utilitarian's defense of a life measured through the calculus of pleasure and pain. The utilitarian measurement produces an ethics, a politics, and an educational model that Dewey strongly rejects.

According to Dewey, a choice must result in the "unifying [and] harmonizing [of] different competing tendencies" (*HNC*, 14:135). On the face of it there would seem to be no reason why the utilitarian choice, understood as a mental event, should fail to achieve this harmonization. But Dewey insists that any model of thought must be linked to a pattern of action: "If ideas, meanings, conceptions, notions . . . are instrumental to an active reorganization of the given environment, to a removable of some specific trouble . . . the test of their validity lies in accomplishing this task. If they succeed in their office, they are reliable, sound, valid, good, true" (*RP*, 169). The utilitarian calculus fails this test. It attempts to control the future success of a choice by predicting the future that a particular choice will actualize. But this effort, in Dewey's view, radically misconstrues the relationship between present and future. Any conception of futurity, any projection of our habit-histories into the future, is meaningful only because of its relationship to an understanding of the present situation. There is an "inability to dominate the future . . . [m]en always build better or worse than they know" (*HNC*, 14:206). The utilitarian calculation involves a hopeless effort to orient action on the basis of future pleasures and pains. The calculation is hopeless because such sensations "depend on our own state of some future moment and upon the surrounding circumstances of that moment. [But] both of these are variables that will change independently of present resolve and action" (14:141).

By seeking to control the uncontrollable, the utilitarian calculus fails the consequentialist, pragmatic test. But it fails, too, in its model of human thought. The utilitarian is persuaded that he or she is thinking about the future when, in fact, he is only thinking, in a way impoverished by his error, of the present. Contrary to what the utilitarian asserts, "we do not think of future losses and expansions." "We think, through imagination, of objects into which in the future some course of action will run, and we are *now* delighted or depressed . . . at what is presented" (*HNC*, 14:140).

In fact, a person's "estimate of future consequences of the agreeable and annoying is . . . of much greater value as an index of what he [or she] now is than as a prediction of future results" (*HNC*, 14:142). But such an estimate is only one way in which people can come to understand the possibilities that the present affords. Utilitarians fail to realize that attention to the present is the manner in which experience generates meaning from the organic histories, the habits, of past and future. Dewey suggests the anti-utilitarian model of thinking which his educational proposals will seek to foster:

> The present, not the future is ours. No shrewdness, no store of information will make it ours. But by constant watchfulness concerning the tendency of acts, by noting disparities between former judgments and actual outcomes, and tracing that part of the disparity that was due to deficiency and excess in disposition, we come to know the meaning of the present acts, and to guide them in the light of that meaning. The moral is to develop conscientiousness, ability to judge the significance of what we are doing . . . by fostering those impulses and habits which experience has shown to make us sensitive, generous, imaginative, impartial in perceiving the tendency of our inchoate dawning activities. (14:144)

The utilitarian attempts to make a choice consistent with his misunderstanding and ends up by developing a perverted set of habits that must be produced to sustain the selected course of action. It will be recalled that, in Dewey's view, habits constitute human character; thus, he is able to conclude that the utilitarian calculus leads to "morbidity, sophistication, isolation from others" (*HNC*, 14:141). A personality shaped by this calculus will subsequently base his or her choices on a deficient sense of the possibilities available. By contrast, Dewey seeks to portray a different temporal sensibility, one conscious of the experience that both past and future become meaningful only in the present.

We began this chapter with the lost public, a public that, in Dewey's view, mistakenly regards itself as a community of autonomous and free individuals. In fact, citizens are largely cut off from the knowledge that they need to relocate their actions within the social histories that frame their habits and provide meaning to their deliberations. In the words of one commentator, "Society has been thoroughly repoliticized in ways that cannot be grasped by traditional liberal categories which distinguish the political from the economic and so occlude the character of a highly politicized economy."[38] Since the self is a site of interaction of social and organic activities, and since the capacity to be mindful, or "to mind" or to think about an issue, are always of the form "what kind of self is in the making, what kind of world is in the making," the absence of an awareness of the nature of political economy and technological and bureaucratic authority engenders mindlessness and the loss of self.

Dewey teaches us that we must free the language of public life from the historical forms that have held it, and thus ourselves, hostage. Understanding that nature is a scene of openings and closings, continuities and disruptions, multiple intersections and redivisions, we come to see our own conscious experience as a dynamic and always provisional recreation of meaning from new patterns of stasis and change. Contemporary society, in Dewey's view, by teaching us to celebrate individualism as atomistic and by persuading us that democratic life means no more than a private vote, is undermining our capacity to think. Indeed, it is only when we come to regard a situation as problematic and malleable, as unsatisfying yet possessed of multiple possibilities of new associations, that we invest that situation with meaning. Only when we remeasure, remark on, a problematic situation do we come to feel what Dewey calls the unmeasurable "significance" of life. But how exactly is this done? How do we come to mind a situation, and how can language serve to "assign" it a significance? How, in short, do we learn to resist either mindless excess or mindless passivity?

6

The Education of Experience

The Politics of
Language and Science

THE LINKAGE OF Dewey's theory of meaning with a model of education starts from an inquiry into how human beings learn. This inquiry centers on Dewey's account of the role of the "sign." As suggested in the previous chapter, Dewey understands conscious experience to emerge from a situation characterized by uncertainty or doubt. Seeking to reconstruct the situation, we project potential associations of events as possible futures in what Dewey calls imaginative rehearsals. But in such moments those aspects of the situation which we reassemble or project are interwoven with the stored meanings that make up the material of our experience. Immediate experience and preexisting habits of interpretation interrogate each other, the first seeking to reorder aspects of the second. The terms of that interrogation, of thinking or consciousness or the having of an idea, are signs: schematic scenarios made up of referential inferences. In Eugene Rochberg-Halton's words, "a qualitative immediacy becomes a mediated sign." Recast in this vocabulary, our moments of thought and decision are a form of experience in which "objects are . . . living signs whose meanings are realized in the transactions we have with them."[1]

Dewey is convinced that our interactions with and transformations of the world are not simply haphazard: we experience certain events as brute occurrence, but we can interpret those events as signs of other events, as producing certain outcomes. When our activity is continuous with nature's invitation to growth, to the possibilities of alteration and reorganization, we draw on inferences, or signs, from which we can learn. Signs offer us the method of experienced intervention. Paraphrasing Dewey's *Logic,* R. W. Sleeper remarks:

> The argument moves from existence to disclosure, from existential relations of involvement to the ordered forms of language, and thence to the formal structures of logical relations. Inference is fundamental, and social discourse, language as a means of communication, depends on it. . . . Dewey works it out by taking the relation of involvement as a causal relation between signs and things signified. Inference is the taking of a sign as evidence of the thing signified. . . . He takes it that the sign-signified relation as an existential causal connection is what every inference aims at, and what it discloses when the signified object is reached.[2]

Dewey's most famous illustration of his thesis involves the learning about the extended inference from heat to pain to avoidance. In 1896 Dewey described the initial episode of a child burning her fingers in a candle flame. In his article, which centers on the search for discriminating sensations, Dewey criticizes the popular model of the event, in which sight, sensory stimulus, response, and memory are regarded as "distinct psychical existences."[3] Dewey argues, rather, that the retreat from the flame and memory of the experience is "simply the completion, or fulfillment of the previous eye-arm-hand coordination and not a mere and not an entirely new occurrence." The thought, or as Dewey might have put it, the minding of "pain," is the result of the need to find an inference, or tool, through which an experience might be avoided in the future. In Dewey's view, therefore, a sign-idea can equally well be described as a behavior, a method, or a theory.

In sum, language and science are collections of signs or symbols which represent rehearsed associations and projections of organic experience. This is why language and science can "mean": "As symbols are related to one another, the important relations are recorded and preserved as meaning" (*PP,* 152). Dewey argues that language makes up only a part of our experience. To be sure, it makes possible meaning, habit alteration, and imaginative experimentation, but, as is the case of other animals, human behavior consists of an "immense multitude of immediate organic selections, rejections, welcomings, expulsions . . . elations and dejections" that are extralinguistic. Language comes late. It is a "a selected statement of what we wish to retain among all these incipient starts, following ups and breaking off" (EN, 300).

Such extralinguistic behavior is present in those habitual organic responses that are subconsciously present in moments of perception. But the critical point is that such primary organic habits are themselves affected by linguistically produced meanings, or the products of discourse which orient our perceptions and by the habits that they may effect: "Meanings acquired in connection with the use of tools and of language exercise a profound influence upon organic feelings. In the reckoning of this account, are included the changes effected by all the consequences of attitude and habit due to *all* the consequences of tools and language—in short, civilization" (EN, 300).

Thus, the signs of language, embodied in all our cultural practices, including scientific inquiry, can raise our experience to a level of meaning above that of other animals. But they can also savage us: the very mechanisms through which language affects organic responses can operate to pervert our relationship with the world about us. We can wrench signs from shared experience, cut them off from circulation, and selfishly appropriate them. A public unable to develop a shared understanding of its signs will be unable to direct that understanding to public goals. Since, as we have seen, Dewey is convinced that experience works through association, the manipulation of the circumstances of free association is in a very direct sense a crime against meaning. (Dewey went so far as to claim that "association in the sense of connection and combination is a 'law' of everything" [PP, 22]).[4] Democracy, and the education that will secure it, is a form of associated life which points to free association as a common experience.

Recall that for Dewey there is no systematic break in the chain from the inanimate to the human. There is a greater complexity of interactions but no caesura. A perversion at one level is a perversion at all levels of experience:

> Activities which develop, appropriate and enjoy meanings bear the same actualizing relation to psycho-physical affairs that the latter bear to physical characters. They present the consequences of a wider range of interactions, that in which needs, efforts and satisfactions conditioned by association are operative. In this widened and deepened activity, there are both added resources and values, *and added liabilities and defaults*. The actualization of meanings furnishes psycho-physical qualities with their ulterior significance and worth. But is it also confuses and perverts them. The

effects of this corruption are themselves embodied through habits . . . forming one-sided degraded and excessive susceptibilities. . . . These habitual effects become in turn spontaneous, natural, "instinctive"; they form the platform of development and apprehension of further meanings, affecting every subsequent phase of personal and social life. (*EN*, 301–302; emphasis added)

Education in a democracy, in both formal and social senses, amounts to a sustained effort to insure that the distortions Dewey discusses here will be minimized. He seeks "educational procedures by which a normal integration of meanings in organic functions shall be secured and perversions prevented." But what defines "normal integration"? As we have seen, Dewey's axiology, in which language and habit emerge from natural organic interactions, commits him to the mirror image: language and habit profoundly affect our other organic sensibilities. Meanings, or the linguistic assertion of interactions, point toward fresh orientations to the world, and the same is true of scientific discourse, which, as suggested, is only a special case of meaningful language.

The essential fact is that the conditions of symbolic communication and scientific knowledge constitute the world in which we must live and toward which our habits must be oriented—and education's task is to clarify the conditions of this constitution. A successful education is "growth in meaning" because an educated person has internalized the manner in which our habits have been formed by the interaction of knowledge and the organic predispositions that knowledge modifies. Education instructs us that "knowledge of the conditions under which our meanings and our modes of talking and using them organically occur is . . . indispensable" (*EN*, 342).

Language, in Dewey's view, cannot be a private mechanism: it always "implies two selves involved in a conjoint or shared undertaking" (*EN*, 299). The commonality of language, its capacity to incorporate meaning, renders it a political phenomena. James Gouinlock makes this point with acuity: "Language is understood functionally: it is whatever succeeds in creating a community of action. Whatever cries or gestures succeed in effectuating such action thereupon *become* language. The meaning of vocal acts, then, is precisely the interactions which the objects designated by them undergo in the social situation."[5]

But language is not simply an event initiated by the conversants; it is, for Dewey, a transformative experience for each and has an unavoidable impact on its speakers: it "compels one individual to take the standpoint of other individuals and to see and inquire from a standpoint which is not strictly personal but in common to them as participants or 'parties' in a conjoint undertaking." Language, Dewey goes on, "occurs for the sake of determining future agreements in associated behavior, and it is this subsequent behavior which finally settles the actual meaning of the words in question" (*Logic*, 46–47).

The link between communication and collective participation is direct: "To fail to understand is to fail to come into agreement in action; to misunderstand is to set up action at cross purposes" (*EN*, 179). Language ties us together, but it simultaneously ties us to the natural world and to the histories that are unfolding therein. The linkages between hitherto discrete sensations of natural objects which language affords results in the remaking of our direct experience toward one another. We see objects as usable, transportable, exchangeable, and temporally situated: "to perceive is to acknowledge unattained possibilities; it is to refer the present to consequences, apparition to issue, and thereby to behave in deference to events . . . as meaning, future consequences already belong to the thing" (182). Language invites us into the future, as it points to the past consequences and present possibilities of collective behavior. As the mechanism that links people with one another and with nature, it is "the tool of tools" (168).

Dewey's point is that language permits the consequences, or meaning, of human activity, to be more universally shared, known, and employed in fresh domains in the future. Language permits a liberation from the particular instance, followed by a reintegration with an expanded environment.[6] The liberation of meanings from local circumstances has a heuristic effect. The fact that language is consequent on particular conjoined acts teaches us "that qualities which we attribute to objects ought to be imputed to our own way of experiencing them, and that these in turn are due to the force of intercourse and custom. This discovery marks an emancipation; it purifies and remakes the objects of our direct or primary experience" (*EN*, 14). Communication is a two-way mirror: it points us back to the subjectivism of the social circumstances from which it emerged and forward toward the experimental implementation of fresh meanings, which will in turn bring out fresh activity. This is not to claim that meanings are not initially particular to a certain culture. But if meanings are regarded as exhaustively captured through the locality of their origins, the universalist promise remains unrealized: "meanings that are formed on this basis are sure to contain much that is irrelevant, and much that is required for the intelligent control of activity" (*Logic*, 50).

Language, which permits the bracketing of immediate involvement and the assimilation of the life histories of other people, offers us a way to reconstruct our own histories based on the knowledge that we can alter ourselves by altering the civilization about us. But if language is to free the events of experience for meaning, then the conditions in which it develops must be socially nurtured. Political restrictions on both communication and experimentation create artificial restrictions on the process of meaning creation. Even in so-called democracies, Dewey was convinced, most citizens do not grasp that the spread of literacy and the discoveries of science have offered enormous possibilities of reorientation which historic patterns of social organization—now ingrained in their habitual, subconscious behavior—have made them blind to.

Science, Pragmatism, and Politics

Dewey's philosophy points to a politics of extended possibilities, a democratic structure in which funded meanings become accessible to all, and his educational recommendations also attempt to promote this end. But one cannot forever postpone questions about Dewey's politics. In particular, how do we know when the extent of possibilities he celebrates becomes too great? Dewey can criticize a too narrow range of possible futures, but does he offer us advice to prevent an excess of possible choices, making it impossible to act? Answering these questions requires directly confronting Dewey's political writings, for Dewey insists, the measure of a philosophy's success is its worldly consequences. "Philosophy," he writes, "recovers itself when it ceases to be a device for dealing with the problems of philosophers and becomes a method, cultivated by philosophers, for dealing with the problems of men" (*MW*, 10:4). When measured by his own standard, does Dewey's philosophy produce a coherent, principled political position?

A survey of Dewey's writing on domestic and international politics suggests no simple answer to the question. In general terms Dewey's position embodies two connected components. First, a belief that the resolution of the major political crises of the day lay in providing information to the adult populations of democratic regimes. Second, that one could infer the information required from an understanding of historical social habits combined with imaginative rehearsals of the future. Both assumptions are clearly consistent with Dewey's pragmatic philosophy, as presented here. But the test is in the specifics, and here the result of Dewey's prescriptions are uncertain. As he tried to assess events around him, certain aspects of the situation, and thus of his assessment, seemed to catch him unawares. The critical question is whether the results are problematic for Dewey's vision as a whole. While even a summary of Dewey's extensive political involvements lies far beyond the scope of this study, a single and provocative example can suggest certain tensions within Dewey's pragmatic vision.

For nine months in 1937–38 Dewey (who was approaching his eightieth year) chaired an independent commission, which exonerated Leon Trotsky from Stalin's charges against him. Following the hearings in Coyoacan, Mexico, Trotsky characteristically published an attack on the liberal morality of his defenders and a defense of historical materialism. Equally in character, Dewey took no umbrage but responded with a spirited, philosophical attack on Trotsky's theoretical logic.

In his essay on June 1938, entitled *Their Morals and Ours,* Trotsky offered an elegant, if not especially sophisticated defense of Marxist-Leninist strategy. Trotsky wrote: "Dialectical materialism does not know the dualism between means and end. The end flows naturally from the historical movement. Organically, the means are subordinated to the end." The means are social revolution; the end is "the liberation of humanity." Scientific materialism has provided the "laws of the development of society," and one can successfully deduce the means from those laws.[7]

Two months later Dewey responded. He objected not to the communist allegiance to science but to the particular form of scientific logic which Trotsky's argument embodied. "To be scientific about ends," Dewey wrote, "does not mean to read them out of laws, whether the laws are natural or social." More specifically, Dewey objected to the claim by Marxists that their dialectics was exempt from the requirements of inductive procedure: "Since the class struggle is regarded as the only means that will reach the end, and since the view that it is the only means is reached deductively, and not by an inductive examination of the means-consequences in their interdependence, the means, the class struggle, does not need to be critically examined with respect to its actual objective consequences." In Dewey's view Marxists such as Trotsky committed an error of logical reasoning. They deduced their means from a law of social development which they had not measured against its actual capacity to realize its end-in-view (human emancipation). Instead, they had turned means into ends. Thus, they defined the process of class struggle, then and always, as emancipatory: "The professed end—

the end-in-view—the liberation of mankind, is thus subordinated to the class struggle as the means by which it is to be attained."[8]

Dewey's response to Trotsky, read as an isolated polemic, was coherent and consistent. But it must be read, too, against Dewey's earlier celebration of the Soviet Union, the result of a visit in 1928. Dewey's overriding reaction to the Soviet Union was to see the situation there in terms of an educational endeavor. As he remarked in the first report of his visit, "the final significance of what is taking place in Russia is not to be grasped in political or economic terms, but is found in change, of incalculable importance, in the mental and moral disposition of a people, an educational transformation" (*I*, 59). Dewey's positive reaction to what he saw served as testimony to his own faith in the possibilities of a public education, but it suggested too a certain overeagerness to embrace collectivist solutions.

Dewey was acutely aware that his judgments were highly provisional, due to "the narrowness of [his] experience." But certain features of Soviet life struck him as unmistakable—and positive: the dynamic mobility of the population, its capacity for self-reflection, and its effort to employ the social sciences. Dewey applauded the "sense of creative energy that is concerned only with the future," celebrated the "presence of a deliberate and systematic effort at exploration and self-emancipation," and supported the "belief in the reality of a science of society." Above all, Dewey felt himself caught up in the mood engendered by a vast social undertaking that was unfolding as he watched. He regards Russia as "an experiment whose outcome is quite undetermined" (*I*, 29, 113, 146).

The vital contribution and current success of Russian education, in Dewey's view, was that it prepared its citizens for the psychological challenge that such an experiment represented. The Soviets intended this "new mentality" of a "cooperative social type" to "create habits" that dovetailed "in an extraordinary way, both in administrative organization and in aim and spirit, into all other social agencies and interests" (*I*, 57, 61). Russian education provided for such a social experiment, but the causality, in Dewey's opinion, was reciprocal. He concluded that "only in a society based on the cooperative principle can the ideals of educated reformers be adequately carried into practice" (73).

Dewey's theoretical differences with Trotsky may strike a warmer note than this earlier celebration of Soviet pedagogy, but, taken together, they suggest genuine difficulties with his position. It is clear, as a starting point, that Dewey was deeply attracted to moments of social flux, in which social energies seemed to contribute to what were praiseworthy, collectively shared goals and when policies were not yet fixed. He was convinced that the outcome of the tumultuous release of energies he had witnessed would "create its own future society according to its own desires and purposes . . . [it will be] unlike the society which orthodox Marxian formulae call for" (*I*, 58). Contrast such sympathy with Dewey's judgment about America in 1928: "We seem to find everywhere a hardness, a tightness, a devotion to efficiency and prosperity of a mechanical and quantitative sort" (*LW*, 3:134). The language of the comparison is revealing: the absence of identified subjects and the abstraction of expression echo Dewey's naturalistic metaphysics but failed to grasp essential particulars of the situation.

In his enthusiasm for Soviet education Dewey applauded the match between means and ends but failed to ask realistic political questions: What if, for example, the powers organizing the experiment turned it toward other ends?[9] Dewey trusted the political leader turned social experimenter. He applauded the reciprocal fit between social aims and educational means. His later bitter disappointment at the outcome of the Soviet experiment suggests the feelings of a man betrayed by those he had considered fellow social scientists.[10] As Dewey recalled in 1937, he had "looked on the Soviet Union as a social laboratory in which certain experiments would be worked out" (*LW*, 11:335). But the costs for failure were, perhaps, of a different order; very different visions can adopt seductively similar logics of justification.

Dewey, in his philosophy of reflective choice, stressed the importance of history, the fact that human intelligence is subject to the influence of habit and limited by perspective. In Dewey's view, however, the synthesis of experience and imagination would permit people to remake history and enrich their perspective. The difficulty lay in Dewey's confusion of such moments of personal choice and a scientists' inductively derived hypothesis. Even educated citizens can be reluctant, or unable, to remake their politics at every moment; Dewey saw the goal but underestimated the restraining power of residual habit he had so effectively discussed in his philosophical work. Seduced by the specter of wholesale experimentalism in the Soviet Union, Dewey did not see the power structures under the surface claims of "cooperation." Rousseau, one might imagine, would have seen more clearly.

Education for Democracy

Dewey found in the pedagogic enterprise the single most powerful means to alter the habits of citizens. In his view the future of any society hinged upon the education of the young. But if education was undeniably a social process, it was also a natural one, a development of dynamic structures. *Education* was only a word for a certain kind of growth: "In directing the activities of the young, society determines its own future. . . . Since the young at a given time will at some later date compose the society of that period, the latter's nature will largely turn upon the direction children's activities were given at an earlier period. This cumulative movement of action toward a later result is what is meant by growth" (*DE*, 41).

The immaturity of the child is precisely "the *power* to grow" (*DE*, 42), to develop those dispositions we have termed *habits:* "the power to retain from one experience something which is of avail in coping with the difficulties of a later experience . . . [the] power to modify actions" (44). As stated earlier, Dewey identified growth with change. In order to live all organisms have to engage, consciously or not, in constant reorderings of their relations with the environment. In his work on education Dewey repeats the argument, tying it specifically to his understanding of the pedagogic process: "Our net conclusion is that life is development. . . . Translated into its educational equivalents, that means (i) that the educational process has no end beyond itself; it is its own end; and that (ii) the educational process is one of continual reorganizing, reconstructing, transforming" (49).

Dewey intended his account of the educational process at this point to be generic, read out of the natural processes through which organisms live. But the reader will soon notice the similarity of language between this description and the normative, democratic ideal that Dewey sought to promote. This similarity was not accidental: in a two-part argument Dewey attempted to show the congruence of the natural drive toward adjustment and growth with the structures of a democratic politics. Dewey's first claim was that, unless a child can grow up in a democratic society, those generic traits of growth or habitual adjustment will be stunted and frustrated:

> It is assumed that the aim of education is to enable the individuals to continue their education—or that the object and reward of learning is continued capacity for growth. Now this idea cannot be applied to *all* the members of a society except where intercourse of man with man is mutual, and except where there is adequate provision for the reconstruction of social habits and institutions

by means of wide stimulation arising from equitably distributed interests. And this means a democratic society. (*DE*, 100)

Democratic society provides an indispensable framework for democratic education. But in his second argument Dewey posits a reciprocal causality; the sustaining of a democratic polity rests, in turn, on the success of formal education in fostering the requisite democratic sensibilities: "we may produce in schools a projection in type of the society we should like to realize, and by forming minds in accord with it gradually modify the larger and more recalcitrant features of adult society" (*DE*, 317). Borrowing the terminology of a different philosophy, Dewey declared, "Democracy has to be born anew every generation, and education is its midwife" (*MW*, 10:139). In a democracy, as in any society, the maintenance of certain habits of thought and behavior rest on the education of future citizens: "To organize education so that natural active tendencies shall be fully enlisted in doing something, while seeing to it that the doing requires observation, the acquisition of information, and the use of a constructive imagination, is *what most needs to be done to improve social conditions*" (*DE*, 137; emphasis added).

In a democratic state a democratic sensibility is the end or aim of education. The qualities of democracy must be implicit in the educational situation, properly considered and imagined. And so they are: Dewey's description of the educational process as one of "continuous reconstruction" allows him to claim that the ends of democratic behavior—which he describes in the same vocabulary—can be continuous with education itself. Democracy is indeed "an end which grows up within an activity." In this case the activity is education, and the end is a democratic sensibility, which it promotes (*DE*, 78, 106). We are now in a position to understand Dewey's simultaneous claims that education has no ends or aims beyond itself and that "a democratic community [is] more interested than other communities have cause to be in deliberate and systematic education" (87). Democratic communities are precisely the manifestation of the natural drive toward growth, realized in their ability constantly to reconstruct their environment in order to make sense of fresh stimuli. This ability is the end of education.

So far, however, Dewey's argument has been necessarily general. Democracy—the realization of "a form of social life in which interests are mutually interpenetrating, and where progress or readjustment" is critical—rests on the success of an education that readies its future citizens for just such conditions (*DE*, 87). The principal goal is the promotion of democratic habits that promote flexibility, sharing of interests, and a willingness to employ the tools of knowledge, effective communication, and voting in the task of social reconstruction. But one cannot hope to approach such general goals without a much more sophisticated model of democratic sensibilities. As Dewey remarked, "The conception of education as a social process and function has no definite meaning until we define the kind of society we have in mind" (97).

The Meaning of Democracy

"Democracy is no more adequately defined by any merely quantitative conception than a tree is defined by counting the number of cells which constitute it" (*ED,* 230). Dewey passionately believed that one could not construct genuinely democratic societies by mechanistic formulas but, rather, through public responsibility. That sense of responsibility came with the realization that in a democracy the individual habits, and the decisions that emerge from them, were the consequences of social structures whose origins and power were usually unrecognized by citizens. Such a realization would make inescapable a role for each citizen in promoting changes in those structures for which embedded social habits (possibly including one's own) had become a barrier to the communication and planning that could result in more dynamic lives for oneself and one's peers. In this sense the actual policy-making followed in a democracy revealed an ideal means of inculcating habits and, thus, a model for education.

In Dewey's model democratic society citizens would learn to take responsibility for integrating their actions with the well-being of a society:

> Responsibility for the conduct of society and government rests on every member of society. Therefore, every one must receive a training that will enable him to meet this responsibility, giving him just ideas of the condition of the people collectively, and developing those qualities which will ensure his doing a fair share of the work of government. (*ST,* 8:398)

This passage points us back toward the vital role of formal education and projects the goal of the democratic experiment. As already suggested, Dewey believed that a democratic society offered the finest opportunity for human beings to forge lives marked by intelligent judgment, or meaning, and his philosophy of meaning was the product of a certain kind of thinking based on the power of language. Ideally, a democratic state would provide those channels of communication in which that sense of an infinite horizon—of the vast interconnecting world, a part of which we modify by our activities—becomes a sense of communion through one another. When we become the conscious co-authors of our histories through comprehending the influence and latent powers those histories exercise, when we take responsibility for creating fresh histories to expand our present, then we will have realized the democratic community: "Democracy will have come into its own, for democracy is a name for a life of free and enriching communion. It had its seer in Walt Whitman. It will have its consummation when free social inquiry is indissolubly wedded to the art of full and moving communication" (*PP*, 184).

In the previous chapter I argued that Dewey's conception of the democratic ideal does not emerge ex nihilo. It is, on the contrary, an amplification of Dewey's understanding of the process of meaning creation as made possible by an understanding of actual social conditions, or habit-histories. We are the product of such histories: "development of modes of manufacture and commerce, travel, migration, and intercommunication which flowed from the command of science over natural energy." Such histories had universalized certain possibilities of life; in a democratic society it could be "a matter of deliberate effort to sustain and extend them": "We must base our conception upon societies which actually exist, in order to have any assurance that our ideal is a practicable one. But . . . the ideal cannot simply repeat the traits which are actually found. The problem is to extract the desirable traits of forms of community life which actually exist, and employ them to criticize undesirable features and suggest improvement" (*DE*, 87, 83).

Existing societies are still far from able to fulfill this model of constructive criticism, of building a communion of meanings. Measuring our society against an idealized assumed community maps out paths as yet untaken. When we ask: "How numerous and varied are the interests which are consciously shared? How full and free is the interplay with other forms of association?" we begin to realize the extent of our unfulfilled democratic possibilities. To make those possibilities more vivid Dewey suggests the parallel of the ideal family: "There are material, intellectual, aesthetic interests in which all participate and that the progress of one member has worth for the experience of other members—it is readily communicable—and that the family is not an isolated whole, but enters intimately into relationship with . . . all the agencies of culture . . . and that it plays a due part in the political organization and in return receives support from it" (*DE*, 83). In an Aristotelian vein Dewey translates this standard into political terms, arguing that "all the members of the group must have an equable opportunity to receive and to take from others. There must be a large variety of shared undertakings and experiences. Otherwise, the influences which educate some into masters, educate others into slaves" (84): "A society which makes provision for participation in its good of all its members on equal terms and which secures flexible readjustment of its institutions through interaction of the different forms of associated life is in so far democratic" (99).

Working against this readjustment are the unperceived barriers of ignorance and social inequalities which block the process of communication by sealing off the phenomena that determine our habits of life. We are always tempted to make a lazy virtue of apparent necessity and to cling to the familiar. Thereby we isolate ourselves from potentially liberating experience:

> Families which seclude their domestic concerns as if they had no connection with larger life; schools when separated from the interest of home and community . . . [t]he essential point is that isolation makes for rigidity and formal institutionalizing of life. . . . It is a commonplace that an alert and expanding mental life depends upon an enlarging range of contact with the physical environment. But the principle applies even more significantly to the field where we are apt to ignore it—the sphere of social contacts. (*DE,* 86).

Breaking down those barriers that prevent widening circles of social contact, or generating where possible a greater number of shared interests, represent democratic ends-in-view: targets that, if achieved, will result in a more democratic community. The free flow of communication and the collective access to the tools of technology would prepare the way for "greater reliance upon the recognition of mutual interests as a factor in social control, [and] . . . changes in social habit—its continuous readjustment through meeting new situations produced by varied intercourse." Dewey thus concludes that "these two traits are precisely what characterize the democratically constituted society" (86–87).

Dewey's conception of a democratic polity is now in full view; it is a society in which the barriers to the growth of meaning have crumbled:

> A democracy is more than a form of government; it is primarily a mode of associated living, of conjoint communicated experience. The extension in space of the number of individuals who participate in an interest so that each has to refer his own action to

that of others, and to consider the action of others to give point and direction to his own, is equivalent to the breaking down of those barriers of class, race, and national territory which kept men from perceiving the full import of their activity. (*DE*, 87)

This was the task for which formal education had to equip the future citizen of a democratic state.

Formal Education

Dewey's models of schooling are heavily focused on the primary school. In a manner that parallels Rousseau's, Dewey's educational structures start with the infant. A successful primary education will bring home to the young citizen the potential embodied in democratic forms of social organization. Given Dewey's understanding that behavior is consequent upon habitual attitudes that are the product of planned environmental conditioning, the schoolroom will offer that "kind of environment needed to liberate and to organize" the habits of the young in ways supportive of their future shouldering of democratic responsibilities (*DE*, 105). Supreme among these habits will be a predisposition to find in moments of uncertainty an invitation to collective responsibility, reorganization, and inquiry. The schoolroom will situate "the individual as sharer or partner in the associated activity so that he feels its successes his success, its failure as his failure" (14).

Dewey derives some general organizational principles from this democratic standard:

> A society to which stratification into separate classes would be fatal, must see to it that intellectual opportunities are accessible to all on equitable and easy terms. . . . A society which is mobile, which is full of channels for the distribution of a change occurring anywhere, must see to it that its members are educated to personal initiative and adaptability. Otherwise, they will be overwhelmed by the changes in which they are caught and whose significance or connections they do not perceive. (*DE*, 7–8).

Dewey develops these principles in a fascinating if largely ignored work on the structure of the ideal primary school. In introducing his conception, he employs the philosophical terminology with which we are now familiar: the end-in-view of the primary school, he remarks, "is the development of a spirit of social co-operation and community life" (*School*, 14). The spaces of the schoolroom are analogous to Rousseau's circles, "an embryonic society" in which future citizens will sense a collective responsibility for their environment. In contrast to Rousseau's vision, however, Dewey's pupils will grasp the fluidity of knowledge, its tendency to point the student to fresh social experience, to the establishment of new meanings of experience. The students will discover that "knowledge is . . . [not] an immobile solid; it has been liquefied. It is actively moving in all the currents of society itself" (15, 23).[11]

What Dewey tried to achieve was a "school without walls." As his diagrammatic representations suggested, students would find themselves in an environment in which an object was experienced as part of many histories—histories of natural life, technology, and social use. From discrete objects the student could construct fresh histories and discover new meanings. The room in which students were introduced to spinning wool was immediately adjoined to "an industrial museum" and to a library in which children could find Homer's Penelope along with the music of Wagner's *Sentra* (*School,* 79).[12] Teachers encouraged the mixing of academic disciplines, and pupils were to place themselves, as it were, in the middle of the confluence.

Dewey never claimed that his educational model incorporated some kind of neutrality toward the information conveyed in the schoolroom. In his eyes conventional educative techniques, with their emphasis on passive learning, would perpetuate undesirable social habits of mind. Often, he observed, "the bonds which connect subject matter of school study with the habits and ideals of the social group are disguised and covered up" (*DE,* 181). Dewey had no reason to conceal his political intentions: his educational schemes and democratic faith were inseparable.

Thus, the lessons in Dewey's schoolroom had a particular and pointed structure. A reformed education was needed precisely because contemporary humans had developed habits that underrepresented or distorted the very possibilities that their ingenuity had provided. Dewey would stress a kind of idealized economic history, which in his view dealt "with the growth of effective liberties, through command of nature, of the common man" over political economic history, in which this progress was so much less evident (*DE,* 216).[13] History would glorify the heroes who had opened up fresh channels of productive possibility and dynamic change: the student would understand "the sorts of character that help on and that hold back" (*School,* 156) and would acquire "a cultivated imagination for what men have in common and a rebellion at whatever unnecessarily divides them" (*DE,* 121). Believing that a large ground of communality was present in immediate experience, Dewey argued that most divisions were unnecessary. Dewey, no less than Rousseau, accepted the fact that a socially critical education is also a deliberately naive education. The artifice of the teacher is to draw the student into comparisons between the natural interconnections that constitute knowledge and the manner in which contemporary society was breaking down those connections for political and economic purposes.

Dewey's view of the sciences should make it obvious that the logic of inference, of problem solving, would play a vital role in his pedagogic design. Scientific theories involve abstracting from immediate experience, abstractions needed to gain control over events. Such conceptual work, such inquiry, contains, in Dewey's view, a vital lesson for future democratic citizens: "Scientific abstraction and generalization are equivalent to taking the point of view of any man, whatever his location in time and space." Moreover, the abstract nature of scientific concepts was instrumental and moral, "detached for the sake of wider and freer application in later concrete action" (*DE,* 227–28): "The young begin with active occupations having a social origin and use, and proceed to a scientific insight in the materials and laws involved, through assimilating into their more direct experience the ideas and facts communicated by others" (193). The presentation of the history of the sciences would be no more geared toward normative neutrality than that of political history. Schools should teach pupils to see inquiry "used in the interests of a truly shared or associated life" such that its fruits "become the *positive* resources of civilization" (37).

The outlines of Dewey's proposals should now be clear. Taken as a whole, education would "mak[e] the ties which bind persons together more perceptible—which breaks down the barriers of distance between them" (*DE,* 316). But it is not simply ties between people with which Dewey is concerned; the unusual juxtaposition of objects in the classroom would kindle the interest of students: "The word interest suggests, etymologically, what is *between*—that which connects two things otherwise distant" (127). Above all, students would learn the habit of being interested in the world: "To have an interest is to take things as entering into . . . a continuously developing situation, instead of taking them in isolation. . . . It shows that subject matter of learning is identical with all objects, ideas and principles which enter as resources or obstacles into the continuous intentional pursuit of a course of action" (138). The process of education would be a dynamic one in which new connections, histories, and possibilities of object reorganization are constantly interesting the students and drawing them into a sense of responsibility for managing the potentials of their inheritance.

Children's lives grow in meaning in the same way as those of adults, the difference is that the schoolroom provides an optimized, carefully planned, space wherein teachers can encourage and make habitual the learning process: "There is no limit to the meaning which an action may come to possess. It all depends on the context of perceived connections in which it is placed; the reach of imagination in realizing the connections is inexhaustible. . . . With every increase of ability to place our own doings in their time and space connections, our doings gain in significant content. We realize that we are citizens of no mean city in discovering the scene in space of which we are denizens" (DE, 208). Students learn to grasp possibilities of extending the meaning of their experience and, thus, to approach the Protagorian ideal. The child should develop a sense of the interconnectedness of life which implicates his or her own efforts: "the growth of the imagination in flexibility, in scope, and in sympathy, till the life which the individual lives is informed with the life of nature and of society" (School, 56). To develop judgment is to grow into an active self, to discover the location in which one stands and through which one will project the conception of a life.

Dewey focused his pedagogic designs on connectivity, on the sense of wonder and excitement which one can suggest to children as they find themselves experiencing "mindfully," as they become the subjects and re-creators of histories. As always, Dewey's concern was with consummatory experience, on the unity of a moment that springs from art, from informed and skillful doing. This involves "the elimination of all that does not contribute to the mutual organization of the factors of both action and reception . . . the selection of just the aspects and traits that contribute to their interpenetration of one another."[14] He directs us to "inclusive ideal ends" (FC, 33; LW, 10:23), in which the sense of the "extensive and underlying whole" anchors our particular eliminations and selections (AAE, 194). This broad horizon is possible because of what Dewey calls mind. Alexander offers a useful gloss: Dewey's conception of mind refers to all aspects of language use, even to objective systems of meaning embedded in a culture. Education leads us into a habit of constantly interrogating the horizons of mind.

A New Individualism

It is too easy to gain the impression in these passages that Dewey was attempting to undermine the entire vocabulary of private individualism, an effort that would link his work with the latter parts of Rousseau's *Social Contract*. Instead, if Dewey's educational pro-grams achieved their intent, the product would be a new individu-alism, a sense of self enriched by a democratic environment. Dewey reminded his readers that "individualism" *was* a unique manner of acting in and with a world of objects and persons: "Democracy . . . admits that the full significance of personality can be learned by the individual only as it is already presented to him in objective form in society; it admits that the chief stimuli and encouragements to the realization of personality come from society, but it holds, none the less, to the fact that personality cannot be procured for anyone . . . by anyone else" (*ED*, 244).

The realization of this double truth could be a liberating one, a fact to be celebrated, not ignored. Education and communication could bring us to a view of our surroundings such that we might find ourselves through our society. Once again Dewey resorted to a spatial metaphor to bring his point home. In a language deeply at odds with Rousseau's celebration of enclosure, but of equal power, Dewey remarked: "To gain an integrated individuality, each of us needs to cultivate his own garden: but there is no fence about this garden: it is no sharply marked off enclosure. Our garden is the world, in the angle at which it touches our own manner of being. By accepting the corporate and industrial world in which we live, and by thus fulfilling the precondition for integration with it, we, who are also parts of the moving present, create ourselves as we create an unknown future" (*ION*, 5:122). It is easy to misconstrue this passage, like so many in Dewey's corpus. By the word *acceptance* Dewey does not mean mindless or passive celebration but, rather, the reverse. To "accept" is to be mindful of, to allow elements of material knowledge to present themselves to thought. The extraor-dinary juxtaposition of garden and corporate world, for example, is not intended to suggest either a painless fusion of nature and technology nor, more obviously, the view that one must regard them as incompatible. A garden is nature reorganized in experience, and so, too, is the world of manufacturing. The problem for an educated intelligence is to accept and rethink the coexistence of these ele-ments—to keep them in mind.

Dewey was convinced that educating a citizen meant helping peo-ple acquire habits attuned to liberating and reconstructive possibil-ities. This could insure the release of reformative energies in the face of a highly fragmented material culture. Education would point the citizen in a new direction: "Feeling that associates infinity with boundless power, with capacity for expansion that knew no end, with the delight in a progress that has no external limit, would be inexplicable were in not for the fact that interest has shifted from . . . beholding a harmonious and complete scene to interest in transforming an inharmonious one" (*RP*, 12:117).

In Dewey's model of formal education students would develop the habits of mind which would foster a democratic experiment—habits alive to the dynamics of an expanding and ever open world. Gone would be "that belief in a bounded, ordered cosmos, wherein rest is higher than motion"; gone too would be the associated idea of education as "a preparation and of adulthood as a fixed limit" (*RP*, 172, 185). Instead, the democratic polity would embody, indeed symbolize, education as an end, a continuous growth in human possibilities of meaning creation. Dewey offered a fine summary of these interwoven strands of his *paideia*, in which democracy, formal education, growth, meaning, and politics are welded into a dynamic whole:

> When the identity of the moral process with the process of specific growth is realized, the more conscious and formal education of childhood will be seen to be the most economical and efficient means of social advance and reorganization, and it will also be evident that the test of all institutions of adult life is their effect in furthering continued education. Government, business, art, religion, all social institutions have a meaning, a purpose. That purpose is to set free and to develop the capacities of human individuals without respect for race, sex, class or economic status. And this is all one with saying that the test of their value is the extent to which they educate every individual into the full status of his possibility. (12:186)

Dewey well knew that modern democratic societies have fallen far short of this standard. In the schoolroom Dewey hoped to sponsor reforms that would physically remove walls, do away with passive and isolating training, and inculcate a sense of challenge. In the world beyond the schoolroom Dewey's defense of a democratic political education had to face more subtle barriers, but the goal was the same: "communication, sharing, joint participation" (*RP*, 12:197). It rested with democratic society to insure the more widespread transmission of experiences, ideas, emotions, and values. The goal was "to transmit a society built on an industry which is not yet humanized into a society which wields its knowledge in behalf of a democratic culture," and this "requires the courage of an inspired imagination" (*MW*, 10:198).

Barriers to Democracy

Social barriers that frustrate communication and deprive the majority of the capacity to "have in mind" represent a deep challenge to the democratic experiment. But even for those young citizens whose education has predisposed them to recognize such barriers, other obstructions remain. The first is the longevity and authority of certain philosophical models that legitimize stasis. Dewey's metaphysics of experience provided him with the core concept of meaning from which grow his democratic sympathies and educational model. But, simultaneously, it represented Dewey's effort to unmask the ideologies perpetuated by earlier philosophical models: "When philosophy shall have cooperated with the course of events and made clear and coherent the meaning of daily detail, science and emotion will interpenetrate, practice and imagination will embrace" (*RP*, 201). Philosophers alone can make such promises. Moreover, a political sensibility or position that scorns the need for philosophical support is unworthy of serious consideration. Recall Dewey's claim that "any theory of activity in social and moral matters, liberal or otherwise, which is not grounded in a comprehensive philosophy seems to me only the projection of an arbitrary personal preference" ("Nature," 252).[15]

Dewey's argument is not with philosophy itself but, rather, with the traditions of Western metaphysics. Dewey's first target was the poisonous legacy of Platonic philosophy. It "brought . . . the idea of a higher realm of fixed reality . . . and of an inferior world of changing things with which experience and practical matters are concerned." This philosophical dualism "forever after" sanctified a detachment from the "lower realm of change," a realm that Dewey was convinced constituted the inescapable horizon of experience (*QC*, 13, 17). The consequences of this dualism are still with us: despite the pervasive evidence of a natural striving to reshape the world on the basis of experience, "philosophers have denied that common experience is capable of developing from within itself methods which will secure direction for itself and will create inherent standards of judgement and value" (*EN*, 38).

Dewey identifies a second, and equally damaging, philosophical tradition, which he characterized, somewhat vaguely, as sensationalist or mechanistic. Once again such philosophies founder on the dualisms that they needlessly create: "Philosopher[s] ha[ve] a new problem with which to wrestle: What is the relationship of these two 'worlds'? Is the world of value that of ultimate and transcendent

Being from which the world of existence is a derivation or a fall? Or is it but a manifestation of human subjectivity, a factor somehow miraculously supervening upon an order complete and closed in physical structure" (*EN*, 394).

To embrace the first possibility—that existence is an inferior form of the transcendent—leaves man to "wander skeptical and disillusioned." To entertain the second leads to a fruitless search for "some organ of unique character that carries [men] into the superempirical" (*RP*, 124). In either instance the consequences are much as they were in the case of Platonic teaching. In Dewey's reading Plato portrayed the individual unschooled in philosophy as a passive spectator.[16] In this ancient model what people did has little connection with what they knew; in the modern alternative what is done has no link with what is valued.

Dewey's efforts to grasp the quiddity of these philosophical systems were undertaken with more than an academic interest. Dewey restates the Nietzschean position that Western political structures embody, and are parasitic upon, metaphysical positions. Of the Greeks Dewey remarked that "experience afforded . . . no model for a conception of experimental inquiry and of reflection efficacious in action" (*EN*, 93). Dewey found it unsurprising that Plato's metaphysics reified a dislocated, stratified human experience, since Plato's teachings reflected political structures that were in themselves antidemocratic. Likewise, the philosophies of sensationalism represented a final effort to legitimate the stratified society from which they emerged; such philosophy was the last "intellectual product of that feudal organization which is disappearing historically" (*RP*, 172). The persistent effect of such philosophy was a source of deep frustration to Dewey, who regarded sensationalism as a blinding misinterpretation of modernity: "Our material culture . . . is verging upon the collective and the corporate, our moral culture, along with our ideology, is, on the other hand, still saturated with the ideals and values of an individualism derived from the prescientific, pre-technological age" (*ION*, 5:77). Dewey believed that democratic politics could not be grounded on a dualistic metaphysics that privileged either timeless unchanging truth or the separation of positive and normative experience. Such ontologies represented the misguided defense of "a separate and isolated mental world . . . self-sufficient and self-enclosed" (*EN*, 15). Dewey's own philosophical endeavors attempt precisely to break down such enclosures.

In the second part of this chapter I have reviewed Dewey's treatment of an equally devastating barrier to political progress: collective ignorance, which breeds inertia and stunted personal growth. For

Dewey human behavior is essentially habitual; the growth of individual intelligence rests on the capacity to develop self-awareness through language, science, and art. Formal education could only offer a partial aid in this process, inculcating experimental habits of mind. If humans were to continue their education or growth outside the classroom, they would have to carry certain convictions with them. In particular, formal education had to provide an indelible belief that people's habits and aspirations are the product of different histories—ideological, cultural, and technological—which are often out of mind, or, rather, held in isolation from one another and thus not minded. The consequence of this separation is a set of social habits that generate the mismanagement of social policy. It is only "when the patterns that form individuality of thought and desire are in line with actuating social forms, that individuality will be released for creative effort" (*ION*, 5:109).

Dewey spent considerable time outlining the etiology of such misalignments, but in essence his argument is familiar: the industrial revolution made manifest the power of technology to reshape the life of society, yet it had at the same time spawned an individualism that betrayed the democratic possibilities inherent in that very power. A small class of entrepreneurs dominates the "observed horizon," while the vast majority remain ignorant of the "overflowing consequences of remote and inaccessible collective actions" which shape their lives (*PP*, 296–97). That majority is, indeed, a public in Dewey's sense: a group of individuals who have an interest in attempting to structure their environment so as to take better advantage of its possibilities. But the very complexity and anonymity of the environment that the industrial revolution unleashed has become a barrier even to the recognition of those interests: "Indirect, extensive, enduring and serious consequences of conjoint and interacting behavior call a public into existence having a common interest in controlling those consequences. But the machine age has so enormously expanded, multiplied, intensified and complicated the scope of the indirect consequences . . . [that] [t]here are too many publics and too much of public concern for our existing resources to cope with" (126).

Dewey's response to the challenge of rescuing this lost public is grounded in his understanding of human behavior. A proper education would produce citizens alert to the fact that political structures were inadequate to the task of managing public life. Ideally, these citizens would select an end-in-view that would reorient their actions. At a macro level Dewey believed that such an end-in-view must be the public construction of "the Great Community," an open democratic society (*PP*, 147). The "end" of this community is a society that will provide each citizen with sufficient access to information and control to enable him or her to best reconstruct the social habits and political structures that had frustrated the effective pooling of experience. Dewey sought a

> society in which the ever-expanding and intricately ramifying consequences of associated activity shall be known in the full sense of that word, so that an organized, articulate Public comes into being. The highest and most difficult kind of inquiry and a subtle, delicate, vivid and responsive art of communication must take possession of the physical machinery of transmission and circulation and breath life into it. (184)

In this wooly yet eloquent passage Dewey defends his preferred conception of democratic politics: a society in which citizens can employ language intelligently in order to judge the consequences of their collective powers. In such a democracy people will engage in the reflective transformation of their own habits as they transform the environment within which those habits develop. Dewey never suggests that the process is straightforward; he only asks whether his work has brought that goal into view. He wondered if "[Was] it possible for local communities to be stable without being static, progressive without being merely mobile?" He questioned whether "the vast, innumerable and intricate currents of trans-local associations [can] be so banked and conducted that they will pour the generous and abundant meanings of which they are potential bearers" (212). Writing through two world wars, Dewey harbored no illusions, but his faith in the possibilities of democratic life remained unshaken. "If [democracy] turns out in the end a failure," he concluded "it will not be because it is too low a doctrine but because it is too high morally for human nature, at least as that human nature is now educated."[17]

Measuring the Dynamic

Dewey's conception of democratic politics is sustained from within by his model of democratic education. He grounds that model in a conception of human experience and actions, in which there is no bifurcation between the human and the organic. The multiplicities of human experience are a part of the natural world, the world that constitutes and is in turn reconstituted through that experience. This seamless relationship makes meaning possible: the human ability to experience certain events in sequences of continuity and interruption allows a person to "make sense" of the world and to refract its history. In short, Dewey affirms "the extent to which the antecedent reality of the situation admits the possibility of transformation of the situation" by human judgment and activity.

Dewey's theory of democratic education relies completely on his model of human experience. In an undemocratic regime the majority of citizens cannot share in the construction of meaning. Instead, those who have access to the products of scientific knowledge and material technology will shape the habits and aspirations of the rest. As a political system, democracy alone has the potential to nurture the human capacity to share in the adventure of inquiry and to contribute to the shaping of public meanings. In other words, democratic citizens uniquely enjoy access to the physical and cultural resources that will constitute much of their own behavior. Dewey's educational theory indicates how to take advantage of this possibility by readying the citizen for a life of experimentation.

For Dewey socialization results from the uniquely human capacities to learn from experience and to reconstruct the environment. These abilities rest in turn on the capacity of communication, and communication can only take place in concert. Dewey argues that education can produce thoughtful communicators. It can lead citizens to be deeply suspicious of the barriers that block access to historical, scientific, and political knowledge. It can inculcate habits attuned to the possibility of collectively considered pragmatic reform. A proper education can persuade us that stasis is artificial, that isolation is but a moment in which we can reorder and remeasure those bonds of language which connect us. To put the point in Protagorian terms, "systematic and continuous inquiry into all the conditions which affect associations" will provide democratic citizens the opportunity to be mindful measurers of their world (*PP*, 218).

Perhaps one can find the best summary of Dewey's thought in one who (one may surmise) had never read him. Michel Foucault's analysis of the modern episteme locates the promise and perhaps the limit of Dewey's enterprise:

> Actual experience is, in fact, both the space in which all empirical contents are given to experience and the original form that makes them possible in general and designates their primary roots; it does indeed provide a means of communication between the space of the body and the time of culture, between the determinations of nature and the weight of history. . . . Man is . . . always open, never fully delimited, yet constantly traversed—which extends

from a part of himself not reflected in a *cogito* to the act of thought by which he apprehends that part; and which in the inverse direction, extends from that pure apprehension to the empirical clutter . . . the whole silent horizon of which is posited in the sandy stretches of the non-thought.[18]

The congruity between Foucault's depiction and Dewey's epistemology is striking. Recall, for example, Dewey's claim that "in the experience, and in such a way as to qualify what is shiningly apparent, are all the physical features of the environment extending out into space . . . and all the habits and interests extending backward and forward in time of the organism" (*EEL*, 10:323). But Foucault points us toward a difficulty: in Dewey's thoughts on experience, education, and art there is a residual and pervasive anthropomorphism, an assumption that the "unthought," the horizon of mind, stands as the guarantor of the meaning, the aesthetic value, of our intelligent projects. As humans attempt to project, to build, and to reconstruct, this intuited horizon offers surety for the sense of their activity. That horizon is what Dewey calls "a pervasive quality of experience . . . [a] constant sense of things belonging or not belonging . . . the sense of an extensive and underlying whole . . . it is the essence of sanity" (*AAE*, 194–95).[19] In any individual experience one will rule out certain actions—but only so as to maintain the unity of that particular activity, so that each discrete action can be linked together in a temporal and spatial continuity. That continuity represents, in an active and choate form, the intuition of the inchoate continuity, the horizon of meaning, or mind, from which it drew all along.

Dewey locates religious sensibility in the experience of actualizing, through our life projects, the ideal of a unity which would itself fully mesh with mind itself.[20] He interprets the human project of meaning creation as the drive to harmonize the self and the universe of mind so that the inchoate intuition of the latter might be fully revealed in the former. The ideal of that harmonization, or complete interpenetration, is what is sensed in what Dewey calls "an experience." It is achieved in art, work, or play, as a consummation, a fusion of self and horizon which Dewey was prepared to label as a religious moment. But the true measure of Dewey's faith lies perhaps elsewhere, in the Hegelian confidence that such a consummatory experience is a homecoming, an ideal of transparency in which human measure happily dissolves. Confronting the meanings we have forged of the habits and organic histories of which we are the subject and also subject to, Dewey finds, quite literally, a "consummation devoutly to be wished."

What strikes Dewey as tragic are connections not made, meanings allowed to atrophy, mind uncultivated by conscious trial through imaginative projection. He will not countenance the insanity of the thought that mind is radically unwhole, that consciousness orients itself to that which cannot be thought. There is at the heart of Dewey's democratic faith a conviction that integration is the one telos of experience, that inclusivity is the ethic of naturalism. The measuring rod of experience is never fully out of joint with existence, and the meanings experience affords always hold the promise of a consummatory aesthetic. Hegelian to the end, Dewey's faith must undermine, largely through bypassing them, the countermeanings of exteriority, of the radically discontinuous.

"A man's maturity—consists of having found again the seriousness one had as a child, at play."[21] Dewey's pedagogic enterprise might have taken Nietzsche's epigram as its motto. The intense desire to forge connections from the inchoate field of experience, vivid in childhood, is the desire Dewey's pedagogic design is intended to nurture. His intense conviction that such connections could bring human beings into intelligent harmony carries with it hope that the child's play embodies the harmonious measure, the tuning fork, of existence.

7

Thinking to Learn

WHAT KIND OF education does a modern democratic society owe its citizens? There is something uncomfortable about asking this question, as if we were seeking answers that society seems wary of actually heeding. Certainly, reformers are ready to discuss the structures of education and are almost unanimously agreed on the need for more schooling, more coherence of subject matter, and more testing. But those same reformers are less forthcoming about the detailed content of an education, and they are reluctant to connect that content to an account of what constitutes a democratic public life.

What more could or should one ask for beyond an emphasis on "the three Rs?" The implicit answer from contemporary reformers is often "Nothing."[1] This response presupposes that there already exists a sensible consensus about the values we seek in education and that further theorizing is an unnecessary distraction. It is along these lines that David Paris takes it as "presume[d] that open-mindedness, sensitivity to evidence and argument, reflective judgement, and so on are intellectual virtues and are values worthy of promotion by the schools."[2] One is particularly struck in this passage by "and so on," the suggestion of impatience with those who would problematize the otherwise neatly practical program of education reform.

Perhaps the most powerful way of questioning such a view is to grant its premise. In the opening chapter of this work I stressed the methodological confusions and internal inconsistencies of the contemporary reform movement. But let us grant that, through the added attention, resources, and planning at work in the classroom, SAT scores rise and dropout rates fall. Grant, too, that students do a better job of performing on better (nonmultiple choice, substantive subject area) tests. What will such a future citizen be prepared to do? The answer is perhaps best expressed by *the Economist* as it concluded its chiding of current American educational failures. The United States "has not moved on so far or fast enough. The Anglo-Saxon World has done little in the 1980s to catch up with the world leaders in education. The real choice for an investor with an eye to human capital is between the Pacific rim and Germanic Europe. . . . [Skilled workers] will give the Germanic countries a vital edge in the age of human capital."[3] By focusing on the race for skilled workers, one addresses a critical problem for any nation-state. Yet in regarding this race as the focal point of education, and assuming that attention to other issues is secondary at best, one betrays the promise of democratic education.

Freed to construct a polis and to interpret the always ambiguous instruction of the deities, Protagoras challenged the earliest citizens to find in themselves and their experience the measure of all things. But his invitation is fraught with difficulty. How can such citizens educate themselves to measure more effectively? If the standard against which citizens are to hold their judgments is a mirror, how might one give a public definition of that standard? If every citizen is a sovereign measurer, what role remains for a class of educators?

The recovery of the perspective of the ancient Sophists suggests some preliminary answers to these still contemporary questions. Extrapolating from the evidence of Athenian history, Platonic dialogues, and sophistic fragments, one can reconstruct the vital components of an education in self-measurement ideally understood. The Athenian citizen depended on education in political literacy to place himself in relation to a temporal order and negotiate his relationship to the public sphere, of which he was a part. First and foremost this is an education in the interpretation of political speech. For every citizen that education would include the capacity to measure the grammatical, theatrical, and emotive contents of public words against an existing sense of the conditions of private and public life. Such an education would prepare the citizen to act as the judge of elite rhetoric, holding the practitioners of that rhetoric to account.

For its part the elite justified its role in a democratic polis through the instruction it afforded both at the level of preparatory education and in its own political practice. By teaching the tools through which citizens could criticize their own claims to power, in short through the education of its critics, the Sophists and the orators who were their students legitimize that power and that teaching. In the arena of public speech sophistry was pitted against sophistry, and the stratagems of argument were agonistically presented before an audience educated to judge their respective merit. Moreover, it was the citizens who must finally judge, not only between proposals but also between orators. The right of Athenians to fine or even ostracize their own politicians was unique in ancient Greece.

An education in grammar cannot stand alone. The lessons that Clinias receives from the Sophists in Plato's *Euthydemus* would be of limited use in the absence of a sense of the civic identity of the polis against which citizens could judge competing advice. The ancient Greek world afforded a number of institutions through which citizens could explore the character of such an identity: the funeral oration, the theater, and the assembly being perhaps the most important. These institutions, which made possible the experience of public remembrance, imaginative experimentation, and political judgment, temper the otherwise rampant subjectivism of the man as measure doctrine. In particular, citizens are prompted to judge the affairs of their city against the intersecting grids of history and space—the record of the communities past and the constraints of its geographical boundedness.

The Sophists had to defend their practice in epistemological as well as pedagogic terms. Because their claim to educate could not be separated from issues of both the status of knowledge itself and the grounds on which they claimed to know that knowledge, the debate about education was, for the Greeks, necessarily philosophical. In this context it is instructive to link my account of Protagoras's position with the contemporary debate about education. As already suggested, "Protagoras," as we have come to know him, is largely the creation of his critic Plato, whose vision of education famously rests on an anti-Sophistic philosophical foundation. Today we can still encounter educational positions rooted in a Platonic sense of the permanence of ultimate values. Mortimer Adler offers a classic statement of such a position, which he links directly to an educational theory: "The universality and constancy of human nature, the same throughout history, the same in various cultures, the same in different individuals, is the source of the universal and absolute principles of education."[4]

But this form of argument, at least in its secular versions, is unattractive to contemporary American "liberal" or "democratic" theorists.[5] One is more likely to encounter universalist arguments that theorists ground, perhaps paradoxically, in the provisional circumstances of our particular liberal democratic norms. In the United States John Rawls has reinterpreted his theory of justice so as to base it on "fundamental intuitive ideas latent in the public political culture."[6] In Europe Jürgen Habermas has likewise reinterpreted his once transcendental thesis (the claim that an egalitarian structure of free discussion is necessarily implicit in every meaningful speech act), often under the pressure of his best critics. One such figure is Seyla Benhabib, who seeks to rid universalism of its lingering objectivism while retaining an element of that universalism in linguistic terms. But Benhabib's own language embodies a deeply provisional, liberal norm.[7] She offers no ground beyond the immediate experience of modernity.[8]

Two striking features of these contemporary views are their Protagorian echoes and their relative silence on matters of education. If I may summarize a densely articulated position, "democratic universalists" argue that ethical and epistemological claims have no extrapolitical justification. The Sophists, as we have seen, tied the justification of their own teaching methods to a conception of political empowerment. Their argument was that access to a public vocabulary and mastery of its forms alone enabled citizens to measure the public space. But (to move to the second feature) the Athenian conception of the vocabulary of measurement strikes me as richer in pedagogic content than those of Protagoras's modern heirs. Certainly, as the *Euthydemus* indicates, the Sophists' form of instruction is tied to a theory of moral education (as in Rawls) and to a defense of the realm of open political dialogue (as in Habermas). But the Sophists also taught the citizen to measure public speech against the rhetorical and political structures on which that speech depended for its public legitimacy. Side by side with an education in the skills of reading, singing, writing, and war, the Sophists' instruction in the tropes of grammatical and rhetorical speech laid bare the very vehicle through which cultural and political norms were maintained.[9] Educated citizens were able to judge political positions against their experience of the polis-in-speech, its physical and psychological boundaries, its history in myth and memory, its ideals, and its ultimate demands on life and limb. Citizens had access to a vocabulary encompassing religious, cultural, economic, and military affairs. While the range of citizenship strikes the modern liberal as indefensibly small, the range of issues open to the judgment of the educated Athenian citizen was wide, indeed.

My treatments of Jean-Jacques Rousseau and John Dewey provide democratic interpretations for the forms these judgments can take.

Who is capable, Rousseau asked, of separating themselves from themselves so as to reach an understanding of the dynamic relationship between the self and its social and ethical environment? Finding in himself the most immediate candidate, Rousseau put on display the role of connected and unconnected critic, standing at once as a member and a marginalized figure of the worlds he inhabits and creates.[10] Devotee of the theater Rousseau explored the limits of imaginative invention while placing the full weight of his invective against the potential poison of both theater and the imagination. The citizen of Geneva calls his city to account against an idealized standard of itself, as Pericles had once done in Athens.

But, Rousseau teaches that one cannot will out of one's psyche the seductive lures of social jealousy, solitude, and erotic longing which threaten the homogeneity of any community. Rousseau rehearses these lures before us and, in so doing, lays out the multiple and dynamic sites of the self. Onetime darling of the eighteenth-century Parisian world, Rousseau, in the persona of Saint-Preux, dissects the anatomy of commercialism and the vocabulary of transient fashion through which the social market defined bourgeois identity. No Western thinker has made solitude so seminal a focus of his or her mature thought, none painted the charms of sociability in such compelling colors. Cutting across the tensions between solitude and community are the complexities of the erotic. Rousseau develops the Platonic insight that erotic attraction itself is bound up in the impossible effort to possess another identity without eclipsing that attraction, which depends on distance. But eroticism also invites us toward transcendence, toward the celebration of conditions known to be beyond reach. Identities that search to conflate themselves with the unreachable are also sited in temporal terms: memory and projection, which fuse lived experience with the metaphors of lost innocence or imagined Edens, infinitely enrich the already multiple questions of spatial location. To remind ourselves of a now familiar example, Rousseau's Geneva is a location and a history, an imagined Sparta, an emerging Paris, a theatrical sight, a promised refuge, a tragic disappointment. But in all of these "places" Rousseau discovers and rediscovers himself.

Political theorists are constantly reiterating the idea of placing identity at the heart of normative argument and of delineating identity in spatial, if not temporal, terms. The originality of Rousseau's thinking emerges sharply in comparison to the more sophisticated of these contemporary rereadings. Anxious to oppose with equal vehemence the essentialisms of the past and the nihilistic seductions of postmodernist word plays (often interpreted as a kind of rampant relativism), current theorists place the competing pressures that form the human self on a contingent but definite spatial grid. In William Connolly's words: "The political theory of the self provides access to an interconnected set of sites in the self upon which a variety of engagements occur between the dictates of order and that which accepts, resists, evades, endorses and satiates them."[11] Similar vocabulary is pervasive in Charles Taylor's influential conception of human identity. To be fully human, Taylor argues, "is to exist in a space defined by distinctions of worth."[12] In Taylor's view self-interpretation takes place constantly in the renegotiating of influences that make up that space.

The point of casting the issue of self-identity in such terms is to undermine any theory that "privileges" a single view of the self—in particular, any theory that anchors such a view in the assertion of a single truth or form that would define the ideal human condition. Every effort to prescribe a single narrative of existence, these theorists argue, runs aground on the pervasive contingency of, and the lack of any predestined fit in the relationship between, the multiple strands that situate (site) our identity. Thus, Connolly argues, "if the world is not the product of transcendental design, we are likely to encounter resistance in the forms we impose upon it." Social or political life makes the search for such forms a necessity, Connolly acknowledges, but it is always the case that such forms harbor contingency: "human life cannot be without the creation of social forms and . . . every social form will engender that which resists it."[13]

Is that then the contemporary message of the spatial metaphor, this conception of self as contingently placed through an intersection and interpretation of competing forms? The answer is that such a conception represents the descriptive portion of the theory. But theorists such as Connolly tie the idea to the insistence that there is always room to maneuver within any ordered form and to a conviction that, in this realization, one can found a more humane politics. Human beings should neither rail against the contingent nature of social rules (for that produces Nietzschean *ressentiment*) nor be content with them (for that would be to grant them unwarranted authority). We are all to question contingencies and accept that their ever imperfect fit with one another opens up the "space" of such questioning. But the final injuction of such theory, no matter what its postmodernist distinctions between "difference" and "otherness," is remarkably traditional. It is "to create space where differences can be while acknowledging the need for communalities."[14]

In more heroic terms Habermas makes the same point: "What then does universalism mean? Relativizing one's own form of existence to the legitimate claims of other forms of life, according equal rights to aliens and others with all their idiosyncrasies and unintelligibility, not sticking doggedly to the universalization of one's own identity, not marginalizing that which deviates from ones own identity, allowing the sphere of tolerance to become ceaselessly larger than it is today—all this is what moral universalism means today."[15] This is a sophisticated form of special pleading, a form of humane Rousseauism in which the clashing, often tragically incommensurable languages through which he located the sources of identity are rendered ironic or homogenized into open-ended, but never aggressive or paralyzing, narratives.[16] It is an invitation to generosity without judgment, an assumption that the self can embrace the world and yet save the world and itself from vapid homogeneity. But Rousseau, who had seen more of the world from more perspectives than any philosopher of his age, taught how improbable such a model of human progress must be. Nothing takes greater preparation, Rousseau suggests, than the development of the emotional, psychological, and intellectual strength to be a judge of self and other. Thus, Rousseau's own exhaustion, his dreams of the Bastille, and his passion for the company of hermaphroditic plants to limit his psychological driftings. The price of an evolving judgment, with its wrenching shifts in perspective, is near madness.

Rousseau's thoughts on education are not sanguine about "the need to educate with a sensitivity to difference *and* to the need to educate to overcome difference."[17] Rousseau asks the critical question about the nature of such sensitivities and differences. Sensitivity, in Rousseau's view, might properly lead to the desire to overcome either one's hostility or one's allegiance to a particular form of distinction or difference in oneself or another. In some cases one should celebrate difference by liquidating it, in some cases by fighting to preserve it.

Rousseau's answer to the question of when to do what, as we have seen, depends on the historical, geographical, and political conditions within a particular community. Rousseau argues that, in certain instances, education is learning that to overcome or synthesize difference (for example, between Genevan republican virtue and Parisian foppery) is to lose one's sense of self and to invite helpless dependence. Nor is it a question of simply muting those differences that threaten our or others' rights. Any politically authorized language of rights already prejudges as legitimate particular boundaries of difference. But the capacity to judge the legitimacy of boundaries—historical, political, erotic, religious, national, and aesthetic—is the measure of our education. Untutored citizens overcoming their differences while maintaining their "rights" could be seen everywhere: they are Rousseau's Parisians bound together by social envy and private hubris; they are visible today sitting in front of the televised "home shopping club." Alone together, legitimating the wealth that separates them and the market (both cultural and material) which homogenizes their differences, these are modern citizens.[18]

By contrast, Rousseau imagines in *Emile* an education freed from the preexisting temptations of a painless and poisonous *amour-propre,* the sentiment that best characterizes modern socialization. In that work he underlined the critical precondition of any ethical pedagogic project: before citizens could contain within themselves the conflicts and self-denials that make judgment possible, they would have to learn to withstand the temptation to embrace the slavish sleep of property worship and its invitation to narcissistic pride. In Rousseau's view the automatic pursuit of social fashion imprisons most selves in a narrative they had not constructed and could not interpret.

In its place one could teach the achievement of a more anguished, but more virtuous, sense of self-respect (in the sense of earned pride and self-perspective) and a discriminating imagination. But Rousseau also argued that too great a separation between aspiration and possibility could become debilitating to action, that the seduction of the open-ended—even if it leads to the search for ever greater insight—enslaves the mind to the unreachable and makes it the plaything of fashion. To learn to hold apart the boundaries of a necessary distance between desire and attainment is the most difficult of lessons. For many, Rousseau knew, it was too much, and the only path he saw away from mindless subjection to fashion was a mindful and willed accord with the general will.

In the contemporary vocabulary of political theory liberal good sense domesticates the distances that Rousseau himself experienced as tragically debilitating and wondrously inexhaustible. But the education of citizens who can measure their existence is not necessarily a liberal one: as citizens learn to take the measure of themselves, there can be no a priori assumption that a narrative will emerge in which one will find a modus vivendi between difference and sameness, or in which these categories would exhaust the legitimate interpretations of experience. Rousseau should make us uncomfortable about the current theory, with its emphasis on achieving a dialectic synthesis of self and other. Rousseau knew that the self was, in our contemporary phraseology, "multiple," and thus that the dream of reuniting the self around a single ethical or narrative dimension was next to impossible. But the fact of multiplicity does not lead Rousseau to celebrate open-ended free play or to assume that the players can come to agree on the rules of the social game that preserves the freedom of their will.

Rousseau tells stories in which characters celebrate, and even mythologize, the tragic tensions implicit in human relations. His heroes and heroines seek unions with a particular other (through eroticism), the communal other (through the immediate political group), and the imaginary other (through the displacement of self in fiction, drama, and history). But as Derrida suggests in another context, each moment of psychological fusion is haunted by those physical and material absences that alone make it possible. Each overcoming of separation, each move toward the consensual, is also a moment of destruction. Rousseau is far more pessimistic about the human condition than contemporary postmodernists. He does not believe that identity can be understood as a dialectic of the "devalued other" and of "discourses of dignity and self-governance," in which the former is stripped away and the second valorized in the name of radical pluralism.[19] Recalling the vast range of Rousseau's insights affords a sombre generalization: difference is a form of voluntary or involuntary exile from a pluralist community; one can maintain dignity, on occasion, only by self-censorship.

The price is extraordinarily high, and the moments of stasis are few: Rousseau is in constant motion, both physically and within the forms of his writing. But the maintenance of these distances is not contingent; it is the permanent condition of the man as measure of all things. Rousseau can be both a critic of Geneva and its loyal citizen, but only at the price of exile. He could celebrate the lessons of Sparta only by knowingly fictionalizing its recorded history and could construct the Social Contract only because he understood that a politics of egalitarianism was an artificial construction and a losing gamble against the natural history of the species. Rousseau learns to be a measure through a refusal to collapse the incommensurables within his own experience and between that experience and those of others. It is *because* these distances are indispensable that Rousseau does not educate his readers to sanitize them but, rather, to celebrate, fear, and mourn them. Julie, one recalls, can retain her sense of judgment only through the refusal to lose herself in Saint-Preux, but she ultimately finds the weight of separation unbearable. Internally, the roles of lover and mother, judge and religious soul, hold each other in perspicacious but almost hellish balance and end in spiritual and physical suicide.

As he experiments with multiple perspectives, Rousseau reminds us that, without an imposed sense of nonnegotiable limits, human beings will drift with the tide. While self-imposed limits are preferred, others are legitimate, but only when their character is understood and accepted by the citizens involved. Though Rousseau's experimentation with self-location is legion in Western thought, the results are no celebration of openness tempered by a faith in an underlying consensual telos. Indeed, Rousseau's teaching endorses neither branch of this postmodernist *jouissance*.[20] On the issue of openness Rousseau would be amused by the contemporary exhortation to allow "students and teachers to negotiate which courses, if any, are to be required."[21] This, in Rousseau's view, would be to expect students to judge the quality of a knowledge they had yet to encounter. The product of such an education would not be freedom but, instead, its reverse: children incapable of delayed gratification, of schooling their impulses or accumulating knowledge.[22]

The reader will recall that the first moment at which the Tutor "negotiates" with Emile comes at the closing moments of his education. In Rousseau's view the capacity to judge matters of ethical and intellectual substance is the highest mark of any education and cannot represent its initial point of departure. At the same time, Rousseau argues in *The Social Contract* that only constant public exercises in self-denial can maintain a consensual politics. Once untutored self-interest starts monopolizing political discourse, strategic interests will develop, the sense of the public interest will disintegrate, and the framework of community will evaporate.

I noted among many contemporary readers of Rousseau an unwillingness to accept his tragic perspectivism. Rousseau realized that the internalization of the constraints that make judgment possible has pathological effects—thus, his projection of the collapse of Emile's marriage, the disintegration of Geneva, Julie's demise, and perhaps Rousseau's own paranoia. Rousseau knew that all forms of socialization (and thus all educational strategies) produced in subjects "desires they do not want to have" and impulses that they have to reject "at the cost of guilt and anxiety."[23] But through his writings he makes visible to the reader the etiologies of these repressions. Rousseau shows that certain forms of willed self-denial evoke the ecstasies and inseparable sorrows that are the mark of understanding, if one has the strength to sustain them. Rousseau thus deepens the lessons of the Sophists, by taking account of the psychological dimensions of measurement. An educated human being has learned that there are no innocent nor fully open nor fully negotiable perspectives.

It is an ironic feature of intellectual history that Rousseau's contribution to education is constantly marginalized for sins he does not commit. At the same time, John Dewey's thought is celebrated for overcoming those sins, even those close reading indicates that Dewey may have done nothing of the sort. While Rousseau's celebration of man's inherently innocent nature is said to produce a crippling celebration of authority, critics praise Dewey as the figure who led the charge of "anti-essentialism," who "sees no Rousseauian self to be repressed or liberated."[24] In fact, Rousseau employed the conceit of the natural as just that, a conceit. Rousseau was intent on "setting the facts aside" to gain particular temporal and psychological perspectives. As the detailed account of Dewey's epistemology has made clear, Dewey does not put the facts aside; he asks, rather, how facts are constituted for us by the nature of our experience. Certainly, as he pointed out, there is a difference between asserting that human nature supplies the limit conditions for political and educational possibilities and claiming that that nature supplies "the ends of their development."[25] But asserting, as he does, the first of these positions makes Dewey an odd champion of deconstructionists, radical liberals, and fellow travelers.

The recent rediscovery of and praise for Dewey's pedagogic oeuvre is due in part to the ease by which one can assimilate his work with so many contemporary reform programs. Citing Dewey becomes a kind of legitimation game in which theorists bend his celebration of growth, pluralism, and democracy to endorse a particular vision of a pedagogy. But Dewey's intellectual odyssey is only made possible by the philosophical commitments he makes. His defense of experimentalism, his provisional but never final skepticism about the organic continuum embracing the world and human beings, and his conviction that aesthetic gratification was the gift of experience once liberated from political boundaries constitute his "democratic faith." Dewey's defense of democracy as *the* ethically and politically legitimate structure is unthinkable outside the tenets of this faith in the promise of nature.

Richard Rorty's cheery couplings not withstanding, what links the thought of Dewey to other masters of modern thought is not his deconstructivist voice. Rather, that connection stems from Dewey's complex, Hegelian conviction that the history of human experience has intelligible sense. Dewey is equally Hegelian in the belief that meaning could grow toward aesthetic consummation, although he gives Hegel a democratic twist. Only a democratic society constituted by the free exchange of ideas and a commitment to intelligent social planning could liberate our capacity to cultivate meaning from experience. At the core of Dewey's democratic faith is the conviction that the ethical and aesthetic commitments that justify democratic politics and education are themselves anchored in an organic largesse, an originary and natural storehouse of meaning.

One way of clarifying what Dewey has in mind is to compare Dewey's epistemic naturalism with that of Martin Heidegger. In a remarkably gentle passage Heidegger asked about the way a carpenter learns his craft. Knowledge about the technique of carpentry, Heidegger suggested, can never be enough: "If he is to become a true cabinet maker, he makes himself answer and respond above all to the different kinds of wood and to the shapes slumbering within wood—to wood as it enters into man's dwelling with all the hidden riches of its nature. In fact, this relatedness to wood is what maintains the whole craft. Without that relatedness, the craft will never be anything but empty busywork . . . Every handicraft, all human dealings are constantly in that danger."[26] To speak of education is, etymologically, to speak of a drawing out. But this suggests that education itself must have an originary source, a site that the particular act of education must sight and then resituate in each individual. To imagine that the project of education can be defined instrumentally— in the production of one who will be a better calculator, a better reader, or a more disciplined worker—is to imagine that one can define a projection by its destination as opposed to its source. But the destination of education, as Dewey vibrantly affirms, can only be found in its sources. As the carpenter learns that the made object owes its quality to the understanding of the original wood, so every education finds its origin and its essence in the condition of human experience and the manner in which the educator can draw out that experience.

It is in the confidence of an organic presence that Dewey's teaching is most distanced from Rousseau's. Nature is not the absent other but, instead, the inescapable horizon within which human experience grows in meaning and intelligence. The power of Dewey's democratic faith lies in its integrative implications: since human creativity is continuous with organic life, Dewey argued, the dualisms of body and soul, worker and intellectual, truth and experiment, imagination and intelligence, were artificial. Such dualisms privilege a certain aspect of experience in an effort to monopolize for a particular elite the cultural and political benefits that accrue to those who exercise the "superior" aspect. In Dewey's view our own organic experience enables us to endlessly reorder our experience through the social phenomena of language, science, and culture. Dewey argues that we do so morally only when the effects of that reordering empower each of us to do so as coequal experimenters. Education can prepare us to celebrate the power of nature's infinitely interweaving and dynamic associations.

This double aspect of Dewey's teaching—faith and experience—is often too much for his contemporary political champions, but they celebrate him nonetheless, and it is not difficult to see why. Take, for example, Stanley Aronowitz and Henry Giroux's blend of modernism, postmodernism, and critical pedagogy: what they call for is a language and social practice in which "different voices and traditions exist and flourish to the degree that they listen to the voices of others, engage in an ongoing effort to eliminate forms of subjective and objective suffering, and maintain those conditions in which the act of communicating and living extends rather than restricts the creation of democratic life"[27] With the exception of the (strikingly quaint) distinction between subjective and objective, the vocabulary is pure Dewey. In his attack on a class-divided society he urged that all citizens "must have an equitable opportunity to receive and take from others," and "there must be a large variety of shared understandings and experience." Dewey's effort to forge a democratic education as the "intermediary between aimless education and the education of inculcation and indoctrination" (DE, 56) and his invitation to explore a humanism of "expansion that knew no end" (RP, 12: 117) make him the prophet of contemporary democratic reform. As the preceding chapter suggests, the scope of his democratic vision and the sophistication of its integrated dimensions point to Dewey as the seminal democratic theorist.

And yet the very seamlessness of Dewey's vision, the organic sensibility that envelopes it, and the faith that sustains its unity should give his followers pause. It is true that Dewey's naturalism and his political theory give hostages to the idea of marginality, to the question of the idiosyncratic. He writes, after all, of natural traits of "isolation," of the "discrete," and of "whimsical contingency" (EN, 242). But the full force of Dewey's organic epistemology lies in the other direction. As a faith, it proselytizes in favor of the "inclusive" (258). Dewey's acknowledgment of "an encompassing infinity of connections" (HNC, 14: 180), his celebration of what is normal, and his worry about "perversion" (EN, 301) point in the same direction. In chapter 6 I interpreted this last worry as a concern that politics might subvert the free flow of shared experience. But Dewey's tendency to celebrate the integrated space of public dialogue also produces an intolerance for the marginal figure or the fragmented experience. In this sense, it is pedagogic reformers such as Dianne Ravitch who are Dewey's intellectual heirs. He would have endorsed her concern that "the spread of particularism throws into question the very idea of American public education" and applauded a "definition of citizenship and culture that is both expansive and inclusive."[28]

Even those who can accept Dewey's distrust of the unconnected and the marginalized social actor should recall the source of that view. The strength of Dewey's inclusivist commitments rests on a faith that he could read a democratic telos out of organic experience and affirm his interpretation through experiences of aesthetic consummation. Toward the end of his writings Dewey's faith in the unity of experience points to a commitment still more sacred than that to the organic, to a form or order that lies "even below the level of life" (*AAE*, 14). At such moments Dewey's democratic faith calls to mind Václav Havel's conviction that being itself stands as the guarantor of the ethical democratic community.[29]

Thus, there remains a critical tension between Dewey's organic, inclusive democratic faith and the contemporary celebration of democracy as self-justifying. Consider one important example: it is clear that many theorists follow John Dewey in the belief that reform in education depends on the restructuring of a kind of public dialogue. Dewey argued throughout his life that people "associate in many ways, but the only form of association that is truly human . . . is participation in meanings and goods that is affected by communication."[30] Dewey's would-be disciple Rorty urges that we learn to speak with "those who share enough of one's beliefs to make fruitful conversation possible"[31] Benhabib searches for "what would be allowed and perhaps even necessary from the standpoint of continuing and sustaining the practice of moral conversation among us."[32] James Donald calls for the regulative ideal of a "community as unknown, uncentered, always to be constructed in the process of dialogue and self-naming."[33]

I could indefinitely extend the list to little purpose. What is clear is the intuitively appealing and repeatedly reaffirmed centrality of dialogue that theorists draw from Dewey's synthesis of conversation, a commitment to democratic politics, and a model of education. Certainly, their emphasis on the use of public language as a starting point for the construction of a theory of democratic education offers a number of immediate advantages. Intuitively, the idea of exclusion from a debate is obnoxious. To link democratic authority to the promise of entry into a conversation of political rulers is at least rhetorically and psychologically compelling. But the allegiance to Dewey ends at this point. Contemporary theorists are happy to rely on concepts of discursive rationality, which they justify only on the grounds that all should have equal rights of entry into public debate.[34] The only way in which one can ultimately decide whether a particular set of conditions pertaining to public debate is rational is to submit it to public confirmation, to the test of John Rawls's "overlapping consensus."

Dewey, who lived through the aftermath of the civil war and two world wars, believes otherwise. His defense of a democratic education rests on three interlocking and mutually supporting foundations. The first is a passionate appeal to the standard of historical pragmatism: the closure of public debate to many sectors of society rested on mythologies (often religious in nature) created by self-serving elites. Read the history books, Dewey argues, and judge how the power invested in science, rhetoric, and education fares in societies premised on closure and social hierarchy. Second, study your own experience. Think about rival models of how you learn, about how your capacity to judge the world changes, and about those moments of your greatest aesthetic satisfaction. Dewey claims that you will tell the most coherent, compelling story about such experiences in terms he has sketched: the fluidity of knowledge (*School*, 23), the organic quality of language, and the conception of the self as an activity of reacting, knowing, and minding. And the natural home for creating such an identity is, in Dewey's view, the democratic society. The third is Dewey's faith in the universal commensurability of a language and its capacity endlessly to expand to the range of human possibilities without destroying the dignity of the self. Who would not wish to be the recipient, Dewey asks, of the social intelligence stored in the flows of public language and memory?

Rousseau, for one. Language flowing together can make untenable the idiosyncratic and precious self-denials, and self-willed constraints that constitute a life of freedom. Despite D'Alembert, there is no growth in meaning in the synthesis of Paris plus Geneva: Parisian discourse necessarily ruins Geneva's celebration of self-sufficiency. The pious contemporary hope to celebrate diversity together, to rescue respect for Western culture by arguing that it alone tolerates difference, would strike Rousseau as one more chapter in Enlightenment mythology. Calling the balance the division of the public and private—or, in contemporary parlance, the agonistic of "discordant concordances"—makes no difference.[35] Public language, in Foucault's terms, colonizes all that it touches; once society unearths "local knowledges" for public affirmation it destroys them.

Back to School

The transition from a political theory of democratic education to a series of nuts-and-bolts recommendations is perforce an awkward one. One must take a story that embraces ontologies and spatial-temporal matrices and temper it by translation into terms appropriate to the domain of the schoolroom. In the present case I should transpose a vision that evoked Protagoras's measure, Rousseau's dynamic perspectives, and Dewey's faith in organic continuum into a robust pedagogic program. So difficult are translations and transpositions of this kind that political theorists with an interest in education often apologize for the brevity of the results or avoid such transitions altogether.[36] What all such theorists implicitly hope for (present company included) is a process of benign trickle-down. Those who make education their profession are, through some mysterious symbiotic process, to be made aware of our ideas and understand how and when to modify them for practical use. But it is incumbent on the theorist to take the first steps in such a process. I offer what follows as a beginning, as a sketch of instrumentalities toward a paradigm of democratic education. What follows is one translation of the ideas of Protagoras, Rousseau, and Dewey into the context of contemporary American education; other translations, of course, are possible and I welcome them.

The United States is still the land of invention, and there is scarcely a pedagogic idea that someone has not tried somewhere. A few have achieved national recognition: Washington state's Schools for the Twenty-first Century, Theodore Sizer's Coalition of Essential Schools, James Comer's School Development Program, Henry Levin's Accelerated Schools, Nabisco's Next Century Schools, Foxfire, the Whole Language Movement, and the Saturn School of Tomorrow all showcase aspects of successful pedagogic technique as measured by both general criteria (reduced dropout rates and higher test scores than the national average) and their own chosen measures.[37] There is, in fact, no great secret in creating schools that meet preset goals: make the curriculum goals clear; give the autonomy, resources, and incentives for teachers to reach those goals as they see fit; involve the parents in school activities; teach healthy children; involve the community and the students in making the schoolroom a physically and psychologically inviting place; promote students by achievement rather than age; and keep expectations high.[38] The question of why American political culture makes these general principles so difficult to translate into practice continues to frustrate educational reformers, but my present concern is with the defense of certain goals of education: How might one fold the lessons of Protagoras, Rousseau, and Dewey into a curriculum?

The contemporary reform movement, under the auspices of the Office of Educational Research and Improvement, is producing its own "National Educational Goals" and the curriculum to back it up. But the overarching design of these goals indicates the gulf that separates them from the proposals that emerge from the preceding chapters. In particular, the design of the curriculum has been broken down into autonomous areas of learning which reflect the perennial academic distinctions and which have no organized relationship to one another. Seven discrete fields (mathematics, science, history, arts, civics, geography, and English) are being defined by seven separate organizations.[39] Moreover, the draft standards reflect exactly the tensions inherent in our present system. While politicians praise the idea of individual school autonomy, the language of the standards are specific to the nth degree, thus jeopardizing the very autonomy they are supposed to complement. To give one example, the National Standards for Civics and Government will come equipped with lists of key concepts ("defined in glossary"), exact specifications of the "scope of inquiry," and a list of the primary and secondary sources with which every student should be familiar.[40]

The detailed question of pedagogic technique—how best to engage particular students so as to promote their most active and sustained involvement in any curriculum—lies well beyond my competency. But the previous chapters do suggest some thoughts about the role of the teacher in the project of a democratic education. It should be clear that the teacher cannot be a pure conduit for the delivery of parental desires: those desires represent a very particular perspective that guardians can sustain or undermine in their homes. It is always possible that family resources can be engaged to broaden and sustain inquiry. But the teacher's loyalty is ultimately to the pupil, not the parent.

Second, teachers, as Rousseau and Dewey suggest, are the architects of pedagogic space. It is in determining the very shape of the classroom, the groupings of the children, the pacing of projects, and the constraints on subject matter that the teacher will articulate the perspective, from what we termed the *methoria*, the land in between competing contemporary perspectives. Teachers sympathetic to my arguments will distance themselves from the immediate messages of their communities and from the instincts of the untutored child: *methoria* is an artifice of instruction. Nietzsche (in this rare instance following Rousseau) draws the critical conclusion: "An educator never says what he himself thinks, but always only what he thinks of a thing in relation to the requirements of those he educates."[41] The teacher alone must design the spatial-temporal sites in which his or her direction and authority will prepare the way for the students' own transcendence. Rousseau's tutor educates Emile for that moment in which he will finally relinquish authority over the boy, in which the drawing out of education within the boundaries of the Tutor's design must come to a close. Democratic education focuses on the achievement of that moment.

What should such teachers teach? What could be the content of an education for democratic citizens, for those who will be the measure of all things? The preceding chapters lay out the general terrain, a body of material for the consideration of teachers. My reading of this material, however, suggests certain ideas for the design of the school curriculum, especially at the high school level. My suggestion is to move the traditional formal disciplines (English, mathematics, science, and history) from the core to the periphery of the curriculum.[42] The core, by contrast, should focus on public discourse— on its power to name, to authorize, to legitimize, to valorize, to separate, and to collectivize. To prepare citizens to be the measure of all things education will represent a critical encounter with those many public messages that will shape choices and self-ascriptions. Four fields of focus will constitute the core: critical engagement with public rhetoric, active participation in drama, competency in matters of political economy, and exposure to a myriad of disciplines that intersect at the human body. One should not expect that one can blend together the lessons of Protagoras, Rousseau, and Dewey into some elegant balance between the private and public spheres, or the celebration of difference in unity. My suggestions reflect the cross-currents, the tensions between these thinkers, while building on their joint opposition to final ontological certainty.

Consider, first, the field of rhetoric. The topics around which the study of rhetoric will revolve concern public issues that have shaped the lives of both local and national communities. Because they are politically consequential, different streams of the American public discourse perennially compete for legitimacy. At any particular time there is a central discourse—embodied in the distribution of social goods, the patterns of legal constraints, and the schedule of social opportunities—which that discourse legitimates. Co-opted into or else confronting that politically authoritative discourse are a plethora of more local claims made up of individual histories, communal self-understandings, ethnic loyalties, and religious particularities. Where unco-opted, these claims either ignore, compete for entry into, or seek to transform and colonize the core content and thus the frontiers of that central discourse. An education in the forms of public rhetoric can be assembled around the story of the shape of that conversation and its impact on the contemporary citizen.[43]

The encounter with public rhetoric would include historical and current events and would span a number of forms and technologies of communication, including not only the written and spoken word but also media images and computer languages. Students would focus on a number of case studies in which they would examine the relationship between issues, audiences, and media in speech, advertising, song, literature, documentary, demonstration, video, and film. Students would construct their own presentations and recreations of critical debates, employing (so far as economically possible) a variety of media forms. Teachers would lead the analysis of the effectiveness of imagery, metaphor, cadence, and syntax in group discussion. While one focus would be on public issues that have pitted a marginalized group against a preconstituted consensus, teachers would be free to select their own positions in the debate based on their understanding of the children and their community. The question of whether history, sooner or later, gives "victory" to the just, and whether victory is in any case an appropriate result, has no a priori answer.[44] Students will concentrate on dissecting the dynamic relationship between differing forms of rhetoric, the political impact they do or do not create or embody, and the ethical claims that are reforged in the process.

Taken together, for example, the stories of Martin Luther King Jr. and Malcolm X dramatically present two responses to the challenge posed by confronting the core language. The first is co-optation. King offered a translation of civil rights into the core language, into terms that the Constitution had already authorized and legitimated. Hoping to shame the apathy around him by confronting the population with its own performative contradictions, King intended to enlarge, if not revolutionize, the language and practice of civil rights. Malcolm X, by contrast, often damned the core as essentially illegitimate. Translation would destroy his particular and preferred narrative. The choice was either to colonize or to secede, and Malcolm X at times regarded the latter as the more promising path. Pupils, having read, watched, and debated these choices and their historical consequences, would learn to measure for themselves the dilemmas of social exclusion and the limits of constitutionalism.[45]

The outlines of the focus on public speech would emerge around such stories of translation, be they stories of translation sought or declined, of comparative success or failure. Adding an account of the Amish people to that of King and Malcolm X, for example, would enrich the lessons students could derive from the history of contested translations. Despite the apparent similarity of the Amish people's position to that of Malcolm X—namely, a refusal to translate the language of their particular self-understanding into the values of "mainstream" opinion—that mainstream responded in utterly different ways. Students could examine what it is about the language of the two cases which accounts for the different outcome and debate the terms of the historical "resolution" of the issue.[46] The critical question may be posed in Rousseau's terms: When should the wider community protect the cultural and/or political autonomy of a particular group? Students will analyze the claim that exposing Amish children to the company of other high school children would make the choice to remain Amish impossibly more burdensome. Is exposure to the majority's understanding of progress a legitimate state demand? Students recreating the debate will ponder the issue in much the same fashion as Rousseau's Genevese readers were asked to judge the threat of a Parisian cultural invasion.

Debates within the field of public speech need not be so overtly political. For example, the debate over the promise and/or poison offered by computers and the domain of "hypertext" is heating up. In the words of a champion of the new technology, "Interactive computer fiction . . . mixes critic and creator in ways which leave not only fiction, but the whole of literary criticism, never the same again."[47] Students exposed to the rhetorical forms and techniques of hypertextuality will be in a position to debate the possibilities and the losses or silences this new technology creates. The fields of advertising, film, and music naturally afford further content for the examination of contested social values.

The second core focus is the theater. It is clear that there are any number of educative opportunities available in the capacity to perform, view, and criticize a dramatic presentation, but a democratic education of citizen as measure focuses on a few. First, the presentation in dramatic form of speech, dance, or formal drama affords what Rousseau sought in Geneva: the celebration of the self to its own immediate community. Where the student can call on particular preexisting stories (such as religious, ethnic, or national ones), that student can construct a performance around them. Alternatively, students can choose (or create) presentations that express their own instincts, beliefs, or passions.[48] Family or guardians and the immediate community could attend.

Rousseau would not have endorsed the acting out of roles foreign to the student's immediate community. Once again the teacher must decide: Should the students exchange gender or ethnic roles? Should they perform in and out of mask, affording the experiences of identity, concealment, and transfer? Rousseau argued that, in a cosmopolitan center such as Paris, such drama was harmless but that it could undermine the identity of a homogeneous community. Dewey would have welcomed the broader experience such role playing might bring. Broadly speaking, about this, as about other areas of the core, my view is that education in the United States should shift from a Rousseauian emphasis in the starting grades to a Deweyian emphasis as the child matures. That is, early education should not embrace the ambiguities of identity and location which the more mature student will learn to handle. This general principle democratizes Rousseau's own experience, allowing students the sometimes painful chance to stand both inside and outside their immediate communities. Nevertheless, in many instances the teacher may judge that too great an emphasis on role playing across cultures would undermine, not support, the students' capacity to develop self-discipline and confidence. This will be especially true when schools must pluck children from circumstances of domestic chaos and/or poverty.

Self-discipline will come, in part, by requiring that students memorize their lines or their choreography: the transmission of ritual and the spontaneous celebration of particular historical identities are incompatible with the passivity of encountering without internalizing. The requirement to memorize short prose, poetic, or musical passages for solo delivery before classmates and a subsequent discussion illustrating the meaning of the choice would add to one's sense of responsibility for the project. In addition, each student could be asked to present to the class a reading of a work of fiction, offering a background presentation, a selection of excerpts, and an account of his or her reaction to the text. After a semester of such presentations, the students of that particular group would select a few of these texts for the class to read and discuss as a whole, followed by a theatrical presentation of a selected story to a broader audience. Finally, the school could hold, at least twice a year, a general assembly in which students would debate topics of seminal importance to the school in front of teachers, staff, and the interested public.

Now to the third dimension of the core. The development of a literacy in political economy would have a broad focus. For reasons I noted in chapter 1, the intention would not be to produce a vocational literacy but, rather, a capacity to judge public policy. Students would study questions about macro relationships between markets, income distribution, political ideology, technology, the family structure, and employment patterns. Dewey argued most vehemently that illiteracy in these areas makes the citizen incapable of articulating a public interest or grasping the relationship between individual and social goals. But Rousseau, too, following Aristotle, focused on the relationship between economic self-sufficiency (or its absence), the political structure of a community, and the nature of private life. In pursuing these issues, teachers would offer technical knowledge to the student on a need-to-know basis, as both Rousseau and Dewey insisted. Recent developments in educational software technology could make this field dynamic and challenging to students: interactive courses merging computers, video, cd rom, and high-quality sound are already proving effective and popular in pilot trials.[49] While students would be able to work in groups on some aspects, my suggestion would be that each conduct an individual final discussion on the broad issues framed like that in *Euthydemus*. Teachers representing opposing positions on major issues would engage the student in agonistic conversation on topics within political economy. (For especially able students the dialogue might include a third party whose role would be to question the basic assumptions of the other two—but a Socrates is rarely available.)

As a number of educators have already suggested, the intellectual dimensions of this field lend themselves to community projects.[50] Working in groups, students will investigate and then attempt to develop and execute programs that involve local issues. The range of such projects is almost unlimited but would include environmental, housing, educational, tax, and industrial policies. Where possible, such projects should involve the students in dealings with local, and perhaps national, media, local government, and business. Dewey was right to suggest that the "school without walls" could expand its own democratic discourse by the inclusion of parents, churches, local businesses, art and science interests, and local government.

Where financially possible, students might also be able to produce a printed text or a video presentation of their case for the parties involved and attempt to distribute the material to the relevant target audiences. A summary report prepared by the group would set out the theoretical base of the planned intervention, a defense and description of strategies, and an analysis of the results. The school would make such reports available to parents and community.[51]

The fourth area of emphasis would be the body. I interpret this topic, once again, very broadly: How does or should the law constrain or liberate the human body? How do the languages of physiology, sexuality, race relations, sport, and the marketplace of commercial images treat the body? The focus on the body will not necessarily defend currently fashionable obsessions, or fads. Rather, students will study the ways in which social practices endlessly redecorate, repackage, and replace the body. The study of the body in these terms would certainly open up pursuits that have been traditionally grouped under the rubric of science, but the exploration of the biology, chemistry, or neurophysiology of the body would take place in the context of the other lines of critical inquiry, not in isolation from them.

Selecting and organizing the material through which students will investigate the body gives teachers extraordinary room for maneuver. As a component of democratic education, the "body" segment should offer a critical perspective on the ways in which contemporary society manages, portrays, satirizes, and celebrates the body. But as ever, it is the teacher who will negotiate the tension that the models of Rousseau and Dewey create between them. To what degree should investigations of the body focus on self-referential understanding, with a focus on the history and practice of the local culture? Should the model be roughly that of Rousseau's pastoral fête in the Clarence of *La Nouvelle Héloise,* in which the community dances to the rhythms of its immediate agricultural seasons? A historical investigation of American sports, combined with a critical study of its current politics, could center on the immediate context of school and local surroundings. Such a study would offer a plethora of possibilities for further thinking about ethnic history, economics, technology, and theater, thus dovetailing with other elements in the core curriculum. Or should teachers instead direct students to compare the ancient figurines of the Pacific islands, the nudes of Rubens, and the self-portraits of Francis Bacon in order to begin a study of images of the body in art? The answers to these questions will be based on practical as well as pedagogic circumstances. Do teachers and schools have the resources, through access to team teaching and to libraries in print or on disk, to guide such multicultural study? Will such a line of investigation stimulate the students to ask searching questions about their immediate society and its cults of the body? Could such studies build on questions that students themselves developed while considering the body in a more immediate context?

Pedagogically, Rousseau and Dewey are in accord that, no matter what the nature of the material taught, students will retain little of use unless their immediate energies and passions are engaged. In an extraordinarily heterogeneous society such as the United States, only the individual school and teacher can gauge the psychological, intellectual, and cultural backgrounds that will nurture or frustrate their choice of pedagogic paths. There can be no single answer to the challenge of arousing in the contemporary classroom the erotic energies, which Rousseau manages so deftly on behalf of his characters and readers. Reflecting on the teachings of Protagoras, Rousseau, and Dewey, thoughtful teachers will interrogate the theme of the body with stories chosen to enhance self-reflection, criticism, and deepening judgment.

These four broad areas of concentration would lead to a relatively formal examination, which would be taken at a national level by graduating high school seniors. The purpose of such a test (which I refer to below as "General Questions") is to allow a school to determine if a student is ready to graduate with a basic grasp of the critical issues in the national agenda. Today students taking the SAT, for example, face questions like the following: "Select the pair that *best* expresses a relationship similar to that expressed in the original pair: yawn-boredom. a: dream-sleep, b: anger-madness, c: smiles-amusement, d: face-expression, e: impatience-rebellion."[52] While students able to analyze the relationship between rhetoric and ideology might have fun wondering why their predecessors were exposed to such questions, their own education would prepare them to discuss such topics as:

1. What criteria should be used in deciding who should be allowed entry into, and citizenship, of the United States? [Such questions focus on the boundaries of community and citizenship, prompting questions about political allegiance, history and identity.]

2. In what circumstances if any should the state ban or restrict the distribution of books, music, or films? What would follow from adopting the opposite view to the one you defend? [Questions of this type ask future citizens to consider the weight they wish to place on their value judgments and on those of others.]

3. Should the religious beliefs passed on from parents to children be tested by classroom exposure to competing beliefs, both religious and scientific, without the consent of parents? [Questions about the relationship between belief, education, and authority form a vital part of education for a democratic citizen. Questions of this kind have long made up a critical portion of public debate.]

4. How do campaign contribution laws, media access conditions, and the American electoral system shape our public choices? What would you want changed, if anything, and why? [Students are asked to relate the empirical features of contemporary political debate to normative issues of political value. Such questions implicitly raise issues about broader problems of democratic political economy.]

5. How might the state of major economic factors (inflation, money supply, interest rates, trade and employment) affect the decision of informed individuals to purchase or rent a home? Should the market determine who gets to live where? [Major economic decisions shape critical future opportunities and constraints.]

6. Who should determine the amount of federal funds given to subsidize individual or group activities in the field of scientific research, artistic activity, and education? What criteria should the deciding agents use in their decisions? [This type of question asks the candidate to evaluate competing demands for public aid and to examine the relationship between the value of private pursuits and their contribution to the common domain.]

7. What is at stake in the decision to educate American children in languages other than English, or bilingually, or only in English? Who should decide? [Combining issues of community, identity, and authority, questions of linguistic education ask students to investigate the commensurability between political and linguistic identity and to measure their proper relationship.]

8. What constraints should be placed on the ability of parents to determine the biological nature of their children? [Drawing on issues of technology, ethics, and politics, questions about genetic engineering can prompt effective analysis across issue domains.]

One could, of course, indefinitely extend and alter such lists of questions within their cross-disciplinary and normative focus. This focus emerges from the design of the core curriculum itself and the habits of critical inquiry that curriculum has fostered. While the specification of teaching techniques to bring the core and its General Questions to life lies outside my present scope, it is clear that important and successful work along such lines is under way in a number of schools. In particular, the Coalition for Essential Schools, under the leadership of Theodore Sizer, stresses a pedagogic doctrine that expects students to master and display the results of interdisciplinary work in a wide variety of formats. The intention, with which I am in some sympathy, is to enable students "to figure out . . . how we represent ourselves, the meanings and values of such representations—written, designed, somehow shaped—which define us."[53]

I have already indicated that engagement with the traditional disciplines and/or with vocational work would be moved to the periphery of the core curriculum. By this I mean to suggest not that the periphery is secondary, but only that individual students will move, through their aptitude, presentations, investigations, and dramas, toward more specialized work in particular branches of inquiry. There is every reason why choice of an area of specialization should emerge from the core, and not vice versa. The core represents the literacy of a democratic citizen, a citizen who will measure his or her society and self. The core focus allows the teacher to construct a pedagogic space in which he or she will choose how to balance the temptation toward cultural isolation against the tendency to collapse one's preferences into a passive celebration of preexisting main-stream social values. It will also permit the participation, through its particular dynamics, in self-legislating groups brought together around collective endeavor. In this context a student's particular choice of specialty will emerge as one in which his or her individual talents or passion can build on a shared educational experience: there should be no need for tracking within the core subjects, as I have outlined them. I confess to agnosticism with regard to further formal examinations in particular areas of specialization: where appropriate, it seems to me that the relevant professional, business, or academic bodies that represent the post-high school occupations may be in the best position to design such tests.[54]

Naturally, the relationship between the core and the periphery raises issues of school design which blend into the politics of school selection. Following the logic of my proposals, every school would teach the four core fields. Based on local circumstances, certain schools with the requisite facilities would become particular centers of excellence for the more advanced development of special skills. The current tracking that establishes a social hierarchy between pre-college and prevocational training will only be undone (as it should be) when the United States learns from international example that technical education can be in every way as competitive and worthy of respect as college education. Some progress has already been made in the creation of apprenticeship programs, but the United States lags far behind Germany and Denmark, the acknowledged leaders in the field.[55] Nevertheless, a start can be made at the high school level. The resources available to particular communities will, of course, vary: in some instances the more specialized learning op-portunities will be available within the same school as the student attends for his or her core education; in some cases students would join groups at other sites for their activities. In any event, the idea would not be to split up the students along completely separate tracks after they had reached some minimal level of core competence; they would, instead, undertake specialist and core activities simultane-ously in the final years of high school.

We come, finally, to the vexing question of the guidance teachers should provide with regard to the choice of topics and texts. As my discussion of public speech suggests, the choice of topics for study will often be based on the teacher's judgment of his or her students and a determination of those questions that will shape the cultural horizon and self-understandings, of their society. The best teaching is done, naturally, by the passionate. The desire to introduce students to a particular story, for example, is in itself a conviction that the story will strengthen the students' sense of purpose or will open vistas of experience for further exploration. The endless debate between defenders of various "canons" is useful mainly because it reminds us that ideas are worth arguing over. Michael Oakeshott had the best response for those who insist that teachers must teach a particular list of titles: "A culture is not a doctrine or a set of consistent teachings or conclusions about human life. It is not something we can set before ourselves as the subject of learning. . . . A culture . . . is a continuity of feelings, perceptions, ideas, engagements, attitudes and so forth, pulling in different directions, often critical of one another and contingently related to one another so as to compose not a doctrine, but what I would call a controversial encounter."[56]

Teachers should be free to select a balance between texts that celebrate distant worlds, which make stasis uncomfortable, and those that affirm the immediate community of teacher and pupil. On occasion that choice will be less for the sake of balance than for providing an occasion for agon: the opportunity for teacher and student together to confront the seductions, impossibilities, and irresolvable but inescapably clashing perspectives of human experience. There is nothing in such a project that is necessarily therapeutic; the challenge of teaching is to create a strength of judgment able to maintain itself in the turbulence of that agon.

Such broad guidelines, however, do not go quite far enough. While I am convinced that political theorists have paid far too much attention to the extreme cases of public versus private authority in education and not nearly enough to the justification for its basic materials, the ideas I have been considering may have a place in that debate. As the Athenian example, Rousseau, and Dewey all suggest, the exploration of the self-understanding of a community, especially the preparation of democratic citizens who have an equal right to determine its future direction, requires some sense of the limits within which that community can continue to maintain its identity and its space for self-debate. Exposing students to the many ways in which that space has been renegotiated need not resemble Rousseau's recipe for a desperately weak Poland, in which education teaches future citizens to dote heart and soul on their country. But it does follow the suggestion contained in the *Letter to D'Alembert*—namely, that the encouragement of certain impulses risks the very preservation of areas of public identity and debate. These are not the impulses that led a Rousseau into exile, a Thoreau or a Martin Luther King into jail—the impulse to remind a democratic community of its internal inconsistencies. But the desire to silence the reach of public debate by triumphalism privatizes the actors involved and those over whom they have authority. The publicly funded school will not consciously engage in such activity in the design or practice of its curriculum. But triumphalism is not the same thing as censorship: as Rousseau argues, a democratic dialogue that permits, indeed mandates, its own renegotiation must uniquely and properly exercise constraint over the limits of that renegotiation. The litmus test is that educators justify those limits by showing how they contribute to the child's development of a sense of individual self-awareness and judgment. Censorship, or the constraints educators impose on children's pedagogic projects, are an inescapable dimension of enabling those children to develop the skills of measurement.

The question of censorship arises in two specific domains. The first concerns the claims of certain groups for control over the core list of subjects taught at school. Take, for example, the view that one could characterize the language of Western politics as a "phallocentric discourse," a tradition that operates to exclude the female voice, or voice of the "other." The issue for democratic education is whether this other voice seeks critical union with or colonization of the core discourse and, if so, with what consequence. As an issue of contested translation, democratic education will welcome the challenge to the status quo and the recognition of a new speaker. But what follows if teachers render the "male" voice illegitimate by definition, if committed teachers lead students to abandon male-authored works rather than judge them from fresh perspectives? Democratic education could justify such claims of censorship only be indicating the forms of judgment which children could not otherwise attain and by defending the depth and quality of the thinking that would result. In short, educators must take public responsibility for the exclusion of perspectives they seek to silence. Oakeshott wrote of the shallowness of a public discourse that too often "resembles the barking of a dog at its own yelp," about a language "of appetite" that "allows only expression of 'points of view.' "[57] Drawing their students toward more profound adventures of learning and judgment, teachers may need to act as the censors of social noise and, in so doing, may exclude something of high value. There is no escape from this pedagogical conundrum: in raising and resolving such questions of selection and focus, teachers are themselves measuring their world.

What of the other side of the coin, of those communities that try to protect their own space of identity and dialogue from the threat of external destruction? The case of the Amish is instructive. Rather than trying to colonize the core, they wish to be ignored by it. The logic of my argument suggests that public schooling will not support those who absolutely refuse to introduce their children to the vocabulary of the core subjects. The record suggests, however, that the Amish do confront the core discourse, albeit in such a way as to emphasize its ungodliness and materialism. So long as they are able to articulate their critique in terms available to the wider community, the Amish are sufficiently educating their children to satisfy democratic demands. A sufficiently rigorous dialectic is at work, and no physical harm to individuals is involved. Those who argue that the Amish do not educate their children to be the measure of enough things might recall that those children may be more effective at measuring the things about which they learn. Critics might also temper their impatience by recalling a fragment by Hölderin:

> Is there a measure on earth? There is
> None.

Hölderin's question is sobering to democratic education, but it, and I, remain unwilling to affirm his answer. Democratic education returns the self to itself not as the imperious judge of all that it surveys but, rather, in the form of a dynamic, impossibly heterogeneous odyssey of interrogation, loyalty, and risk. "The experience [is] like that of watching a storm rise to its height. . . . There are a series of waves; suggestions reaching out and being broken in a clash, or being carried onwards."[58] There are meaner metaphors by which to live.

Notes

Introduction

1. One might argue that "right" or a moral or natural law is what legitimates government, not just majoritarian will. Nevertheless, the American constitution in its entirety is subject to unlimited popular revision.

2. Friedrich Nietzsche, *The Will to Power*, ed. and trans. Walter Kaufmann (New York: Vintage Books, 1967), par. 888; hereafter cited in the text.

3. Cynthia Farrar, *The Origins of Democratic Thinking* (Cambridge: Cambridge University Press, 1988), 262–63. The issue of employing the masculine or the feminine personal pronoun is an awkward one. Not so, of course, when one is citing Greek sources, or the work of Rousseau, in which gender is often clearly marked. In general, I have tried to indicate gender where appropriate. The reader should otherwise assume gender neutrality.

4. Democritus, Fragments (B33); also cited in Farrar, *Origins of Democratic Thinking*, 254.

5. Josiah Ober, *Mass and Elite in Democratic Athens* (Princeton: Princeton University Press, 1989), 191.

6. John Dewey, *The Public and Its Problems* (New York: Henry Holt and Co., 1927), 184.

7. I am indebted to Thomas Langston for bringing these passages to my attention. Langston discusses their role in American politics in a book on the president in American politics (Baltimore: Johns Hopkins University Press, forthcoming).

1: The Politics of Reform

1. One of a number of current initiatives is "Education for Democracy International," a coalition of university, publishing, and professional teaching forces currently involved in Poland, Hungary, Czechoslovakia, and Rumania.

2. Mortimer Adler, *Reforming Education* (New York: Collier Books, 1990), 17.

3. While there is some evidence that racism is less overtly present in American society than in the past, the attribution of causality to the public school is far from proved. For the evidence, see Herbert McClosky and John Zaller, *The American Ethos: Public Attitudes Toward Capitalism and Democracy* (Cambridge: Harvard University Press, 1984).

4. For a general historical survey, see Diane Ravitch, *The Troubled Crusade: American Education, 1945–1990* (New York: Basic Books, 1983). On America's recent performance in teaching literacy, see Irwin S. Kirsch and Ann Jugebult, *Literacy: Profiles of America's Young Adults*, National Assessment of Educational Progress, report no. 16-PL-02 (Princeton: Educational Testing Service, 1986). On numeracy, see the International Association for the Evaluation of Educational Achievement, *Science Achievement in Seventeen Nations* (New York: Pergamon Press, 1988). For the general data, see the annual surveys contained in *The National Report Card* (Princeton: Educational Testing Service).

5. See David Kearns and Denis Doyle, *Winning the Brain Race* (San Francisco: Institute for Contemporary Studies, 1988).

6. For a poignant reconstruction of the challenge faced by teachers and children in such a situation, see Tracy Kidder, *Among Schoolchildren* (Boston: Houghton Mifflin Co., 1989).

7. One striking example of success against the odds is the experiment in East Harlem, New York. Details are provided in Raymond J. Domanico, "Model for Choice: A Report on Manhattan's District 4," *Education Policy Paper*, no. 1 (New York: Manhattan Institute for Policy Research, 1989). Gallup opinion polls indicate public preferences about the salaries that ought to be paid to various professions. In 1984 teachers were placed far below lawyers and just above clergy on the list. Seventy-six percent of the public believed that a salary of more than $40,000 was appropriate for lawyers. Just 42 percent had the same view about teachers. See Stanley M. Elam, *The Twenty-second Annual Gallup Poll of the Public's Attitudes Toward the Public School*, printed in *Phi Delta Kappa*, September, 1990, 48.

8. The citation is from Adler, who still hopes to ground an education for democracy in Aristotelian principles (see Adler, *Reforming Education*, 61, 241, 254).

9. J. A. Schumpeter *Capitalism, Socialism and Democracy* (London: Allen & Unwin, 1943), 242, 269.

10. For a flavor of these convictions, see the issue "Math and Science Education" in *Forum for Applied Research and Public Policy* (1992). For a full-scale treatment along the same lines, see David Kearns and Denis Doyle, *Winning the Brain Race*. Kearns was onetime under secretary of education and chairman and CEO of Xerox Corporation, Denis Doyle a senior research fellow, Hudson Institute.

11. Kearns and Doyle, *Winning the Brain Race*, 5.

12. Perhaps the most noted contribution of neo-Marxists to the educational debate comes from Samuel Bowles and Herbert Gintis, *Schooling in Capitalist America* (New York: Basic Books, 1976). Their work, with its scathing attacks on the idea that American education is meritocratic, is largely ignored within

the mainstream of educational debate. Perhaps Elizabeth Kelly's manuscript *Public Knowledge, Education, and Democracy* (Boulder, Colo.: Westview Press, forthcoming), which imports Jurgen Habermas's conception of public discourse to aspects of American education, will renergize a socialist perspective. For discussion of the postmodern theorists, and bibliographical details, see chapter 7. The remainder of the present chapter discusses mainstream authors: those who are often cited by policymakers or senior representatives of the teaching profession.

13. Amy Gutmann, *Democratic Education* (Princeton: Princeton University Press, 1987). Later I discuss recent work by Benjamin Barber and forthcoming writing from Stephen Macedo. I have found no references in the American literature to James Tarrant's *Democracy and Education* (Aldershot, U.K.: Gower Publishing Co., 1989), which attacks market models of education more directly than does Gutmann. The terms *liberal* and *democratic* are naturally imprecise. I mean roughly to characterize those theorists who are concerned with issues of private and public discrimination and repression and who champion a particular conception of liberty drawn from the works of John Locke and John Stuart Mill.

14. The best-known work on these issues remains Robert Bellah et al., *Habits of the Heart* (Berkeley: University of California Press, 1985). For a treatment of the effects of communication technologies, see Kenneth Gergen, *The Saturated Self* (New York: Basic Books, 1991).

15. Witness the extraordinary success of Allan Bloom's *The Closing of the American Mind* (New York: Simon and Schuster, 1987). Bloom's evocation of a golden age in education was restricted to a handful of elite universities, but many readers found in Bloom the storyteller of their own lost innocence.

16. This much-cited figure was first presented by Chester Finn in his book *Taking Charge* (New York: Basic Books, 1991).

17. Finn, *Taking Charge*, 32, 296, 34.

18. This evocation of the theorist Michel Foucault may strike readers who are familiar with Foucault's work on asylums, prisons, and schools as overdrawn. But the emphasis on more and more schooling slides into recommendations for constant surveillance. See, for example, the language in which Laurence Steinberg describes the problems of single-parent families: "monitoring is less vigilant," Steinberg points out, due to "limited human resources." "Communities of Families and Education," in *Education and the American Family*, ed. William J. Weston (New York: New York University Press, 1989), 162.

19. Finn, *Taking Charge*, 24–25, 169.

20. For details of the original blueprint, see *Boston University's Report on the Chelsea Public Schools: A Model for Excellence in Urban Education* (Boston: Boston University, 1989).

21. James Coleman, "The Family, the Community, and the Future of Education" in Weston, *Education and the American Family*, 181.

22. I will return to the issue of "choice." Both major political parties support choice within the public school system, although only Republicans have supported the extension of choice to private secular and parochial schools.

23. Once again, support for national standards and testing is bipartisan, although by no means universal. The "Goals 2000" educational reform bill introduced by Education Secretary Riley in April 1993 continues the previous administration's commitment to the development of a national system of standards and assessments.

24. The case for the longer school year is made succinctly in Michael J. Barrett, "The Case for More School Days," *Atlantic*, November 1990.

25. Many critics point out that it costs far more to educate a child in a public rather than a private school. See, for example, John R. Lott, Jr., "Why Is Education Publicly Provided?" *Cato Journal* 7 (Fall 1987): 475–501, 476. For further discussion of the article, see Stephen Macedo, *Educating for Liberty: Private Freedom and Public Schooling* (unpubl. MS).

26. For detailed discussion of the issue of school choice, see *Choice and Control in American Education*, ed. William Clune and John White, 2 vols. (London: Falmer Press, 1990); and *School Choice*, Carnegie Foundation for the Advance of Teaching (Princeton, N.J., 1993).

27. These consequences are much in evidence in the United Kingdom, which has since 1988 introduced a number of reforms enabling public schools to "opt out" of local educational authority control. At the time of writing the new curriculum and testing apparatus is in chaos, boycotted by teachers nationwide (see *New York Times*, August 1, 1993).

28. The best case for these proposals can be found in the "Address of Dr. John Brademas" to the Annual Convention of the National School Boards Association," San Francisco, California, April 13, 1991. The author would like to thank Dr. Brademas for making available a manuscript copy of his remarks.

29. As one conservative policy analyst put it: Riley "is not a real reformer . . . except for the choice issue, he's really not that different from Lamar Alexander." Allyson M. Tucker, manager for the Center for Educational Policy at the Heritage Foundation, quoted in *Education Week* 12.no. 16 (January 13, 1993).

30. These remarks are to be found in Thomas Pangle's "Reflections on Democratic Education from the Perspective of the Founding," prepared for the 1990 Annual Meeting of the American Political Science Association.

31. Nathan Tarcov, *Locke's Education for Liberty* (Chicago; University of Chicago Press, 1984), 71–72.

32. Stephen Macedo, "Educating for Liberty: Private Freedom and Public Schooling" (MS, 1991), 43.

33. See, for example, the opposing views on whether the Amish should or should not be allowed to opt out of publicly accredited schooling. Shelley Burtt defends the first position in a paper, "In Praise of Yoder," presented at the 1992 Annual Meeting of the American Political Science Association, Chicago; Amy Gutmann the second in *Democratic Education*.

34. One remaining defender of the acid solvent of neutrality is Bruce Ackerman. His convictions lead him to the family hearth itself, but not to praise it: Ackerman argues that parents have a responsibility to be neutral toward the good in the education of their children. Bruce A. Ackerman,

Social Justice and the Liberal State (New Haven: Yale University Press, 1980).
35. Macedo, Educating for Liberty, 44.
36. William Galston. "Civic Education in the Liberal State," in Liberalism and the Moral Life, ed. Nancy Rosenblaum (Cambridge: Harvard University Press, 1989), 101. Galston joins Macedo in seeking to reset the balance between state and family. He argues that there is no need "for public authority to take an interest in how children think about different ways of life."
37. Jean Bethke Elshtain, Power Trips and Other Journeys (Madison: University of Wisconsin Press, 1990), 89, 92.
38. Naturally, the literature on democratic theory as a whole is vast. A concise and critical discussion of mid-century theorists can be found in Carole Pateman's Participation and Democratic Theory (Cambridge: Cambridge University Press, 1970), chap. 1.
39. Robert Dahl, A Preface to Democratic Theory (Chicago: University of Chicago Press, 1956), 76.
40. George Kateb, "Democratic Individuality and the Meaning of Rights" (MS, 1989), 36.
41. Presumably, it is this same "educative force" that in turn provides the "overlapping consensus" or the "deepest convictions" identified by contemporary theorists as constituting the core democratic political intuitions of American citizens. The terms are taken from John Rawls, "The Idea of an Overlapping Consensus," Philosophy and Public Affairs 17 (1988); and Gutmann, Democratic Education, 47.
42. Schumpeter, Capitalism, Socialism and Democracy, 269.
43. Gutmann, Democratic Education, 46.
44. For a different critique of Gutmann's work, see Kelly, Public Knowledge, Education, and Democracy, 13–136. Kelly is right to argue that "the neo-rationalist approach evades critical political questions of power, conflict, and social antagonism," 136.
45. Gutmann, Democratic Education, 65–70, 31, 29.
46. Ibid., 41.
47. Benjamin Barber, Strong Democracy (Berkeley: University of California Press, 1984), 122, 120.
48. For a sense of this variety, see George H. Wood, Schools That Work (New York: Dutton, 1992); and Jonathan Kozol, Savage Inequalities (New York: Crown Publishers, 1991).
49. Arthur G. Powell, Eleanor Farrar, and David K. Cohen, eds., The Shopping Mall High School (Boston: Houghton Mifflin Co., 1985), 41. See also Theodore Sizer, Horace's School (Houghton Mifflin Co., 1992), 91. Sizer describes the average high school curriculum as "a riot of programs."
50. Powell, Farrar, and Cohen, Shopping Mall High School, 39–40.
51. Ibid., 11, 126.
52. One piece of empirical data that most frustrates reformers is the Gallup Poll finding that the majority of parents are content with the offerings and performance of their local public high schools. Apparently, the choices they offer are not unpopular nor overly sparse. See Twenty-second Gallup Poll.

53. Ibid. Seventy-two percent of parents believe that the public school their eldest child attends is worthy of an A or B rating. Only 7 percent of public school parents believe that poor curriculum or standards are the most critical problem with the schools, 51, 53.

54. In Cambridge, Massachusetts, a considerable effort has been made to educate the consumer—to the cost of $100,000 per annum. But such funding is required and regulated by public authority. Elsewhere, the evidence suggests that low-income families are poor information consumers. See Michael Olivas, "Information Access Inequalities: A Fatal Flaw in Educational Voucher Plans," *Journal of Law and Education* (October 1981): 449–50.

55. To give one example, data from the famous public choice experiment in Harlem, New York, shows no indication of increased parental involvement. See Wayne Riddle and James Stedman, *Public School Choice: Recent Developments and Analysis of Issues* (Congressional Research Service, 1989), 19.

56. For an indication of the complexity of the issue, see Weston, *Education and the Family*, 32–65.

57. John Chubb and Terry Moe, *Politics, Markets, and America's Schools* (Washington, D.C.: Brookings Institution, 1990).

58. For further discussion, see Henry M. Levin, "Education as a Public and Private Good," in *Public Values, Private Schools*, ed. Neal Devins (London: Falmer Press, 1984), 223. For the statistics, and their connection to the debate about "choice" programs, see Henry M. Levin, "The Theory of Choice Applied to Education," in *Choice and Control in American Education*, ed. William H. Clune and John F. White, 1:275 (London: Farmer Press, 1990). My own views on the issue can be found in "Political Theory, Educational Practice," *PS* (September 1991): 498–501; and "Choice: The Silver Bullet in Education?" (MS, Vanderbilt Institute for Public Policy Studies, Fall 1991).

59. Kearns and Doyle, *Winning the Brain Race*, 73. Amy Gutmann places this tension at the heart of her objections to voucher schemes, in *Democratic Education*, 69.

60. The image was presented to the author during an interview with Chester Finn in Washington, D.C., July 1991. The arguments behind the idea are defended in his book *Taking Charge*.

61. For a bibliography critical of test worship, see Sizer, *Horace's School*, 236.

62. For more discussion of contemporary efforts to establish national curricula goals, see the final chapter.

63. Cited in *New York Times*, July 15, 1992.

64. Kearns and Doyle, *Winning the Brain Race*, 82.

65. For many examples of such proposals, see Sizer, *Horace's School*.

66. For a typical statement to this effect, see the "Secretary's Commission on Achieving Necessary Skills (Scans)," *What Work Requires of Schools* (Washington, D.C.: U.S. Department of Labor, 1991).

67. Joe Spring, "Education and the Sony War," in *Taking Sides: Clashing Views on Controversial Educational Issues*, ed. James Wm. Noll (Guilford: Dushkin Publishing Group, 1991), 128.

68. Valerie A. Personick, "Industry Output and Employment: A Slower

Trend for the Nineties," *Monthly Labor Review* 112 (November 1989): 34–38. This issue presents more detailed breakdowns of labor projects, which can also be found in *The Occupational Outlook Handbook*, U.S. Department of Labor, Bureau of Labor Statistics, Bulletin 2350, April 1990.

69. George Silvestri and John Lukasiewicz, "Projections of Occupational Employment, 1988–2000," *Monthly Labor Review* 112 (November 1989): 60.

70. It is not surprising that the school discussed by Jonathan Kozol places a heavy emphasis on preparation for McDonald's: only one in twenty four will graduate from any college, and McDonald's, together with other fast-food chains, are heavy employers. Kozol, *Savage Inequalities*, 45.

71. Lawrence Mischel and David M. Frankel, *The State of Working America* (Armonk, N.Y.: M. E. Sharpe, Inc. 1991), Economic Policy Institute, 123.

72. Ibid., 127.

73. David Paris, "Schools, Scapegoats and Skills: Educational Reform and the Economy" (MS, 1992), 7, 8.

74. Congressional Research Service (CRS) report for Congress, "Economic Benefits of Education," Lind LeGrande, December 13, 1988.

75. Cited in Wood, *Schools That Work*, xix.

76. There is not much evidence that higher scores correlate to the literacy skills for which businesses are pleading. Moreover, as a number of studies indicate, "we simply do not have the kind of evidence that would tell us how workers educated in a certain way are able to perform certain jobs better because they had developed certain skills through education." Paris, *Schools, Scapegoats and Skills*, 15. On the first point, see Kearns and Doyle, *Winning the Brain Race*.

77. Chubb and Moe, *Politics, Markets and America's Schools*, 218.

78. See the discussion of the draft proposals for a "civics" curriculum in chapter 7.

79. In this passage I am indebted to comments from Jean Elshtain.

80. For the figures and discussion, see Kearns and Doyle, *Winning the Brain Race*, 83.

81. Both Finn and Kearns, among many others, incorporate these proposals into their plans, couched, of course, in tones of regret and comfort for the families who cannot share time with their children.

82. Kearns and Doyle, *Winning the Brain Race*, 93.

83. Chubb and Moe complain that "democracy cannot remedy the mismatch between what parents and students want and what public schools provide." My response is that this is as it should be. John Chubb and Terry Moe, "An Institutional Perspective on Schools" (paper prepared for the Annual Meeting of the American Political Science Association, San Francisco, 1990), 7.

2: The Buried Triangle

1. A.H.M. Jones, *Athenian Democracy* (Oxford: Oxford University Press, 1977), 41. For a discussion of why this might be so, see M. I. Finley, *Democracy*

Ancient and Modern (New Brunswick, N.J., and London: Rutgers University Press, 1973), 28; or Nicole Loraux, *The Invention of Athens* (Cambridge: Harvard University Press, 1986), 177–78.

2. Thucydides, *The History of the Peloponnesian War*, bk. 2, 35–36. Werner Jaeger's choice of the title *Paideia* for his three-volume account of Greek thought and culture attests to the role of education as the common denominator of ancient Hellenic sensibility. See Werner Jaeger, *Paideia: The Ideals of Greek Culture*, trans. Gilbert Highet, 3 vols. (Oxford: Oxford University Press, 1971).

3. The representative citation is from Stephen Holmes, "Aristippus In and Out of Athens," *American Political Science Review* 73 (March 1979): 113–28. For critical comment, see J. Peter Euben, *The Tragedy of Political Theory* (Princeton: Princeton University Press, 1990), 5–11. For another warning against employing the example of ancient Athens for improving contemporary democracy, see di Athanasios Moulakis, "The Greeks and Democratic Theory: Moses I. Finley's *Democracy Ancient and Modern Revisited*," in *Rivista internazionale di fiosofia del diritto*, 4th ser., 68 (January–March 1991): 44–84: "To the Greeks, Democracy was a regime, advantageous and attractive to some, less so to others, but not an ideal." "What western civilization has found of greater and lasting value, are the reflections that the vicissitudes of ancient democracy . . . gave rise to," 49, 50.

4. See Cynthia Farrar, *The Origins of Democratic Thinking* (Cambridge: Cambridge University Press, 1988), 81ff. I am not, of course, suggesting that the greater availability of Protagoras's own texts would solve interpretive issues, only that the hermeneutic situation would be altered.

5. For discussion of Protagoras's actions in Thurii, see J. V. Muir, "Protagoras and Education at Thourioi," *Greece and Rome* 29 (1982): 20.

6. Richard Rorty, "The Historiography of Philosophy: Four Genres," *Philosophy in History: Essays on the Historiography of Philosophy*, ed. Richard Rorty, John Schneewind, and Quentin Skinner (Cambridge: Cambridge University Press, 1984), 49–75. For a sympathetic discussion of Rorty's approach in the context of classical scholarship, see Edward Schiappa, *Protagoras and Logos: A Study in Greek Philosophy and Rhetoric* (Columbia: University of South Carolina Press, 1991), 65–68.

7. Schiappa, who intends to provide a historical reconstruction, argues that the Older Sophists "were defending a new humanistic rationalism." The Sophists would have been surprised. For the most part, however, Schiappa's "four hermeneutical principles . . . *ipsissima verba* primacy, triangulation, linguistic density, and resonance," provides a useful model. Schiappa, *Protagoras and Logos*, 56, 21.

8. Hans-Georg Gadamer, *Truth and Method* (New York: Crossroad Publishing Co., 1982), 266, 262 (translation altered). Since the best defense of a method is its practice, I avoid a long discussion of the rival methodologies. Interested readers can return to Leo Strauss for a strong if deeply idiosyncratic defense of the timelessness of great ideas. See Leo Strauss, *Natural Right and History* (Chicago: University of Chicago Press, 1953), 23–24. For its part the literature defending a deep contextualism is enormous. For a

statement clearer than most of the position, see Quentin Skinner, "Meaning and Understanding in the History of Ideas," in *History and Theory* 8 (1969): 3–53.

9. Loraux, *Invention of Athens*, 7–8.

10. Contrast this approach with the (over) confidence of those ready to assert direct intellectual lineages. For an example, consider Patrick Colby's remark that Protagoras's theory "is the rationalization and materialism of contemporary western societies." Patrick Colby, *Socrates and the Sophistic Enlightenment* (Lewisburg: Bucknell University Press, 1987), 17. Or see Susan Jarratt's conclusion that, "as sociologists of knowledge, the sophists anticipate writing across the curriculum programs." Susan Jarratt, *Rereading the Sophists* (Carbondale: Southern Illinois University Press, 1991), 97.

11. J. Peter Euben, "Political Education and Democratic Discourse" (paper delivered for the 1990 Annual Meeting of the American Political Science Association), 20; hereafter cited as Euben 1990b.

12. J. Ober, *Mass and Elite in Democratic Athens* (Princeton: Princeton University Press, 1989), 79.

13. Pay for participation on the juries was introduced in the 450s B.C. and for attendance at the assembly in the 390s. There is considerably debate about the financial attractiveness of the fees but some agreement that they were anything but negligible for the poorer citizen. For these details of the constitutional structure of Athens, see R. K. Sinclair, *Democracy and Participation in Athens* (Cambridge: Cambridge University Press, 1988), 20–23 and 129. For extended discussion of the nature of the Ekklesia and further comments on the issue of pay, see M. H. Hansen, *The Athenian Democracy in the Age of Demosthenes* (Cambridge, Mass.: Basil Blackwell, 1991), 125–60.

14. Ibid., 144.

15. Gregory Vlastos, Ισονομία πολιτική, "Isonomia politike," *Isonomia: Studien zur Glecheitsvorstellung im griechischen Denken* (Berlin: 1964): 29; hereafter cited as "Isonomia Politike."

16. Loraux, *Invention of Athens*, 187.

17. Euben, *Tragedy of Political Theory*, 269. It is worth recalling the subject matter of Aeschylean drama: matricide and blood-drinking furies make odd teachers of liberal tolerance.

18. Ibid., 46, 55, 56.

19. Jarratt, *Rereading the Sophists*, 89.

20. G. B. Kerferd, *The Sophistic Movement* (Cambridge: Cambridge University Press, 1981), 144. Schiappa echoes Kerefed's confident assertion, in *Protagoras and Logos*, 170.

21. Eric Havelock, *The Liberal Temper in Greek Politics* (New Haven: Yale University Press, 1957), 230.

22. What material exists was collected in *Die Fragmente der Vorsokratiker,* ed. Diels Kranz, and has been translated into English (with revisions) as *The Older Sophists,* ed. Rosamond Kent Sprague (Columbia: University of South Carolina Press, 1972). There are a few hundred lines of Gorgias and Antiphon, the anonymous fifth-century B.C. sophistic treatise *Dissoi Logoi* and the late-fifth- or early-fourth-century treatise, the *Anonymus Iamblichi*, of

similar brevity. Much of what remains is of Platonic and thus necessarily problematic origins. I will employ in-text citations for Plato's works, making reference to his *Euthydemus, Protagoras, Gorgias, Meno, Theaetetus,* and *Republic.* For translations I have consulted the editions indicated below (see n. 24). All line references are to the standard editions of the Greek text, including the Oxford Classical texts.

23. Michel Foucault, *Discipline and Punish* (New York: Vintage Books 1979), 217.

24. English-speaking readers unfamiliar with the history of the Sophists or the very limited surviving textual records are well served by the works of Schiappa, Sprague, Kerferd, and Guthrie. Schiappa, *Protagoras and Logos;* Sprague, *Older Sophists;* Kerferd, *Sophistic Movement;* Guthrie, *The Sophists* (Cambridge: Cambridge University Press, 1971). Important rereadings of the Sophists are to be found in Nietzsche, for whom they are the exemplars of those who "*know*" their own morality." Friedrich Nietzsche, *The Will to Power,* ed. and trans. Walter Kaufmann (New York: Vintage Books, 1967), para. 429. Among contemporary accounts, those of Colby, Havelock, Jarratt, Untersteiner, and Crowley are the most provocative, if on occasion also the most transparently instrumental. With Colby's noted exception, these scholars attempt to employ the Sophists as foreparents of a liberal or radical democratic pedagogics. Colby, *Socrates and the Sophistic Enlightenment;* Havelock, *Liberal Temper;* Jarratt, *Rereading the Sophists;* Mario Untersteiner, *The Sophists,* trans. Kathleen Freeman (Oxford: Basil Blackwell, 1954); Sharon Crowley, "A Plea for the Revival of Sophistry," *Rhetorical Review* 7 (1989): 318–34. Among the innumerable classicists who have interpreted those Platonic texts that directly concern the Sophists, I am most indebted to Gregory Vlastos, Miles Burnyeat, C.C.W. Taylor, Cynthia Farrar, J. de Romilly, Thomas H. Chance, and Michel Narcy. Of the many essential works of Vlastos, I have had most occasion to employ his introduction to Martin Ostwald's translation of *Plato's Protagoras* (New York: Bobbs-Merrill Co., 1956). See also Cynthia Farrar, *Origins of Democratic Thinking: Plato Protagoras,* trans. C.C.W. Taylor (Oxford; Clarendon Press, 1976); *The Theaetetus of Plato,* ed. and trans. Myles Burnyeat (orig. trans. M. J. Levett) (Indianapolis: Hackett Publishing Co., 1990); Jacqueline de Romilly, *Magic and Rhetoric in Ancient Greece* (Cambridge: Harvard University Press, 1974); Thomas H. Chance, *Plato's Euthydemus: Analysis of What Is and Is Not Philosophy* (Berkeley: University of California Press, 1992); and Michel Narcy, *La Philosophie et son double: un commentaire sur l'Euthydème de Platon* (Paris: Libraire Philosophique J. Vrin, 1984).

25. Colby, *Socrates and the Sophistic Enlightenment,* 70.

26. Taylor, *Plato Protagoras,* 101.

27. For a more detailed discussion of the problem, see G. B. Kerford, "Plato's Doctrine of Justice and Virtue in the *Protagoras,*" *Journal of Hellenic Studies* 73 (1953): 42–45; and Taylor, *Plato Protagoras,* 79–82., Farrar, *Origins of Democratic Thinking,* 82–84. The issue of gifts granted by the gods to men is raised again by Hesiod, in *Theogony and Works and Days,* trans. M. L. West

(Oxford: Oxford University Press, 1988). In Hesiod's account the gifts are anything but beneficial.

28. Such comparisons are not a rare feature of the Platonic corpus. See, for example, *Statesman*, 298.

29. Farrar, *Origins of Democratic Thinking*, 84.

30. Farrar argues for a kind of trickle-down theory: the Sophists educate the politicians, who educate the people. But it is clear from the text that Protagoras is here speaking of the formal education of young citizens, an education done best by the rich who can afford a long period of formal training for their sons. *Protagoras*, 325–27; Farrar, *Origins of Democratic Thinking*, 87.

31. Colby, *Socrates and the Sophistic Enlightenment*, 50.

32. In fact, the text can be read as conflating social and formal education. Protagoras opens his remarks by making "justice, moderation, being holy ... manly excellence" a condition of citizenship (*Protagoras*, 325a). He speaks of Athens as a city that "compels them [the citizens] to learn the laws and to model their lives upon them" (326c). But he fuses this assertion into a discussion of the formal education that is most likely to be achieved only by the sons of the well-to-do.

33. The critical reforms were those instituted circa 458 by Pericles and Ephialtes, which provided the poor with a stipend for participation in public affairs (see Guthrie, *Sophists*, 19).

34. Ober details "the interaction between the elite's desire to compete and to impress and the masses' authorization of his displaying a symbol that indeed impressed them." Ober, *Mass and Elite*, 244.

35. Vlastos disagrees: "Nothing in the process described in the Great Speech requires either learner or teacher to think for oneself, or even to think. . . ." Vlastos, Introduction to Ostwald, *Plato's Protagoras*, xx–xxi. This is, at least, an idiosyncratic reading of 323a. Moreover, it would be difficult to maintain that such activities as jury service, historically undertaken by all citizens, could have been conducted thoughtlessly, or by pure mimesis. Certainly, the Athenians didn't think so. Those six-thousand citizens who had been picked by lot to serve in the People's Court swore not only to vote "in consonance with my sense of what is most just" but also to "listen impartially to accusers and defenders alike" (cited in Demosthenes, 24.149–51). It might be more plausible to argue that the antidemocratic sentiments of 317a have more to do with Plato's agenda than that of Protagoras.

36. Taylor, *Plato Protagoras*, 103.

37. See Burnyeat, *Theaetetus of Plato*, 22.

38. In the *Theaetetus* the relationship between the status of moral approval and the requirements of education are explicitly stated (Theaetetus, 167a).

39. The ambiguity is extended in Socrates's own gloss on Protagoras's remark, in which he suggests that what the Sophist is teaching his pupil is to "make men good members of their city" (*Protagoras*, 319a).

40. Burnyeat, *Theaetetus of Plato*, 23. Burnyeat adopts the most familiar translation of the measure doctrine. Schiappa notes that *anthropos* "can refer

to an individual human or to humanity as a collective." Schiappa offers the following translation: "Of everything and anything the measure [truly is] human(ity)." Schiappa, *Protagoras and Logos*, 120.

41. Schiappa, *Protagoras and Logos*, 126.

42. Ibid., 25–26.

43. Vlastos, Introduction to Ostwald, *Plato's Protagoras*, xxii; emphasis added. Vlastos emphasizes that what is at stake in the *Protagoras* is not ontological subjectivism ("everything is for any given person such as it appears for that person") so much as ethical subjectivism ("the doctrine that goodness, justice, piety, and the like, are for each such as they appear to each"), xvi–xvii.

44. Taylor, *Plato Protagoras*, 102.

45. The inverse also applies: it is possible to interpret what the doctor does as a version of the skill attributed to the politician. Foods that are edible (and thus objectively "better") are preferred by the successfully treated patient to foods that are unhealthy. For details of this argument, see Plato, *Theaetetus*, trans. John McDowell (Oxford: Clarendon Press, 1973), 166–67.

46. The Great Speech "make[s] it clear that in Protagoras' view the social traditions of Athens or any other city reflect a universal ethical truth, viz. that the basic social virtues are justice and soundness of mind." Taylor, *Plato Protagoras*, 101.

47. Analysis in Schiappa, which in turn draws on the work of Charles Kahn, suggests that many of the distinctions made in modern philosophy—for example between the uses of the verb *to be* as describing either the fact of an existence or the nature of that which exists, postdate Protagoras. Accordingly, Schiappa translates the "man is measure" fragment as arguing that humanity is the measure "of that which is, that it is the case, of that which is not, that it is not the case," implying only a veridical interpretation of the verb *to be*. The experience or measurement of a thing is an open question, dependent on the standard that happens to be controlling for any particular person at any particular time. See Charles Kahn, "The Greek Verb 'to be' and the Concept of Being," *Foundations of Language* 2 (1966): 245–65. Schiappa, *Protagoras and Logos*, 117–33. In a democratic polis the controlling standard for the measurement of political problems will be communal; thus, Protagoras's education was focused on public rhetoric.

48. Burnyeat briefly acknowledges this possibility. See Burnyeat, *Theaetetus of Plato*, 26.

49. Farrar, *Origins of Democratic Thinking*, 74.

50. Thucydides, *Peloponnesian War*, bk. 3, 37–49.

51. For the details of these democratic constraints, see M. H. Hansen, *The Athenian Democracy in the Age of Demosthenes*, 205–12.

52. This is the difficulty with many of the textual commentaries. Even G. B. Kerferd, who argues for a complete separation of judgments about values and those about advantage, says nothing about the criteria of measurement of advantage itself. Kerferd, "Plato's Account," 20–26.

53. For discussion of this fusion, see Alasdair MacIntyre, *Whose Justice?*

Which Rationality? (Notre Dame: University of Notre Dame Press, 1988), 26–28.

54. Loraux, *Invention of Athens*, 196.

55. Ibid., 22.

56. Thucydides, *Peloponnesian War*, bk. 2, 43. Other sources for the same argument are found in Lysias 24–26; and Gorgias, cited in Sprague, *Older Sophists*, 48–49 (DK B 6). For Loraux's discussion of this passage, see Loraux, *Invention of Athens*, 101.

57. Loraux, *Invention of Athens*, 14.

58. Gregory Vlastos, "Isonomia politike," 29.

59. Thucydides, *The Peloponnesian War*, Bk. 2, 40.

60. Ibid., bk. 2, 37. The translation is that of Gregory Vlastos, with the omission of his explanatory notation and his inclusion of the original Greek. For his text, see Vlastos, "Isonomia Politike," 29–30.

61. For discussion and the citation of supporting interpretations, see Loraux, *Invention of Athens*, 186–89. In these readings Plato's "send up" of the Periclean oration in the *Menexenus* represents the most accurate reading of Thucydides's antidemocratic message.

62. Planudes on Hermogenes, cited in Sprague, *Older Sophists*, 48–49.

63. Lysias 2.2. The translation is Loraux's..

64. This is not to say that the *epitaphioi* were silent on the subject of the physical constraints of Athenian identity. In Loraux's words, "In the *epitaphioi*, it is an essential characteristic of the city that it has a periphery." Loraux, *Invention of Athens*, 331.

65. *Nothing to Do with Dionysus. Athenian Drama in its Social Context.* Ed. John J. Winkler and Froma I. Zeitlin (Princeton: Princeton University Press, 1990), 148.

66. Euben, *Tragedy of Political Theory*, 154.

67. Winkler, *Nothing to Do*, 337.

68. Euben, *Tragedy of Political Theory*, 56 and 161.

69. Liddell and Scott, *Greek-English Lexicon*, 1180.

70. Ober, *Mass and Elite*, 268.

71. Thucydides, *Peloponnesian War*, bk. 2, 39.

72. Plato, *Gorgias*, rev. text with introd. and comm. by E. R. Dodds, (Oxford: Clarendon Press, 1959), 210.

73. Deborah Steiner, *The Tyrant's Writ: Myths and Images of Writing in Ancient Greece* (Princeton: Princeton University Press, 1994), 192.

74. Herodotus, *Histories*, bk. 1, 153, and bk. 1, 191.

75. Cited in Sprague, *Older Sophists*, 53.

76. De Romilly, *Magic and Rhetoric*, 32.

77. Plato describes the followers of Protagoras as "spellbound." *Protagoras*, 315a.

78. De Romilly, *Magic and Rhetoric*, 38.

79. George Grote, *A History of Greece* (London: John Murray, 1870), 5:82.

80. Xenophon, *Hellenica*, bk. 2, chap. 2, sec. 24.

81. For a second example of this usage, see Plato's *Laws*, 8586.

82. Surprising because the *Euthydemus* does not enjoy a particularly favored place in the Platonic canon. Until very recently neither philosophers nor classicists have regarded the *Euthydemus* as a dialogue of the first importance. R. K. Sprague, whose work on the dialogue is the best known of recent studies, opens her translation of the work thus: "That the *Euthydemus* has not always found favor is not surprising; it lacks the poetry characteristic of the *Symposium* or *Phaedrus*, it contains no speaker with the eloquence of Protagoras or Callicles, it says next to nothing of the soul or the ideal state." Rosamond Kent Sprague, intro., *Euthydemus*, trans. R. K. Sprague (Indianapolis: Bobbs-Merrill Co., 1965). Her work on the dialogue is *Plato's Use of Fallacy: A Study of the Euthydemus and Some Other Dialogues* (London: Routledge and Kegan Paul, 1962).

83. The most recent work on the *Euthydemus* strongly reaffirms this reading. See Chance, *Plato's Euthydemus*, 21.

84. The quotations are from Hawtrey's commentary. R.S.W. Hawtrey, *Commentary on Plato's Euthydemus* (Philadelphia: American Philosophical Society, 1981), 1; hereafter cited as "Hawtrey.".

85. Narcy, *Le Philosophie et son double*.

86. See Leo Strauss, *Studies in Platonic Political Philosophy* (Chicago: University of Chicago Press, 1983), 74.

87. An examination of Socrates's exchange with Clinias indicates that the latter is offered either a single alternative or a leading question to respond to. In Socrates's retelling of the encounter to Crito, Clinias does take the initiative, but this same fact leads Crito to question the acuity of Socrates's memory (290e).

88. Narcy, *Le Philosophie et son double*, 140. Hawtrey's assertion that "the dramatic structure of the *Euthydemus* . . . is unusually clear" is a mistake. Hawtrey, 18.

89. Plato's deliberate linkage between sophistic rhetoric and violence is found again in the *Protagoras*. In his Great Speech Protagoras on six occasions speaks of *anankazo*, the verb for "using force" or "compelling." Cited in Colby, *Socrates and the Sophistic Enlightenment*, 64.

90. Socrates makes the same account of his position in the *Republic* (472a), when he introduces the paradox of the philosopher king. Since the present example occurs when Socrates is attempting to define the kingly art, the parallel is unlikely to be a coincidence.

91. See Sprague, *Older Sophists*, ix.

92. Transience was the common fate of the Sophists. They are described in the *Timaeus* as having "the habit of wandering from city to city and having no settled home of their own." *Timaeus*, 19e. Protagoras was born in Abdera, a city in the far northeast of Greece, Gorgias in Leontini in Sicily. For details, see Guthrie, *Sophists*, 262 and 269.

93. The interpretation of these two sophisms is the subject of considerable debate in the literature. The standard interpretations nevertheless support the suggestion that Clinias is trapped between antithetical positions. Narcy, characteristically, disputes this: relying on a disputed textual emendation, he suggests that Euthydemus tries to help Clinias to see Dionysodorus's trap.

I believe Narcy's analysis will be rejected by other scholars since it relies on a forced reading of Clinias's response, at 277a8.

94. See Hawtrey, 152–53, for a discussion of the language Plato employs in this passage.

95. Rosamond Kent Sprague, *Plato's Philosopher-King* (Columbia: University of South Carolina Press, 1976), 50–56.

96. Ibid., 53.

97. Plato's *Republic* takes up the same theme in far greater detail and offers a famous defense for the coherence of a kingly art. The judgment of Socrates's "failure" in the *Euthydemus* is based only on the context of eristic debate which informs this particular text. But it is that rhetorical context that is of interest to democratic education.

98. I am not in any sense either critiquing or defending Plato's teaching of the soul, nor his Idea of the Good. Rather, I am pointing out that Plato's teaching parallels that of the Sophists. Both argue that there is an entity that is all-knowing, and both defend a model of teaching. For Plato the dialectic enables perception to trigger ideas of the real latent in the soul. The Sophists argue that man's judgment at any moment is the measure of all things: education can alter man's awareness of the critical tool of that judgment, namely language. I do maintain, however, following Plato, that the two teachings are politically irreconcilable.

99. As Narcy points out of Socrates and the Sophists, "ils parlent la même langue" or "c'est une langue inapte à distinguer de façon stable individu et le genre, le prédique de predicable, le sujet de son attribute." Narcy, *Le Philosophie et son double*, 126.

100. The standard assumption is that the "stranger" is intended to be a portrait of Isocrates. For references to the literature that discusses the issue, see Sprague, *Older Sophists*, 63.

101. I am indebted to Paul Conkin for this phrase.

102. De Romilly is specifically referring to Gorgias. See de Romilly, *Magic and Rhetoric*, 16.

103. Gorgias, "On the Nonexistent or On Nature," in Sprague, *Older Sophists*, 43.

3: Rousseau and the Education of Restraint

1. The principal works are collected in the *Oeuvres complètes*, ed. B. Gagnebin and M. Raymond (Paris: Bibliothèque de la Pleiade, 1959–69), 4 vols; and the *Correspondance Complète de Jean-Jacques Rousseau*, ed. R. A. Leigh, 44 vols. (Geneva and Oxford: 1965–85).

2. Contemporary interest in Rousseau's writings on education is hard to find. The exception is Allan Bloom's introductory essay to his translation of *Emile*. But this treatment, elegant and perceptive, is inevitably a highly incomplete treatment of Rousseau's educational writings. More important, Bloom reads Rousseau with a theoretical searchlight that is intended to place Rousseau in a very particular Socratic perspective.

3. The distinction is made by Melzer: "Rousseau never quite says what I say he means." See Arthur Melzer, *The Natural Goodness of Man: On the System of Rousseau's Thought* (Chicago: University of Chicago Press, 1990), 176.

4. "The festival [in the *Nouvelle Héloise*] expresses in the 'existential' realm of emotion, what the *Social Contract* formulates in the theoretical realm of law." Jean Starobinski, *Jean-Jacques Rousseau. Transparency and Obstruction*, trans. Arthur Goldhammer (Chicago: University of Chicago Press, 1988), 96.

5. Robert J. Morrissey, who wrote the introduction to the English translation of Starobinski's work, stresses Starobinski's intellectual debt to the contemporary German theories of reading of which Hans-Georg Gadamer is so critical a part. Starobinski, *Jean-Jacques Rousseau*, xv. Of particular relevance here is Gadamer's concept of *Wirkungsgeschichte*, or "effective history," the view that all interpretations involve the fusion of horizons between the reader and text within a shared continuum of historical temporality. For more detailed discussion of these issues, see Jean Starobinski, *L'oeil vivant*, vol. 2: *La Relation critique* (Paris: Gallimard, 1970). The classic work of Gadamer on the subject is his book *Truth and Method* (New York: Crossroad, 1982); see, in particular, 235–78. I do not mean to suggest that Starobinski's style of reading can in any way be assimilated to that of Gadamer's, only that there are important affinities.

6. Starobinski, *Jean-Jacques Rousseau*, xxii; emphasis added. Starobinski offers an equally compelling reading of Rousseau's idiosyncratic literary journey: Rousseau must "make himself transparent, to experience transparency from within, while making sure that he remains visible to others, impressed though they may be in an opaque world," 43.

7. Arthur Melzer, *Natural Goodness of Man*, 90.

8. Jacques Derrida, *Of Grammatology*, trans. Gayatri Spivak (Baltimore: Johns Hopkins University Press, 1974). See, for example, 142, in which Starobinski's analysis of Rousseau's decision to write himself into absence is the critical starting point for Derrida's own reading.

9. Starobinski, *Jean-Jacques Rousseau*, 267.

10. The remark about "innate perversity" is Edmund Wilson's, in the preface to his translation of *The Confessions of Jean-Jacques Rousseau* (New York: Alfred A. Knopf, 1928), x. For a more mild suggestion that nevertheless suggests the partial vision of Rousseau, recall Judith Shklar's description of Rousseau as "the Homer of the losers." See her essay "Jean-Jacques Rousseau and Equality," *Daedalus* 107, no. 3 (Summer 1978): 24. Contemporary critics of Rousseau were less prone to think his idiosyncratic teachings harmless. His books were banned and burned; the king of France wanted him locked up in the lunatic asylum of Bicetre. See Rober Wokler, *Rousseau on Society, Politics, Music and Language: The Historical Interpretation of His Early Writings* (New York: Garland Publishing, 1987), 27.

11. J. M. Cohen, ed., notes in *The Confessions of Jean-Jacques Rousseau* (New York: Penguin Books, 1953), 53.

12. Wilson, preface to *Confessions*, x.

13. Hereafter all primary texts will be abbreviated. See the list of abbreviations.

14. A. Meiklejohn, *Education between Two Worlds* (New York: Harper and Brothers, 1942), 41.

15. Ibid., 85.

16. Benjamin Barber, *Strong Democracy* (Berkeley: University of California Press, 1984), 232.

17. Ibid., 233.

18. Carole Pateman, *Participation and Democratic Theory* (Cambridge: Cambridge University Press, 1970), 25.

19. Pateman simply refuses to believe Rousseau: ". . . the self-sustaining nature of the participatory political system should make it an exception to his view that all governments tend in the end to 'degenerate.'" Ibid., 25.

20. Barber, *Strong Democracy*, 233. It is, of course, possible that Rousseau misconstrued his own most powerful insights or cast them in a context best corrected. But the claim that this is so must rest on a separate argument about psychology and politics.

21. One could plausibly argue that Rousseau's increasing paranoia served something of the same purpose, cutting him off from society altogether.

22. The passage, from book 8, is discussed and cited by Derrida, *Of Grammatology*, 155ff.

23. See W. Boyd, *The Educational Theory of Jean-Jacques Rousseau* (New York: Russell and Russell, 1963), 293.

24. Rousseau frequently toys with the uncertain fictional status of *Emile:* Sophie, he suggests, is "not an imaginary being," but "whether it is believed to be true or not, it makes little difference," *E*, 402.

25. Reference to Rousseau's *Second Discourse* suggests how central a role solitude plays in Rousseau's reconstruction of innocence. In this important respect Rousseau has preserved the parallelism between Emile and the man of nature. The "solitary" savage, "perhaps never recognizing anyone individually," has as little sense of identity as Emile (*SD*, 110, 137).

26. This point must be borne in mind prior to any negative judgment as regards the Tutor's manipulation of Emile—a manipulation that Rousseau makes no effort to conceal. Generations of readers have been upset by the tutor's strategy: Davidson remarks that "freedom . . . has no content save in a world wherein each individual spirit is through its own essential activity, freely related to all other spirits." "Faust," he remarks, "is only a grown up Emile." T. Davidson, *Rousseau and Education according to Nature* (1898; New York: Charles Scribner's Sons, 1971), 213, 229. As fully evidenced by the *Reveries*, Rousseau would not reject Davidson's definition; the question was whether such freedom was possible for men in the modern age and, if not, to what extent they could come close.

27. Would Descartes's successors "be more fortunate: will their system last longer? No . . . they are beginning to waiver; they will fall as well, they are the work of man." *Lettres morales*, in *OC*, 4:1096.

28. For Rousseau's intellectual relationship with the Enlightenment, see

T. Marshall's outstanding essay on the subject. Marshall discusses the way in which Rousseau's opposition "is based on thinking over the problem for moral stability posed by the fleeting currents of Enlightened opinions." T. Marshall, "Rousseau and the Enlightenment," *Trent Rousseau Papers* (Ottawa: Ottawa University Press, 1980), 42.

29. Even before he can introduce a romantic element to *Emile,* Rousseau makes considerable efforts to forge emotional links between the reader and Emile. Accounts of his tribulations, for example, dilute so far as possible the necessarily impossible conditions of his enforced isolation. When Rousseau invites the reader to "judge [Emile] by comparisons" by letting him "mix with other children and do as he pleases" (*E,* 161), the invitation is attractive but necessarily rhetorical. Because other children have been spoiled, Emile's education to the age of fifteen must be largely a solitary one.

30. The relationship and, indeed, unity of intent between *Emile* and the *Social Contract* is asserted by their author (who wrote them during the same period) but not satisfactorily explained by the commentators of whom I am aware. For example, Masters argues that "both are intended to free the individual from a dependence on other men qua individuals"—but, if this is true, they must do so in a dramatically different and unexplained manner. Ellenberg asserts that "Emile is educated to virtuous citizenship . . . [in] a miniature body politic"—but Emile, the man of nature, cannot simply be equated with the denatured citizen of the *Social Contract.* Roddier observes that *Emile* and the *Social Contract* emerge from "the same intellectual progress, even though they are centered on two apparently opposing themes"—but the only concrete parallelism Roddier identifies is the inflexibility of the Tutor's will and the general will, ignoring that the second is at least partly the creation of citizens. Chateau argues that the "goal of Emile . . . remains social reformation," but his assertion that this might occur through a "kind of confederation of families" run by Emiles illegitimately imports *La nouvelle Héloise* into what has to be an explanation of *Emile.* Vial, onetime inspector general of public education in France, offers an explanation that at least is internally coherent: "the pedagogy and politics of Rousseau . . . complement one another, or rather they are each but two forms of the moral problem which was Rousseau's constant preoccupation." Pierre Burgelin, the editor of *Emile* for the Pleiade edition, argues that "the incompatibility between man and citizen is nothing but an unhappy historical accident. In the authentic development of his essence, man must rediscover the citizen even if, as risks being the case for Emile, he does not find a country in which to reunite them." *OC,* 4:cvi. But Rousseau never suggests that the incompatibility was an accident. Almost alone Burgelin has the honesty to admit that the problem may be insoluble. He asks how "the individualism of Emile will be joined to the Spartan city of the Social Contract?" and reminds us that Emile will remain a "friendly stranger" in the public realm. R. Masters, *The Political Philosophy of Rousseau* (Princeton: Princeton University Press, 1968), 42. S. Ellenberg, *Rousseau's Political Philosophy: An Interpretation from Within* (Ithaca: Cornell University Press, 1976), 139. H. Roddier, "Education

et politique chez Jean-Jacques Rousseau," in *Jean-Jacques Rousseau et son oeuvre: problems et recherches* (Paris: C. Klincksieck, 1964), 190. J. Chateau, *Jean-Jacques Rousseau, sa philosophie de l'education* (Paris: Vrin, 1962), 239f. F. Vial, *La Doctrine d'education de Jean-Jacques Rousseau* (Paris: Librarie Delagare, 1920), 59. P. Burgelin, *La Philosophie de l'existence de Jean-Jacques Rousseau* (Paris: Press Universitaires de France, 1952), 504. Rousseau's claims about the relationships between his works are somewhat inconsistent; nevertheless, his argument that *Emile* and the *Two Discourses* "inseparable and together form a single whole" is not contradicted by other testimony and thus deserves attention. *Second Letter to Malesherbes*, in *OC*, 1:1136.

31. Since to some degree Emile embodies the savage (albeit a savage who must live in contemporary society), our argument would lead us to expect to find affinities between the psychological conditions of the savage and the moderns. Rousseau suggests as much when he describes modernity as bringing us to "the extreme point which closes the circle and touches the point from which we started" (*SD*, 177). The savage could not be described as free because free human beings are conscious of the fact of their freedom (114). Contemporary man was in the same condition: self-awareness had been surrendered, and man had once again become "nothing" (177). The parallelism, however, cannot be pushed too far. Rousseau is quite prepared to invoke the savage in the shape of a condemning ghost who would not "bend his head for the yoke that civilized man wears without a murmur" (164). It is an "immense space" that separates the peaceful savage from those whose strength and felicity has been enervated through the pursuit of goods superfluous to their needs (178).

32. Emile is trained as a carpenter because the trade can be "practiced at home." Rousseau contrasts the skill of carpentry with those professions Locke recommends: embroidery, gilding, and varnishing. Rousseau might have added that these trades each serve to embellish the unadorned item and are only necessary in a society whose members are seeking to be praised by their neighbor (*Emile*, 201).

33. Some twenty years earlier Rousseau had written in *Project for the Education of Saint-Marie:* "Too much care cannot be taken to give him a knowledge of men, so that he can . . . make use of them for his purpose" (*MEW*, 31).

34. Rousseau's discussion of pity in the *Second Discourse* is further complicated by his critique of Bernard Mandeville's treatment of pity in the *Fable of the Bees*. Mandeville's fable contrasts pity and virtue, while Rousseau attempts to construct virtue from pity. Nevertheless, Rousseau appears to accept Mandeville's contention that pity is a natural and universal human disposition. See *Fable of the Bees*, ed. F. B. Kaye (Oxford: Clarendon Press, 1924), 287–89.

35. "This is precisely how all *amour-propre* works; it subjugates the self in response to opinion and creates a second self which in turn subjects other men to these prejudices." Judith Shklar, *Men and Citizens* (Cambridge: Cambridge University Press, 1969), 90.

36. Rousseau does not here consider the alternative—namely, that pity

for others humbles the self-love of the pitier—in part because he reserves this possibility for use in the education of women.

37. Commentators sympathetic to Rousseau's account downplay the difficulty that Rousseau continually stresses. See N.J.H. Dent, *Rousseau* (Oxford: Basil Blackwell, 1988).

38. The question of why Plato's philosopher kings would wish to reenter society is legion: no obvious reason is provided. But Rousseau is not interested in the development of a judgment of Ideas or a training in the dialectic for the sake of that end. Emile is to be taught to measure the visible world, its rhetoric, its habits, and its myths.

39. The comment is accurate as regards *Emile*. But there is no necessary connection between stable society and stable marriages. Given the immense difficulty of grounding the latter on permanent psychological foundations, Rousseau vacillates between establishing the conditions necessary to promote those foundations (in the *Letter to D'Alembert*) and abandoning the whole effort (in *Political Economy*). See J. Schwartz, *The Sexual Politics of Jean-Jacques Rousseau* (Chicago: University of Chicago Press, 1984), 72.

40. See *Emile et Sophie, ou les Solitaires*, in *OC*, 4:900–910. The closing sections of Rousseau's text are lost, and accounts of them are contradictory. But Emile either deserts Sophie permanently or commits polygamy with her and a Spanish woman on a desert island. For a discussion of the textual issues, see *OC*, 4:clxi–clxvii..

41. There has been a debate between Rousseau scholars about the status that should be accorded to *La nouvelle Héloise* in the context of Rousseau's corpus as a whole. Leigh argues that it "is a novel, not a section of an unwritten treatise on ethics or politics." Shklar and Charvet dissent, seeing the work as an integral part of Rousseau's teaching. Since Rousseau had argued in the *First Discourse* (*FD*, 52f.) that the education of women was of crucial importance, and since he argues that the novel alone remains an organ of education in a corrupt society, (*NH*, in *OC*, 2:5f.), Leigh's argument appears to be splitting hairs. (Leigh's comments can be found following an article of Charvet's in *Rousseau after Two Hundred Years*, ed. R. A. Leigh [Cambridge: Cambridge University Press, 1982], 147.)

42. Philonenko calls this "the most decisive phrase in the *Nouvelle Héloise*." (A. Philonenko, *Jean-Jacques Rousseau et la pensée du mahleur* (Paris: Librarie Philosophique, J. Vrin, 1984), 2:25.

43. Claire's observations of her cousin Julie reinforce the conclusion that Saint-Preux is correct. She remarks that Julie was "born to rule" and calls her "empire" the "most absolute that I know" (*NH*, 2:409). Julie is a more effective ruler even than Wolmar, for she rules the hearts of all around her, even the laborers at Clarence (2:465).

44. In the same letter she boasts to her former lover that she and Wolmar "see each other as we are," but this is simply false. Wolmar subsequently admits to Claire that no "human eye," himself included, can pierce the veil that surrounds the intentions of his wife (*NH*, 2:509, 373).

45. The extraordinary popularity of the work in eighteenth-century Europe suggests that such identification was a standard reaction.

46. It is instructive to compare Emile's disdainful judgment of urban society with Saint-Preux's experience in Paris. Initially, Saint-Preux appears to react exactly as Emile, writing to Julie that "everything is absurd" (*NH*, 2:231). "The Parisian must leave his soul at the door and take up another one with the colors of the house." But Saint-Preux falls victim to the very absurdity he is able to discuss. Placing the specious values of his drinking companions above his own, Saint-Preux comes to grief in a Paris brothel.

47. Philonenko, contemplating this possibility, suggests that "the child of Saint-Preux would have been Emile." Philonenko, *Jean-Jacques Rousseau*, 2:44.

48. Although Schwartz fails to see that Wolmar's aims must remain only partially fulfilled, he accurately captures the nature of Julie's burden: "When . . . [she] considers her irrepressible love for Saint-Preux, the prospect of constant struggle frightens her; when she considers herself cured of her love for him, the prospect of a life from which struggle would be eternally absent bores her." Schwartz, *Sexual Politics*, 139. Realizing that she still loves Saint-Preux, Julie welcomes the approach of death, suggesting that boredom is more to be feared than the fear of struggle.

4: The Education of the Sovereign

1. C. E. Vaughan, *Jean-Jacques Rousseau: The Political Writings* (Cambridge: Basil Blackwell, 1952), 2:294.

2. See also *Lettres écrits de la Montagne, OC*, 3:828.

3. Rousseau used the geometric metaphor again in his private correspondence, equating the placing of men beneath the law with "squaring the circle." Letter to the Marquis de Mirabeau (1767), in *CC*, 33:240.

4. The state's "*essential* task, the point of departure and the basis of all government, is the task of education." E. Cassirer, *The Question of Jean-Jacques Rousseau*, ed. and trans. Peter Gay, (Indiana: University of Indiana Press, 1963), 62; emphasis added.

5. Rousseau's discussion of classical virtue stresses the spontaneity of its acquisition: in his imaginative reconstruction the Spartan has no conception of what it would mean not to be virtuous. As we have suggested, Emile's behavior up to the point where he must agree to leave Sophie has just this quality, and Rousseau's designs for Poland and Corsica attempt to duplicate circumstances in which citizens do not have to struggle to be virtuous. In general, however, Rousseau rejects the idea that such unconsciously possessed attributes represent virtue in the highest sense. What is worthy of man must be the consequence of a struggle, and the concept of struggle is inextricably linked to that of the possibility of choice. Nor is this only true of Emile and Sophie, or Julie and Saint-Preux. The ancient Corsicans "had no virtues; since, having no vices to overcome, it *cost them nothing* to be good." *Corsica*, 296; emphasis added. For the same reason, the savage in *The Second Discourse* had "neither vices nor virtues." *SD*, 128. In this sense, spontaneous patriotism is not, strictly speaking, a virtue. For more discussion of Rousseau's

ambivalence on the issue of virtue and struggle, see the conclusion of the present chapter.

6. In this context Rousseau is critical of D'Helvetius's claim that "a strong and pure virtue" depended on a "deep knowledge" of morality and politics. *Notes sur de l'esprit,* in *OC,* 4:1126.

7. For a sophisticated analysis of the issues posed by such intervention, see P. Coleman, *Rousseau's Political Imagination* (Geneva: Droz, 1984), 106. Coleman's account of the *Letter to D'Alembert* deserves greater attention than it has received.

8. Rousseau faces the same challenge that the Tutor had experienced with Emile: the citizens of Geneva, like the young man, would have to be made conscious of their own psychological condition in order that they may continue to exercise self-control.

9. The audience of Rousseau's opera, *The Village Soothsayer,* was supposed to react with disgust when confronted with the machinations of its antihero. Instead, "his deeds were thought charming because men who looked on themselves as honest folk recognized themselves in him feature by feature." Preface to *Narcisse,* 101.

10. Rousseau is careful to stress "how far it is from them [the Genevans] to the Lacadaemonians" and refuses to endorse any effort to indulge in wholesale importation of Spartan institutions. *Letter,* 134.

11. On the basis of this passage Miller concludes that "Rousseau's Geneva is clearly a place where the antinomies posed at the outset of *Emile* are resolved." (In *Emile* Rousseau had suggested that "one must choose between making a man and a citizen, for one cannot make both at the same time" *Emile,* 39). Since *Emile* was written after the *Letter to D'Alembert,* on which Miller relies, his conclusion is questionable, but our interpretation is sympathetic to Miller's reading. James Miller, *Rousseau: Dreamer of Democracy* (New Haven: Yale University Press, 1984), 46.

12. Tronchin had reminded Rousseau that the circles of Geneva were far from the ideal schools of citizenship which they appear to be in the text. Rousseau knew this full well but defended even existing institutions on the usual grounds that innovation would be for the worse. *CC,* 5:242.

13. Rousseau's sexual politics are extremely complex, as Joel Schwartz has convincingly demonstrated. Recall Schwartz's claim that "Rousseau praises sexual differentiation because it can make a non-exploitative society possible"—it is this feature of sexual desire which interests Rousseau in the case of Geneva. Schwartz, *The Sexual Politics of Jean-Jacques Rousseau* (Chicago: University of Chicago Press, 1984), 6. It is instructive to compare Rousseau's defense of the separation of the sex roles with Jean Baudrillard's strikingly similar discussion of "seduction," which he valorizes as the truly feminine "play . . . of the strategy of appearances." Both thinkers are convinced that unlimited sexual "liberation" represents only a pyrrhic victory for the feminine: in Baudrillard's words, "Proliferation is close to total destruction." Jean Baudrillard, *Revenge of the Crystal,* ed. and trans. Paul Foss and Julian Pefanis (London: Pluto Press, 1990), 131, 129.

14. To T. Lenieps. Rousseau remarked that "in every land men are the

sort that women make them: that is of necessity, it is inevitable, it is the law of nature." *CC*, 5:213.

15. Miller argues that the circles constitute "a distinctly modern space where a political education can occur in public." Miller, *Rousseau*, 34.

16. Coleman, *Rousseau's Political Imagination*, 146.

17. The claim is made in Rousseau's *Letters from the Mountain*, a fact that leads some commentators to dismiss it as a desperate attempt at self-defense. *Mountain*, in *OC*, 3:809f. But Fralin makes a convincing argument that many crucial features of the *Social Contract*, including Rousseau's opposition to any form of indirect representation, are explicable only on the basis of his attachment to Genevois institutions: "the parallels between the city and the claims of the Genevan Bourgeoisie are indeed striking." R. Fralin, *Rousseau and Representation* (New York: Columbia University Press, 1978), 135.

18. Riley argues that this represents a "paradox of willed non-voluntarism" which "cannot be defended." P. Riley, "A Possible Explanation of Rousseau's General Will," *American Political Science Review* 64, no. 1 (March 1970): 87. Paterman argues in response that, since the citizens can always "reassess their 'beginning,'" "it makes sense to speak of social life as a voluntary scheme." C. Paterman, *The Problem of Political Obligation* (Berkeley: University of California Press, 1985), 154f.

19. The problem is recurrent in Western thought. Once the founding contract has been signed, its co-authors will be legitimated by the signed contract. But how can that signing retroactively legitimate those cosigners as having the authority to sign themselves into that authority? For a useful discussion of the views of Hannah Arendt and Jacques Derrida on this problem, see Bonnie Honig, "Declarations of Independence," *American Political Science Review*, 85, no. 1 (March 1991): 97–113.

20. In the context of a very different argument, Cell also suggests that the citizen has such a choice of perspectives. H. Cell, "Breaking Rousseau's Chains," *Trent Papers* (Ottawa: Ottawa University Press, 1980), 166ff.

21. For an argument suggesting that Rousseau's discomfort with "partial societies" was a consequence of weaknesses in his theory of the general will, see A. Levine, *The Politics of Autonomy: A Kantian Reading of Rousseau's Social Contract* (Amherst: University of Massachusetts Press, 1976), 105. Levine accuses Rousseau of creating an artificial distinction between private and general wills in order to ban partial societies on the grounds that they represent neither one.

22. This condition gives Rousseau considerable trouble. Following the passage quoted, Rousseau states that "the law can very well enact that there will be privileges . . . [it] can create several classes of citizens, and even designate the qualities determining who has a right to these classes." *SC*, 66. It is not literally true, *pace* Rousseau's claim, that "every authentic act of the general will, obligates or favors all citizens equally" (63). Rousseau had written more accurately when he asserted that "the sovereign . . . cannot impose on the subjects any burden that is useless to the community" (62). Charvet's fine analysis of these passages points out that Rousseau "systematically confuses" conditions of equal rights, universality, and generality.

J. Charvet, *The Social Problem in the Philosophy of Rousseau* (Cambridge: Cambridge University Press, 1974), 131.

23. Of all those commentaries on the *Social Contract* which are known to me, Paterman alone argues that the work lays out a program of autonomously generated civic education. "The logic of the participatory process itself has an educative effect . . . individuals are gradually educated to think in terms of the general will." Paterman, *Problem of Political Obligation,* 156. Paterman stresses the fact that a substantial measure of material equality is a necessary precondition for the success of the educative process: only so can their wills be considered unconstrained (155). Paterman's brief but suggestive remarks offer support for our present analysis. In an otherwise critical account of Rousseau's *Social Contract,* Rang concedes that Rousseau is concerned with the way in which a "public education" can develop "the political intelligence and moral conscience of each citizen." M. Rang, "L'Education publique et la formation des citoyons chez Jean-Jacques Rousseau," *Etudes sur le Contract Social Jean-Jacques Rousseau* (Paris: Publication de l'Universite de Dijon, Société des Belles Lettres, 1964), 30:262.

24. Rousseau can thus argue that the demands of the general will are "derived from each man's preference for himself and consequently from the nature of man." *SC,* 62.

25. Opaque to the point where many readers have been content to ignore it! (For example, in *Etudes sur le Contract Social,* a collection of essays running to some several hundred pages, not a single effort is made to decipher Rousseau's meaning). In his essay Riley makes a brief reference to the voting procedure with no attempt to decipher it. More substantial attention has been paid in the commentaries of A. Philonenko, *Jean-Jacques Rousseau et la pensée du malheur* (Paris: Librarie Philosophique, J. Vrin, 1984), 3 vols., 3:30–33; Charvet, *The Social Problem,* 127; and Dent, *Rousseau: An Introduction to His Psychological, Social, and Political Theory* (New York: Basil Blackwell, 1989), 204. The most complete attempt to explain the voting procedure is in J. Hall, *Rousseau: An Introduction to His Political Philosophy* (London: Macmillan, 1973), 127–36. The literature on the general will is vast. A number of readings are plausible: Viroli stresses the double role of Republican ideals of rational justification and the contractarian vocabulary of the maintenance of civic harmony. The general will, in this account, enables men to abide by the dictates of natural law. M. Viroli, *Jean-Jacques Rousseau and the "Well-Ordered Society"* (New York: Cambridge University Press, 1988), 13. Dent offers a communitarian reading. The general will operated only when "I am looking for the accord of someone who is looking for accord with me." In Dent's view the loss of will to seek social harmony marks the collapse of the general will. Dent, *Rousseau,* 166.

26. The most coherent account of these passages known to me in Arthur Melzer's. In Melzer's view the general will is simply an extension of men's natural selfishness in a situation in which selfishness has become contradictory and enslaving. To be made unselfish becomes the most "selfish" solution. "Rousseau believes that his principles of political right constitute an empirical description of the universal and self-evident rules of human cooperation."

See Arthur Melzer, *The Natural Goodness of Man: On the System of Rousseau's Thought* (Chicago: University of Chicago Press, 1990), 168.

27. These difficulties are dealt with later in the text in ways that are quite perfunctory and have nothing to do with the lawgiver, whose role they are supposed to justify. But Rousseau was not one to despair in half-measures.

28. This vote, which takes place once the characteristics of the general will are no longer in the majority, is not however meaningless. As Judith Shklar reminded me, such a vote evidences Rousseau's conviction that a majority of the citizens, sooner or later, will reject the artificially created common identity. The natural man in every citizen will reassert himself, and the state will disintegrate.

29. In a work that stresses the individualistic elements of Rousseau's thought, Perkins goes so far as to claim that to "will generally" the individual must rediscover "the meaning and value of his private self." M. Perkins, *Jean-Jacques Rousseau: On the Individual and Society* (Lexington: University Press of Kentucky, 1974), 267.

30. The citizens are reduced "to a condition of being which is nothing but a kind of empty void." R. Polin, *Le Sens de l'égalité et de l'inégalité chez Jean-Jacques Rousseau*, in the Dijon Papers.

31. Emile's tutor does much the same—allowing Emile to believe that he is master of his own will, while in fact he always chooses to do what the tutor has preordained. The likeness between the two authority figures has been convincingly argued. Shklar, *Men and Citizens*, 155. Nevertheless, Emile was given an education fitting to a child who is naturally helpless, who is not denatured as the citizen must be. Moreover, the child and citizen enjoy very different degrees of freedom. (See the following text).

32. The standard account in English is still Roger Masters, *The Political Philosophy of Rousseau* (Princeton: Princeton University Press, 1968), 335ff.

33. As Noone reminds us: "Autonomy is an ambiguous term. As applied to a political group it signifies a competence to authorize laws . . . [as regards the individual] it is a voluntary, non-prudential acceptance of the law even against inclination. Self-imposition must never be confused with self-authorization." J. Noone, *Rousseau's Social Contract: A Conceptual Analysis* (Athens: University of Georgia Press, 1984), 34. Self-authorization remains the cornerstone of Rousseau's social contract, but the task of self-imposition becomes instinctive if the lawgiver is successful.

34. Rousseau called the lawgiver "an extraordinary man." *SC*, 68. But his readers have not agreed. Philonenko sees the lawgiver's task as a "desperate effort" to remedy the defects of all possible forms of government. Philonenko, 3:55. Shklar calls the lawgiver a "wooden, one dimensional figure." Shklar, *Men and Citizens*, 155. Not surprisingly, Carole Pateman fails to mention the lawgiver at all.

35. Rousseau's reluctance to countenance change has been frequently noted. In *Letters from the Mountain* he conveyed his feelings succinctly: "when in doubt, stop every innovation large or small" (*Mountain*, 3:873).

36. A close study of *Letters from the Mountain* indicates that Rousseau saw himself in the role of calling Geneva back to its political traditions, not

recasting them afresh. The constitution he defended was far from fully democratic and certainly did not include the rights Rousseau grants to the popular assembly in the *Social Contract*. For a discussion of the issue, see Candaux's introduction to the *Lettres écrites de la Montagne, OC*, 4:clxii. The tortuous history of the struggles between the Genevese bourgeois and the patriciate is summarized in Fralin, *Rousseau and Representation* (New York: Columbia University Press, 1978), 135. He makes the point that the *conseil general* was composed of "no more than 1,500 of a total population of perhaps 25,000." Moreover, Rousseau refused to support legislation that would have given even this body the legislative initiative. Rousseau supported the right of the *petit conseil* to veto popular efforts to change the law.

37. Rousseau wrote to Mlle. Henriette: "You think that the sole alleviation of the painful feeling tormenting you is to withdraw from yourself. But I, on the contrary, believe that you should draw closer within yourself" (*CC*, letter no. 2076, dated May 7, 1764).

38. In his classic work on the subject Starobinski traces the ways in which this dream recurs throughout the texts of Rousseau. Starobinski argues that, above all else, Rousseau wished to remove those obstacles that blocked immediate access to the nature of others and to an awareness of oneself: "the restoration of a compromised transparency." This chapter has suggested that transparency is not a luxury all can afford to pursue, but Starobinski's claim with regard to Rousseau himself is beautifully sustained. J. Starobinski, *Jean-Jacques Rousseau*, 14.

39. On January 4, 1762, Rousseau wrote to M. De Malesherbes: "The kind of happiness I need is not so much that of doing what I want as not doing what I do not want to do. . . . I have fancied a hundred times that I should not have been too unhappy in the Bastille, since I would have nothing to do but to stay there." *CC*, 1132. The prospect of immanent death produced similar thoughts of quiescence and felicity. For discussion of Rousseau's intimations of mortality, see Elizabeth Kelly, *Public Knowledge, Education, and Democracy* (Boulder: Westview Press, 1994), 149.

40. Also cited in ibid., 111.

41. Writers sympathetic to Rousseau's attack on the bourgeois, and his egalitarianism, simply refuse to accept the pessimism that pervades Rousseau's recommendations. Colletti, in an otherwise perceptive treatment, argues that Rousseau "unwittingly criticizes social relationships as such . . . [and] finds himself driven, against his intentions, to counterpose life in solitude and life in society." L. Colletti, *From Rousseau to Lenin* (New York: Monthly Review Press, 1972), 164.

42. Starobinski, *Jean-Jacques Rousseau*, 157.

5: Dewey and the Vocabulary of Growth

1. To substantiate this claim would require another book. Suffice to say that the "Profession of Faith of the Savoyard Vicar," that section of *Emile* in which Rousseau comes closest to presenting a metaphysics, is fraught with

interpretive problems, inconsistencies with Rousseau's other works, and questions regarding Rousseau's own loyalty to the doctrines he puts in the vicar's mouth. For further discussion, see Arthur Melzer, *The Natural Goodness of Man: On the System of Rousseau's Thought* (Chicago: University of Chicago Press, 1990), 30.

2. Hereafter, titles of all primary texts are abbreviated. See the list of abbreviations in the front of the book.

3. This conglomerate phrase is intended to convey something of Dewey's rejection of the Cartesian divide of self and world, a division extensively discussed below. It is not intended to suggest any further philosophical allegiance.

4. G. W. F. Hegel, *The Philosophy of Right*, trans. T. M. Knox (Oxford: Oxford University Press, 1967), 125.

5. Dewey's conception of such syntheses bears some obvious similarities with Rousseau's thought: in particular, when Rousseau designs a pedagogic project for Geneva. But there are important differences: social life and nature are, in Dewey's thought, to be arrayed on a continuum, not bifurcated as they are in so many of Rousseau's writings.

6. The few references to Dewey are peripheral to Gutmann's argument and are not designed to illuminate Dewey's own. See, for example, Amy Gutmann, *Democratic Education* (Princeton: Princeton University Press, 1987), 13.

7. Steven M. Cahn, ed., *New Studies in the Philosophy of John Dewey*, (Hanover, N.H.: University Press of New England, 1977), 4. In the same volume Frederick Olufson complains of the "barren avenues" of Dewey's prose and the "highly ambiguous" status of his educational thought. (In ibid., 172f.).

8. E. D. Hirsch, Jr., *Cultural Literacy* (Boston: Houghton Mifflin Co., 1987), 119, 192.

9. I. L. Horowitz, ed., *Sociology and Pragmatism: The Higher Learning in America* (New York: Cambridge University Press, 1966), 405; and M. Oakeshott, *Experience and Its Modes* (Cambridge: Cambridge University Press, 1933), 396.

10. A. H. Somjee, *The Political Theory of John Dewey* (New York: Teachers College Press, Columbia University, 1968), 178.

11. J. Gouinlock, *Excellence in Public Discourse: John Stuart Mill, John Dewey, and Social Intelligence* (New York: Teachers College Press, Columbia University, 1986).

12. Alfonso Daminco, *Individuality and Community: The Social and Political Thought of John Dewey* (Gainesville: University Presses of Florida, 1978).

13. For the initial reference, see Richard Rorty, *Philosophy and the Mirror of Nature* (Princeton: Princeton University Press, 1979), 368. For a summary with bibliographical references of the following controversy, see Robert Westbrook, *John Dewey and American Democracy* (Ithaca: Cornell University Press, 1991), 540–41.

14. James Gouinlock, *John Dewey's Philosophy of Value* (New York: Humanities Press, 1972); Thomas Alexander, *John Dewey's Theory of Art, Experience and Nature: The Horizons of Feeling* (Albany: State University of New York,

1987); R. W. Sleeper, *The Necessity of Pragmatism* (New Haven: Yale University Press, 1986); Sandra B. Rosenthal, *Speculative Pragmatism* (Amherst: University of Massachusetts Press, 1986); Larry A. Hickman, *John Dewey's Pragmatic Technology* (Bloomington: Indiana University Press, 1990). The transformation of Dewey's standing is well captured in Hickman's assertion that "it is a widely accepted view among progressional philosophers that the most innovative and influential philosophers of the twentieth century are Wittgenstein, Heidegger and Dewey." Hickman, *John Dewey's Pragmatic Technology*, 199. As Alexander notes, the publication of John Dewey's complete works by Southern Illinois University Press has itself done much to revive interest in Dewey's philosophy. Recently Robert Westbrook has written an intellectual biography of Dewey. A Herculean effort of synthesis, this is the only work that has attempted to integrate Dewey's often opaque philosophy, political theory, and educational views. (See chap. 1, n. 2.) Note should also be taken of *John Dewey: Critical Assessments*, ed. J. E. Tiles (London: Routledge, 1992), 4 vols.

15. H. L. Mencken to A. G. Keller, April 22, 1940; Lewis Mumford, *The Golden Day*, 3d ed. (New York: Dover, 1968), 131. Both remarks are cited by Westbrook, who himself remarks that Dewey is "often damnably opaque." Westbrook, *John Dewey and American Democracy*, 501, 381, 144.

16. Daminco, *Individuality and Community*, 29.

17. Rosenthal, *Speculative Pragmatism*, 22.

18. J. Dewey, *Liberalism and Social Action* (New York: G. P. Putnam's Sons, 1935), 61. I am not implying that this is Dewey's only definition of philosophy.

19. Sleeper, *Necessity of Pragmatism*, 61.

20. Ibid., 120.

21. It is important to note Dewey's choice of language here: nature is an affair of constraints and movements of overcoming, of expansion. A politics that attempts to ignore this seminal condition will frustrate those human capacities that embody it.

22. T. M. Alexander, *John Dewey's Theory*, 110.

23. And compare his formal definition later in the chapter: "consciousness is the meaning of events in the course of remaking" *EN*, 308.

24. Alexander states that "consciousness . . . is characterized by an immediate focus of intensive concern, a proximate sense of context, and a tacitly felt horizon which provides the ultimate determining ground of meaning." *John Dewey's Theory*, xix. Dewey insists that consciousness could not operate without this essential sense—but the sense itself is formed out of habitual patterns of past behavior in the world which we are conscious of only when they are disturbed. Undisturbed patterns of interaction with the environment are characterized in Dewey's terminology as "mind." *EN*, 303.

25. Alexander, *John Dewey's Theory*, 113.

26. One commentator suggests usefully that "Dewey considered knowledge itself a matter of association of associations." See Robert J. Vichot, "John Dewey and the Pragmatist Foundation of American Political Realism: Social Interaction and Public Discourse" (paper presented at the American Political Science Association meeting, 1989), 17.

27. As Gouinlock puts it: "man's contact with nature is removed from sheer immediacy into significance." *John Dewey's Philosophy*, 89.

28. As Paul Conkin reminds me, Dewey's use of *behave* is inconsistent: in this context a more precise word would have been *act*.

29. Alexander, *John Dewey's Theory*, 128.

30. Complex to the point that the present reading can only be regarded as an introduction. For a more technical discussion, see Sandra Rosenthal, *Speculative Pragmatism*, chap. 2.

31. In his writings on art Dewey remarks that, "although there is a bounding horizon, it moves as we move. We are never wholly free from this sense of something that lies beyond." *AE*, 193.

32. This emphasis on action is worth stressing. Only an act can establish a new history, which can represent a source of knowledge. But this is not to say that other forms of meaning do not exist: "apart from considerations of use and history there are no original and inherent differences between valid meanings and meanings occurring in revelry, desiring, fearing, remembering." Dewey concludes that "the matter of the history to which a given thing belongs is just the matter with which knowledge is concerned." *EN*, 339, 322f.

33. Notable exceptions are Hickman, *John Dewey's Pragmatic Technology;* and Rosenthal, *Speculative Pragmatism*.

34. Dewey stresses the concept of relationships throughout his account; see *QC*, in *LW*, 4:100.

35. On the greater complexity of the human environment compared with that faced by the scientist, see *QC*, 4:216. The criteria of repeatability is stressed in *EN*, 49.

36. Hickman, *John Dewey's Pragmatic Technology*, 19.

37. Letter from John Dewey to Arthur F. Bentley, April 9, 1951, cited in Hickman, *John Dewey's Pragmatic Technology*, 4.

38. Timothy V. Kufman-Osborn, "Modernity and the Politics of Meaning" (paper delivered at the annual meeting of the American Political Science Association, Atlanta, 1989), 4.

6: The Education of Experience

1. Eugene Rochberg-Halton, *Meaning and Modernity: Social Theory in the Pragmatic Attitude* (Chicago: University of Chicago Press, 1986), 12 and 185.

2. R. W. Sleeper, *The Necessity of Pragmatism* (New Haven: Yale University Press, 1986), 143. On inferences, see also Hickman, *John Dewey's Pragmatic Technology*, 116–17. Hickman stresses Dewey's conviction that inferences are behavioral; they are "productive activity" in which "new entities are created," 117.

3. J. J. McDermott, ed., *The Philosophy of John Dewey* (Chicago: University of Chicago Press, 1981).

4. For further discussion of this issue, see Roberto J. Vichot, "John Dewey and the Pragmatist Foundation of American Political Realism: Social Inter-

course and Public Discourse" (paper presented at the American Political Science Association meeting, Atlanta, 1989), 17, 23. I am indebted to this article for the citation from Dewey.

5. James Gouinlock, *John Dewey's Philosophy of Value* (New York: Humanities Press, 1972), 88.

6. Dewey's examples are homely ones. A traffic officer's signal, "liberated from the contingencies of its prior use," may be studied by experts and produce "a new and improved system of semaphores." *EN,* 193.

7. Trotsky's essay and Dewey's rejoinder can be found in a collection of the same title: *Their Morals and Ours,* ed. D. Salner (New York: Pathfinder Press, 1977), 49, 48.

8. Ibid., 71, 73, 71, 70.

9. Ironically, Dewey's omission is akin to that he accuses Trotsky of. Is the development through education of a mass collectivist mentality the only path to social emancipation? In 1928 Dewey was willing to believe that it might be.

10. In 1937 Dewey remarked that "the revelations have been a bitter disillusionment to me personally." *LW,* 11:335.

11. While a detailed comparison between Dewey's conception of knowledge and Michel Foucault's model of a discipline lies outside this study, the similarities are striking. What most differentiates the two is the normative tone: Foucault sees disciplines as liquid flows inscribing themselves on the body, subjecting and subjugating the body as a vehicle for their growth. Dewey sees the same thing but regards the individual as more active in his or her capacity to redirect, reassemble, and reconstruct the knowledge/disciplines to which he or she is subject.

12. This example, which is taken entirely from Dewey's text, indicates how muddleheaded are certain of the recent attacks on his educational work. Hirsch, one of those who accuses Dewey of promoting a kind of irresponsible philistinism strives to establish just the kind of educated sensibility that his primary school offered. See Edward D. Hirsch, Jr., *Cultural Literacy* (Boston: Houghton Mifflin Co., 1987), 121.

13. Dewey's work in education betrays a certain ambiguity of purpose. Although he suggests in these passages that young students be presented with a purified knowledge, elsewhere he appears to lean toward a greater realism. Thus, we find him remarking the following: "if we Americans manifest a kind of infantilism, it is because our schooling so largely evades serious consideration of the deeper issues of social life; for it is only through induction into realities that the mind can be matured." *ION,* in *LW,* 5:102.

14. Hickman, *John Dewey's Pragmatic Technology,* 48.

15. Also quoted in Gouinlock, *Excellence in Public Discourse,* 113.

16. In his useful introduction to *Quest for Certainty,* Stephen Toulmin recalls that "the primary meaning of *theoria*" was "being an onlooker" (*QC,* xiv).

17. John Dewey, *Construction and Criticism* (New York: Columbia University Press, 1930).

18. Michel Foucault, *The Order of Things* (New York: Random House, 1973), 321–23.

19. See Alexander's extensive discussion of this and related passages, 250–66, in Thomas Alexander, *John Dewey's Theory of Art, Experience and Nature* (Albany: State University of New York, 1987).

20. See, for example, Rosenthal, *Speculative Pragmatism*, 193.

21. Friedrich Nietzsche, *Beyond Good and Evil*, trans. Walter Kaufmann (New York: Random House, 1989), 83.

7: *Thinking to Learn*

1. "I will be satisfied if we can teach children to read, write and calculate." Arthur Schlesinger, Jr., "Toward a Divisive Diversity," *Wall Street Journal*, June 25, 1991. For a similar view from the academy, see James Q. Wilson in "Reforming the Schools," *Commentary* 92, no. 6 (December 1991).

2. David C. Paris, "Moral Education and the 'Tie that Binds' in Liberal Political Theory," *American Political Science Review* 85, no. 3 (1991): 889.

3. "A Survey of Education," *Economist*, November 21, 1992.

4. Adler, *Reforming Education*, 58.

5. Philosophers sympathetic to the compromises of liberal democracy but faithful to the Platonic example have tended to stress Socratic dialectic rather than Plato's metaphysics of ideal forms in their work. For a sophisticated example, see Thomas Pangle, *The Ennobling of Democracy* (Baltimore: Johns Hopkins University Press, 1992).

6. John Rawls, "The Idea of an Overlapping Consensus," *Philosophy and Public Affairs* 17 (1988): 17.

7. Benhabib defends a "historically self-conscious universalism." "The principles of universal respect and egalitarian reciprocity are our philosophical clarification of the constituents of the moral view from within the hermeneutic horizon of modernity." Seyla Benhabib, "In the Shadow of Aristotle and Hegel: Communicative Ethics and Current Controversies in Practical Philosophy," *philosophical forum* 21, nos. 1–2 (Fall–Winter 1989–90): 8.

8. While such theorists do not endorse the full-blown anti-universalism of Richard Rorty, they come close to accepting that "there is nothing to be said about either truth or rationality apart from descriptions of the familiar procedures of justification that a given society—ours—uses in one or another area of inquiry." Metaphysics gives way to an "account of the value of co-operative human inquiry," which "has only an ethical base." Richard Rorty, "Solidarity or Objectivity?" in *Anti-theory in Ethics and Moral Conservatism*, ed. Stanley Clarke and Evan Simpson (Albany: State University of New York Press, 1989), 169–70.

9. In the case of John Rawls's conception of justice, the trope of the "original position" which formalizes his intuitions is itself quite opaque. That my sense of justice should be captured most exactly through a process of self-blinding suggests an oedipal movement that Rawls nevertheless appears to regard as persuasive. See John Rawls, *A Theory of Justice* (Oxford: Oxford University Press, 1971).

10. Michael Walzer suggests that the role of philosopher, connected critic, and political leader are mutually incompatible, or at least that they must be conceptually distinguished. Rousseau's life and work suggest that a combination of the first two, at least, is possible. See Michael Walzer, "Philosophy and Democracy" in *What Should Political Theory be Now?* ed. John S. Nelson (Albany: State University of New York Press, 1983).

11. William Connolly, *Political Theory and Modernity* (Oxford: Basil Blackwell, 1988), 71.

12. Charles Taylor, *Human Agency and Language* (Cambridge: Cambridge University Press, 1985), 3. Taylor further refines this language in later work, but the spatial metaphors remain. See, for example, his assertion that "we take it as basic that the human agent exists in a space of questions." In Charles Taylor, *Sources of the Self* (Cambridge: Harvard University Press, 1989), 27.

13. Connolly, *Political Theory and Modernity*, 145, 161.

14. Ibid., 167.

15. "ethics, politics and history: an interview with jurgen habermas conducted by jean-marc ferry" (*sic*), *Philosophy and Social Criticism* 14, nos. 3–4 (1988): 436.

16. A final example comes from James Donald, whose postmodernist treatment of education warns us not to be driven by a "performative political ideal" and simultaneously joins the chorus in seeking to privilege" a kernel of shared values and beliefs: empathy, sensitivity to difference, tolerance and mutual respect." James Donald, *Sentimental Education* (London: Verso, 1992), 167.

17. Benjamin Barber, *An Aristocracy of Everyone* (New York: Ballantine Books, 1992), 134. I am in sympathy with many of the points Barber makes in this book; his levelheaded look at the culture and practice of American education and his sympathy toward the insights of Rousseau and Dewey are attractive. I differ on two essential points: first, Barber is impatient with theoretical reasoning. Against Allan Bloom's impassioned Platonism one finds a sketchy view that the philosophical support for education must "stop" "somewhere" between "orthodoxy and cant," 123. At the same time, Barber claims that "justice and democracy are . . . illusions," 124. I am convinced we must lay out our democratic convictions rigorously: I do not believe that theory and democratic education are natural enemies. Second, as the quotation I cite makes clear, I find Barber too ready to embrace the formula of *e pluribus unum*. (Barber translates this tag into the image of a national quilt in which many patches are sown together, 130. I am unsure how one can be "sensitive" to difference by "overcoming it.")

18. The classic description of this phenomena is still David Riesman's *The Lonely Crowd: A Study of the Changing American Character* (New Haven: Yale University Press, 1961).

19. Stanley Aronowitz and Henry Giroux, *postmodern education* (Minneapolis: University of Minnesota Press, 1991), 128–29.

20. The reader might expect that postmodernism and liberal consensus have little in common, but increasingly, the reverse is the case. Even Michel

Foucault, just before his death, warned that "one must be against nonconsensuality." Foucault, "Politics and Ethics: An Interview," in *The Foucault Reader*, ed. Paul Rabinow (New York: Pantheon Books, 1984), 379.

21. Aronowitz and Giroux, *postmodern education*, 21.

22. Interestingly, Foucault comes close to endorsing Rousseau's view on this point. See Rabinow, *Foucault Reader*, 169.

23. Donald, *Sentimental Education*, 94.

24. Ibid., 175.

25. John Dewey, *Democracy and Education* (New York: Macmillan, 1986), 101.

26. Martin Heidegger, *What Is Called Thinking?* trans. J. Glenn Grey (New York: Harper and Row, 1968), 14–15.

27. Aronowitz and Giroux, *postmodern education*, 188–89.

28. Dianne Ravitch, "Multiculturalism," *American Scholar* (Summer 1990).

29. Václav Havel, *Living in Truth* (London: Faber and Faber, 1986), 157, 174. Havel's thought is itself deeply indebted to the work of Martin Heidegger.

30. John Dewey, *Art as Experience* (New York: Perigee Printing, 1980), 244.

31. Rorty, *Solidarity or Objectivity*, 177.

32. Benhabib, *In the Shadow of Aristotle and Hegel*, 13.

33. Donald, *Sentimental Education*, 166. I employed the model of democratic education as conversation in a paper ("Towards a Theory of Democratic Education") presented at the American Political Science Association annual meeting, Atlanta, 1989.

34. Scholars of what has come to be known as "communicative ethics" will rightly argue that this assertion greatly simplifies their efforts to justify a particular set of conditions as constitutive of a "legitimate" public discourse. The point is that such efforts make no final appeal to transcendental justifications, nor do they recognize incommensurable arenas of public speech.

35. Connolly, *Political Theory and Modernity*, 170.

36. An example of elegant avoidance is found in Pangle, *Ennobling of Democracy*. Almost no indication is given about how the model of Socratic reasoning might be brought to life in the classroom. For a sense of the apologetic approach, see Barber, *An Aristocracy of Everyone:* "Like most books on education, this one is two-fifths analysis, two-fifths criticism, and one-tenth polemic. (Am I too kind to myself?) This leaves but a tenth or so of the manuscript for constructive proposals," 230.

37. This particular list, with the exception of Foxfire and the Whole Language models, comes from President Bush's "Education 2000" proposals.

38. It is, of course, not quite so simple. Nevertheless, the vast "effective schools" literature is close to consensus on these points. For a summary along these lines, see *New York Times*, July 15, 1992. For more detailed discussion, see Edward B. Fiske, *Why Do Some Schools Work?* (New York: Simon and Schuster, 1991).

39. See U.S. Department of Education, "World Class Standards for American Education" (Washington, D.C.: USGPO, 1992). President Clinton's "Goals 2000" educational program does not appreciably alter President

Bush's "Education 2000" plans for voluntary national standards in the core disciplines. I am one of many consultants on one of the panels (for civic education) but, obviously, have no responsibility for the resulting document.

40. Center for Civic Education, "Draft National Standards for Civics and Government" (Calabasas, Calif.: 1992), 8.

41. Friedrich Nietzsche, *The Will to Power*, ed. and trans. Walter Kaufmann (New York: Vintage Books, 1967), 512.

42. The most recent major overhaul of a Western national curriculum, that instituted by the National Education Reform Act of 1988 in Great Britain, retains and indeed strengthens the division of the curriculum into these discrete subjects.

43. See E. E. Schattschneider, *The Semisovereign People: A Realist View of Democracy in America*, 1st ed. (New York: Holt, Rinehart and Winston, 1960).

44. For example, John Dewey's organic naturalism produces too one-sided a translation. For Dewey the public discourse, suitably purged of the lingering effects of class, nationality, and race, is the only legitimate source of self-discovery. But Dewey's splendid animus toward social barriers that block self-awareness illegitimately tars all particular discourses with the stain of irrationality. To confront the public discourse is not necessarily to embrace it. George Kateb may be right to suggest that in certain cases "there will be mutual recognition, but there need not be very much mutuality beyond that." See Dewey, *Democracy and Education*, 87; George Kateb, "Democratic Individuality and the Meaning of Rights" (unpub. MS, 1989), 11.

45. New tools available to teachers are helping to bring historical debates to life. While a teacher may conjure great excitement from the printed word alone, there is no reason why educators should banish from the schoolroom technologies that attract children outside it.

46. Later I take up the question of whether certain challenges to the core must be excluded absolutely from core legitimation.

47. Richard Lanham, "Extraordinary Convergence," in *The Politics of Liberal Education*, ed. Darryl J. Gless and Barbara Hernstein Smith (Durham, N.C.: Duke University Press, 1992), 38.

48. In certain cases the content of at least one dramatic presentation may be dictated by events. In a number of more disadvantaged or volatile educational communities, role playing can enable students to defuse the most immediately violent of their passions. One such program, which uses just such role playing, is the "Second Step Program." For a description, see *USA Today*, November 18, 1992. The article reminds us that some 280,000 students are physically attacked by one another in the United States each month.

49. America's largest producer of interactive educational software is Jostens Learning Corporation. To date, much of this software has been aimed at the primary and middle school areas, but this is changing. Lucas Arts Learning has developed an interactive course: "GTV: a Geographical Perspective on American History" for grades 5 through 12, which is currently purchased by more than five thousand schools.

50. See Theodore Sizer, *Horace's School*, chaps. 3 and 4. I am indebted to Sizer and his colleagues for a number of the pragmatic features of these

suggestions, in particular the multiple forms of projects undertaken by the students and the stress on forging connections between them. I have also learned from discussions of the Foxfire and Whole Language programs. The literature on these topics is extensive: for an introduction, see, respectively, J. Puckett, *Foxfire Reconsidered* (Chicago: University of Chicago Press, 1989); and the discussion and bibliography in *School Administrator* (May 1992): 20–26.

51. I am sympathetic to Benjamin Barber's call for compulsory community service on the part of high school students so long as the projects are directed at the community level. Such an approach should keep the center of authority in the school, as opposed to an external political body; it could offer a clear academic content; and its particular structure could be developed by the students. At the time of writing Congress has passed initial legislation offering university tuition support for high school students who conduct national service. My concern here is the obvious economic bias built into such plans: Why should the economically disadvantaged alone have to serve their way into college? For Barber's view, see Barber, *Strong Democracy*, chap. 7.

52. The example is provided in "National Tests: What Other Countries Expect Their Students to Know" (Washington, D.C.: National Endowment for the Humanities, 1991), 3.

53. Sizer, *Horace's School,* 106.

54. I would hope, of course, that such organizations would make decisions based on the accumulated school records of the student, which would include work in the specialized areas, as well as on the basis of the general questions.

55. More detailed information on the current state of American vocational training is available from the National Center for Research in Vocational Training at the University of California, Berkeley. A summary of the Danish programs can be found in *USA Today,* January 27, 1993.

56. Timothy Fuller, ed., *Michael Oakeshott on Education* (New Haven: Yale University Press, 1989), 28.

57. Ibid., 41.

58. Dewey, *Art as Experience,* 38.

Index

to *Emile,* 113, 119; and Hobbes, 114; ideal of freedom in, 115; Lawgiver compared to Emile's Tutor, 119; model of educated judgment in, 114–16; origins of, 113–14; public and private selves in, 117–18; voting difficulties concerning, 117–18
Socrates, 32, 36, 38, 48–56, 61; contrasted with Sophists, 49–53; protreptics of, 49, 54
Socratic virtues, 8
Solon, 117
Somjee, A. H., 130
Sophists, xiv, 30–32, 35, 37, 47, 49–59, 184–86, 192; educational principles of, 37, 50, 55–58; and the elite, 35, 184; techniques of, 51; limits of language and, 58; Nietzsche's view of, xii; relation to democratic politics of, 32–33, 35–36, 184; virtue conception of, 53. *See also Euthydemus;* Socrates protreptics of
sport, 204–5
Sprague, Rosamond Kent, 55
Spring, Joel, 18–19
Starobinski, Jean, 61–63, 123
Steiner, Deborah, 47
Strauss, Leo, 226n.86

Tarcov, Nathan, 216n.31
taxes, 5–6, 22
Taylor, C. C. W., 222n.26, 223n.36, 224n.44
Taylor, Charles, 180
teaching, 11, 22, 32, 49–50, 52, 123–25, 198–205, 208–11; and ethnic

issues, 203–5; Nietzsche's advice on, 199; pedagogic technique in, 199, 207; public speech, focus on, 201–2; selection of texts, 209–11. *See also* Dewey, John, teaching methods advocated by; proposals for democratic education; Rousseau, teachers and teaching
Theaetetus, 36–39, 42; ambiguity in, 38; doctrine of appearance in, 38; "man as measure" standard in, 38
Themistocles, 48
Theory translated into practice, 198
Thoreau, Henry David, 210
Thucydides, 41, 43–44
Tronchin, Rousseau's letter to, 109
Trotsky, Leon, 162–63

United States Department of Labor, 19

video, 201, 204
virtue, 7–8, 32, 34–35, 39, 53, 66, 68, 73, 111, 189
Vlastos, Gregory, 30, 43
Voltaire, 80, 106
vouchers. *See* educational reform

Wagner, Richard, 171
Washington, George, xvii
Westbrook, Robert, 239–40nn.13. 14
Whole Language Movement, 198
Wilson, Edmund, 228nn.10, 12
Wittgenstein, Ludwig, 131

Xenophon, 48, 52
Xerxes, 48

Zeus, myth of, 33

Library of Congress Cataloging-in-Publication Data

Steiner, David M.
    A theory of democratic education / David M. Steiner.
       p.   cm.
    Includes bibliographical references and index.
    ISBN 0-8018-4842-3
    1. Education—Philosophy.   2. Education—Political
aspects.   3. Educational change.   4. Political science.   I. Title
LB14.7.S73   1994
370'.1—dc20   93-49707